CORRESPONDENCE

BETWEEN

GOETHE AND CARLYLE

CORRESPONDENCE

BETWEEN

GOETHE AND CARLYLE

Goethe

EDITED BY

CHARLES ELIOT NORTON

A Marandell Book
COOPER SQUARE PUBLISHERS, INC.
NEW YORK
1970

Originally Published 1887
Published by Cooper Square Publishers, Inc.
59 Fourth Avenue, New York, N. Y. 10003
Standard Book Number 8154-0321-6
Library of Congress Catalog Card No. 71-114084

Printed in the United States of America

PREFACE

In the following Correspondence the letters of
Goethe have been printed from the originals
now in the possession of Mrs. Alexander
Carlyle. These letters had been done up in
a parcel, and packed away by Carlyle, some
thirty years before his death, in a box which
was afterwards used exclusively for papers
connected with Cromwell. Under these papers
they were buried; Carlyle forgot where he had
put them, and they were not found until the
contents of the box were sorted shortly after
his death.

The letters of Carlyle are printed from a
careful copy of the originals now preserved
in the Goethe Archives at Weimar. These

copies were furnished by the gracious permission of H.R.H. the Grand Duchess of Weimar, to whom for this favour the gratitude of every reader of this volume is due.

CHARLES ELIOT NORTON.

CAMBRIDGE, MASSACHUSETTS,
January 1887.

INTRODUCTION

CARLYLE was in his twenty-ninth year when, in June 1824, he first wrote to Goethe, sending him his Translation, then just published, of *Wilhelm Meister's Apprenticeship*. He had not yet attained to any definite position in the world of letters; his writing hitherto had been tentative, much of it mere hackwork, and had attracted little attention. His name was not known outside a narrow circle; he had not yet acquired full possession of his own powers, nor was he at peace with himself. For ten years he had been engaged in constant and severe spiritual wrestlings; his soul, begirt by doubts, was painfully struggling to be free. The predominant tendencies of contemporary English thought were hateful to him; Philosophy in its true sense was all but extinct in England; the standard of ideal aims was hardly held high by any one of the popular writers. Carlyle had laid aside the creed of his fathers, and, dependent for guidance only upon the strength of his own moral principles, was adrift without other chart or compass.

It was in this condition, perplexed and baffled as to his true path, that Carlyle fell in with Madame de Staël's famous book on Germany. His interest was aroused by it. From her animated, if somewhat shallow and imperfect accounts of the speculations of the living German Poets and Philosophers, he learned to look towards Germany for a spiritual light that he had not found in the modern French and English writers.[1] He became eager to study German, that he might investigate for himself. But German Books and German Masters were alike scarce in Edinburgh. Edward Irving

---

[1] "I still remember," says Carlyle in his Letter to Goethe of 3d November 1829, "that it was the desire to read Werner's Mineralogical Doctrines in the original, that first set me on studying German; where truly I found a mine, far different from any of the Freyberg ones!" But it was Madame de Staël's book that kindled his enthusiasm.

had given him a dictionary, but a grammar had
to be procured from London.

It happened fortunately that about this time
Carlyle met with a young man named Jardine, who had been his schoolfellow at Annan,
and who was then, in 1819, settled in Edinburgh, having returned from Göttingen, where
he had resided for a short time as tutor to a
young Irishman. Jardine gave Carlyle some
German lessons in return for lessons in French.[1]
Carlyle, writing in 1866, describes Jardine as
"a feeble enough, but pleasant and friendly
creature, with something of *skin-deep* geniality
even, which marked him for 'harmless master-
ship in the superficial.'" Carlyle made rapid
progress, and was soon able to read German
books. These were procured for him from Germany, by his kind friend Mr. Swan, a merchant
of Kirkcaldy, who had dealings with Hamburg.
"I well remember," writes Carlyle in 1866,
"the arrival of the *Schiller Werke* sheets at
Mainhill (and my impatience till the Annan

---

[1] See *Early Letters of Thomas Carlyle* (Macmillan and
Co., 1886), i. 209, 227.

Bookbinder had done with them) : they had come from Lübeck I perceived. . . . This *Schiller* and *Archenholtz's Seven-Years' War* were my first really German Books."

Schiller's high, earnest, and yet simple nature, the ideal purity and elevation of his works, the free and generous feeling that pervades them, no less than the circumstances of his life, attracted Carlyle. But Schiller's range was limited, and the longed-for light on the mystery of life was not to be obtained from him.

Wilhelm Meister he procured soon afterwards from the University Library at Edinburgh. In Goethe he quickly recognised one who could "reveal many highest things to him," and under whose teaching his doubts were to melt away, leaving clear convictions in their stead. In Goethe's works there was as it were a mirror which revealed to him the lineaments of his own genius. Of all the influences that helped Carlyle to an understanding and mastery of himself, those exerted by Goethe were the most potent ; and he remained for the rest of Carlyle's life

a teacher whom he reverenced. Writing long
afterwards of this period, especially of the year
1826, Carlyle says, "This year I found that I
had conquered all my scepticisms, agonising
doubtings, fearful wrestlings with the foul and
vile and soul-murdering Mud-gods of my
Epoch ; had escaped, as from a worse than
Tartarus, with all its Phlegethons and Stygian
quagmires ; and was emerging, free in spirit,
into the eternal blue of ether,—where, blessed
be Heaven, I have, for the spiritual part, ever
since lived. . . . What my pious joy and gratitude then was, let the pious soul figure. In a
fine and veritable sense, I, poor, obscure, without outlook, almost without worldly hope, had
become independent of the world ;—what was
death itself, from the world, to what I had come
through ? I understood well what the old
Christian people meant by their 'Conversion,' by
God's Infinite Mercy to them :—I had, in effect,
gained an immense victory ; and, for a number
of years, had, in spite of nerves and chagrins,
a constant inward happiness that was quite
royal and supreme ; in which all temporal evil

was transient and insignificant; and which essentially remains with me still, though far oftener *eclipsed*, and lying deeper *down*, than then. Once more, thank Heaven for its highest gift. I then felt, and still feel, endlessly indebted to *Goethe* in the business; he, in his fashion, I perceived, had travelled the steep rocky road before me,—the first of the moderns."[1]

Carlyle, writing to Miss Welsh, 6th April 1823, says: Goethe's "feelings are various as the hues of Earth and Sky, but his intellect is the Sun which illuminates and overrules them all. He does not yield himself to his emotions, but uses them rather as things for his judgment to scrutinise and apply to purpose. I think Goethe the only living model of a great writer. . . . It is one of my finest day-dreams to see him ere I die." And again, 15th April 1824: " The English have begun to speak about him of late years; but no light has yet been thrown upon him, 'no light but only darkness visible.' The syllables *Goethe* excite an idea as vague and

---

[1] Carlyle's *Reminiscences* (Macmillan and Co., 1887), ii. 179, 180.

monstrous as the word *Gorgon* or *Chimæra*."
The needed light was soon to be thrown upon
the Poet and his works.

The first literary use to which Carlyle
turned his knowledge of German was in the
writing of his *Life of Schiller*.[1] This, begun
in 1822, appeared in the *London Magazine* in
1823-24; and was printed, as a separate volume,
without Carlyle's name, in the spring of 1825.
In his Preface to the Second Edition (1845),
he speaks of it disparagingly, as a book he
would prefer to suppress ; but it is an excellent
piece of work, written with sympathy, simplicity
and clear insight ; the best Life of Schiller then
extant, and, in English at any rate, there has
been no better since. It was still only half
finished when he began the translation of
Meister's Apprenticeship,—a book by no means
wholly after his own heart, but which from its
large and genial view of life, from the variety
of observation of human nature recorded in it,

[1] Carlyle had indeed written an article on *Faust* before
this date (*New Edinburgh Review*, April 1822), but it is a
comparatively crude production, and Carlyle did not consider it
worthy of a place in his Collected Works.

and from the picture it afforded of the author's mind, held him with strong attraction. In his essay on "Goethe's Works" published just after Goethe's death (*Foreign Quarterly Review*, 1832), he says: "Many years ago on finishing our first perusal of *Wilhelm Meister*, with a very mixed sentiment in other respects, we could not but feel that here lay more insight into the elements of human nature, and a more poetically perfect combining of these, than in all the other fictitious literature of our generation." Thirty-four years later, in his Reminiscences of Edward Irving, he relates how, "*Schiller* done, I began [to translate] *Wilhelm Meister*, a task I liked perhaps rather better, too scanty as my knowledge of the element, and even of the language still was. Two years before, I had at length, after some repulsions, got into the heart of *Wilhelm Meister*, and eagerly read it through ;—my sally out, after finishing, along the vacant streets of Edinburgh (a windless Scotch-misty Sunday night) is still vivid to me : 'Grand, surely, harmoniously built together, far-seeing, wise and true : when, for many years, or almost in my life before, have I read such a book?' Which I was now, really in part as a kind of duty, conscientiously translating for my countrymen, if they would read it,— as a select few of them have ever since kept doing. I finished it the next Spring, . . ."

In 1824, when this correspondence began, Goethe was seventy-five years old ; a hale and vigorous man. His intellectual interests were as wide as ever, his curiosity unabated, his sympathies unchilled by age. His position had long been unique, and he was now at the height of his renown. Carlyle's letter and his translation of *Meister's Apprenticeship* gave Goethe pleasure, as the expression of a genuine admiration coming from a region from which he had hitherto received little appreciation or even recognition. The letter and book were the more welcome as they seemed to fall in with a project which Goethe had much at heart at this time, namely, the bringing about of a better understanding amongst nations by means of a universal

World-Literature,—the establishing of an exchange between different countries of their
highest mental products; so that all might
at once share in whatever great intellectual
work any one nation might produce. Thus
would mutual understanding be substituted
for the traditional misconceptions of ignorance; a sense of common obligation arise,
and universal tolerance lead to happier relations among the various families of men. In
this work, to which his first publications contributed, Carlyle was soon to show himself the
chief agent between Germany and England,
and Goethe soon recognised in him the ablest
of his fellow-workers.[1]

[1] The influence of Carlyle's writings from 1823 to 1832 in
arousing in England an interest in German literature is hardly
to be over-estimated, whether in its immediate or remote
effects. The following is a list of his writings on German
subjects during these years :—*Life of Schiller*, 1823-24 ; *Wilhelm Meister's Apprenticeship*, 1824 ; *German Romance, Jean
Paul Friedrich Richter, State of German Literature*, 1827 ;
Werner, Goethe's Helena, Goethe, Heyne, 1828; *German
Playwrights, Novalis*, 1829 ; *Jean Paul's Review of Madame
de Staël's Allemagne, Jean Paul Friedrich Richter Again*,
1830 ; *Luther's Psalm, Schiller, The Nibelungen Lied,
German Literature of the XIV. and XV. Centuries, Taylor's*

Nearly forty years after Goethe's death, Carlyle, recalling the events of his early life, wrote as follows of this Correspondence :—" In answer to *German Romance* there had latterly come an actual long *Letter* from Weimar, from the Great Goethe's self, who was evidently taking interest in me. By and by there arrived, at Leith, by Hamburg, a little Fir Box (which still exists here in beautifully *transfigured* shape) containing the daintiest collection of pretty little gifts and memorials to both of us,— the very arrangement and packing of which we found to be poetic and a study. Something of real romance and glory lay for us in this fine Goethe item. That Leith Box (which I instantly went down for in person, and *tore*, as it were, almost by main force, through the Custom-house and its formalities, in few hours, instead of days, and came home with in triumph) was the first of several such that followed at due intervals, and of a Correspondence (not

Historic Survey of German Poetry, 1831 ; *Goethe's Portrait, Schiller, Goethe, and Madame de Staël, Death of Goethe, Goethe's Works, The Tale* (*Das Mährchen*), *Novelle*, 1832.

in itself momentous at all, but to us then an æthereal and quasi-celestial thing), which lasted steadily till Goethe's death. His *Letters*, ten or twelve, perhaps more, are all extant, carefully reposited among my *pretiosa*, but, for many years past, I know not now where.[1] Pretty gifts of his,—that little steel brooch, 'never to be worn,' so She had vowed, 'except when a man of genius was present,' etc. etc."[2]

The stimulus and encouragement of Goethe's sympathy and regard, expressed as they were in simple, cordial and delightful modes, were invaluable to Carlyle. They came to him when he had as yet received no real recognition from his own people, whose acknowledgment of his worth was slowly and grudgingly given. For this neglect Goethe's appreciation and friendship made amends. They confirmed the young writer's faith in himself. Goethe's

---

[1] The parcel which contained these letters, all carefully arranged, was labelled, in Carlyle's hand: " GOETHE.   Tied up so, perhaps about 1834 ; shifted now, without opening (12th January 1852), into another receptacle, with an additional wrappage."

[2] From an unpublished manuscript, written in 1869.

discriminating eye had discerned what no other had discovered — that here was a man who rested on an original foundation, and had the capacity to develop in himself the essentials of what was good and beautiful.

CORRESPONDENCE

BETWEEN

GOETHE AND CARLYLE

I.—CARLYLE to GOETHE.

4 MYDDELTON TERRACE,[1] PENTONVILLE,
LONDON, 24th June 1824.

PERMIT me, Sir, in soliciting your acceptance of this Translation[2] to return you my sincere thanks for the profit which, in common with many millions, I have derived from the Original.

That you will honour this imperfect copy of your work with a perusal I do not hope: but the thought that some portion of my existence

---

[1] Edward Irving's house, to which Carlyle had been welcomed on his first arrival in London early in June.

[2] *Wilhelm Meister's Apprenticeship* (3 vols. Edinburgh, 1824).

has been connected with that of the Man whose intellect and mind I most admire, is pleasing to my imagination ; nor will I neglect the present opportunity of communing with you even in this slight and transitory manner. Four years ago, when I read your *Faust* among the mountains of my native Scotland, I could not but fancy I might one day see you, and pour out before you, as before a Father, the woes and wanderings of a heart whose mysteries you seemed so thoroughly to comprehend, and could so beautifully represent. The hope of meeting you is still among my dreams. Many saints have been expunged from my literary Calendar since I first knew you; but your name still stands there, in characters more bright than ever. That your life may be long, long spared, for the solace and instruction of this and future generations, is the earnest prayer of, Sir, your most devoted servant, THOMAS CARLYLE.

P.S.—As the conveyance is uncertain, a line signifying that you have received this packet would be peculiarly acceptable.

II.—GOETHE to CARLYLE.

[*30th October* 1824.]

Wenn ich, mein werthester Herr, die glückliche Ankunft Ihrer willkommenen Sendung
nicht ungesäumt anzeigte, so war die Ursache,
dass ich nicht einen leeren Empfangschein
ausstellen, sondern über Ihre mir so ehrenvolle
Arbeit auch irgend ein geprüftes Wort beyzufügen die Absicht hatte.

Meine hohen Jahre jedoch, mit so vielen
unabwendbaren Obliegenheiten immerfort be-
laden, hinderten mich an einer ruhigen
Vergleichung Ihrer Bearbeitung mit dem
Originaltext, welches vielleicht für mich eine
schwerere Aufgabe seyn möchte, als für irgend
einen dritten der deutschen und englischen
Lite[ratur] gründlich Befreundeten. Gegenwärtig aber da ich eine Gelegenheit sehe
durch die Herren Grafen Bentinck gegenwärtiges Schreiben sicher nach London zu
bringen, und zugleich beiden Theilen eine angenehme Bekanntschaft zu verschaffen, so ver-
säume nicht meinen Dank für Ihre so innige
Theilnahme an meinen literarischen Arbeiten
sowohl, als an den Schicksalen meines Lebens

hierdurch treulich auszusprechen, und Sie um
Fortsetzung derselben auch für die Zukunft
angelegentlich zu ersuchen.   Vielleicht erfahre
ich in der Folge noch manches von Ihnen, und
übersende zugleich mit diesem eine Reihe von
Gedichten, welche schwerlich zu Ihnen gekommen sind, von denen ich aber hoffen darf, dass
sie Ihnen einiges Interesse abgewinnen werden.

Mit den aufrichtigsten Wünschen
ergebenst,

J. W. v. Goethe.[1]

Weimar, 30 Octbr. 1824.

[Translation.]

If I did not, my dear Sir, promptly inform
you of the safe arrival of your welcome present,
the reason was, that I had not the intention
of writing a mere acknowledgment, but of adding thereto some deliberate words concerning
your work which does me such honour.   My
advanced years, continually burdened with
many indispensable duties, have, however,
prevented me from leisurely comparing your

---

[1] The Italics here, and at the endings of the Goethe
Letters which follow, mark the words which are in the original
in Goethe's own handwriting.

translation with the original; which might perhaps prove a harder task for me than for some third person thoroughly at home in German and English Literature. But now, since I have an opportunity of sending the present letter safely to London, by favour of the Lords Bentinck, and at the same time of bringing about an acquaintance agreeable to both parties, I do not delay to express my sincere thanks for your hearty sympathy in my literary work, as well as in the incidents of my life, and to beg earnestly for a continuance of it in the future. Perhaps I shall hereafter come to know much of you. Meanwhile I send together with this a set of poems, which you can hardly have seen, but which I venture to hope may prove of some interest to you.[1]

With the sincerest good wishes,

Most truly yours,

J. W. v. GOETHE.

WEIMAR, 30*th October* 1824.

---

[1] " The ' *Reihe von Gedichten* which I can hardly have seen,' are a Court Mask by himself, and a printed copy of verses to him on his last birthday and cure from sickness, by one Meyer." —*Note by Carlyle to a copy of this Letter.*

Carlyle writes to Miss Welsh, 20th December 1824:

" The other twilight, the lackey of one Lord Bentinck came with a lackey's knock to the door, and delivered me a little blue parcel, requiring for it a receipt under my hand.   I opened it somewhat eagerly, and found two small pamphlets with ornamental covers, and—a letter from— Goethe !   Conceive my satisfaction : it was almost like a message from Fairy Land ; I could scarcely think that *this was* the real hand and signature of that mysterious personage, whose name had floated through my fancy, like a sort of spell, since boyhood ; whose thoughts had come to me in maturer years with almost the impressiveness of revelations.   But what says the letter ?   Kind nothings, in a simple patriarchal style, extremely to my taste.   I will copy it, for it is in a character that you cannot read ; and send it to you with the original, which you are to keep as the most precious of your literary relics.   Only the last line and the signature are in Goethe's hand : I understand he *constantly* employs an amanuensis.   Do you transcribe my copy, and your own translation of it, into the blank leaf of that German paper, before you lay it by ; that the same sheet may contain some traces of him whom I most venerate and her whom I most love in this strangest of all possible worlds."

III.—CARLYLE to GOETHE.

EDINBURGH, 21 COMLEY BANK,
15th April 1827.

RESPECTED SIR—It is now above two years since Lord Bentinck's Servant delivered me at

London the packet from Weimar, containing
your kind Letter and Present; of both which,
to say that they were heartily gratifying to me,
would be saying little; for I received them and
keep them with a regard which can belong to
nothing else.   To me they are memorials of
one whom I never saw, yet whose voice came
to me from afar, with counsel and help, in my
utmost need.   For if I have been delivered
from darkness into any measure of light, if I
know aught of myself and my duties and destination, it is to the study of your writings more
than to any other circumstance that I owe this;
it is you more than any other man that I should
always thank and reverence with the feeling of
a Disciple to his Master, nay of a Son to his
spiritual Father.   This is no idle compliment,
but a heartfelt truth; and humble as it is I
feel that the knowledge of such truths must be
more pleasing to you than all other glory.

The Books,[1] which I here take the liberty to

---

[1] The *Life of Schiller* (London, 1825); and *German
Romance* (4 vols. Edinburgh, 1827).   Vol. iv. of this edition
contains *Wilhelm Meister's Travels.*

offer you, are the poor product of endeavours, obstructed by sickness and many other causes ; and in themselves little worthy of your acceptance : but perhaps they may find some favour for my sake, and interest you likewise as evidences of the progress of German Literature in England.   Hitherto it has not been injustice but ignorance that has blinded us in this matter : at all events a different state of things seems approaching ; with respect to yourself, it is at hand, or rather has already come. This *Wanderjahre*, which I reckon somewhat better translated than its forerunner, I in many quarters hear deeply, if not loudly, praised ; and even the character with which I have prefaced it, appears to excite not objection but partial compliance, or at worst, hesitation and inquiry.

Of the *Lehrjahre* also I am happy to give a much more flattering account than I could have anticipated at first.   Above a thousand copies of the Book are already in the hands of the public ; loved also, with more or less insight, by all persons of any culture ; and, what it has many times interested me to observe, with a

degree of estimation determined not less by
the intellectual force than by the moral earnestness of the reader. One of its warmest admirers known to me is a lady of rank, and
intensely religious.[1]

I may mention further that, some weeks
ago, a stranger London bookseller applied to
me to translate your *Dichtung und Wahrheit;*
a proposal which I have perhaps only post-
poned, not rejected.

All this warrants me to believe that your
name and doctrines will ere long be English as
well as German; and certainly there are few
things which I have more satisfaction in contemplating than the fact that to this result my
own efforts have contributed; that I have
assisted in conquering for you a new province
of mental empire; and for my countrymen a
new treasure of wisdom which I myself have
found so precious. One day, it may be, if there
is any gift in me, I shall send you some Work
of my own; and along with it, you will deserve

---

[1] Mrs. Strachey. See Carlyle's *Reminiscences* (Macmillan
and Co., 1887), ii. 102, 123.

far deeper thanks than those of Hilaria to her friendly Artist.[1]

About six months ago I was married : my young wife, who sympathises with me in most things, agrees also in my admiration of you ; and would have me, in her name, beg of you to accept this purse, the work, as I can testify, of dainty fingers and true love ; that so something, which she had handled and which had been hers, might be in your hands and be yours.   In this little point I have engaged that you would gratify her.   She knows you in your own language ; and her first criticism was the following, expressed with some surprise: "This Goethe is a greater genius than Schiller, though he does not make me cry!"   A better judgment than many which have been pronounced with more formality.

May I hope to hear, by Post, that this packet has arrived safely, and that health and blessings are still continued to you ?   *Frey ist das Herz, doch ist der Fuss gebunden.*[2]   My wishes are

---

[1] See *Wilhelm Meister* (Library Edition, 1871), ii. 261, 262.

[2] Compare "*Nicht ist der Geist, doch ist der Fuss gebunden.*" —*Goethe's Werke* (Cotta, 1827), iv. 103.

joined with those of the world that you may be long spared to see good, and do good.—I am ever, Respected Sir, your humble servant and thankful Scholar,   THOMAS CARLYLE.

If you stand in any relation with Mr. Tieck, it would give me pleasure to assure him of my esteem. Except him and Richter, who has left us, there is no other of these Novelists, whom I ought not to beg your pardon for placing you beside, even as their King.

IV.—GOETHE to CARLYLE.

[*17th May* 1827.]

Dass die angenehme Sendung, begleitet von einem freundlichen Schreiben, abgesendet von Edinburg den 15^n April über Hamburg, den 15^n May bey mir angekommen und mich in guter Gesundheit, für meine Freunde beschäftigt, angetroffen hat, solches vermelde eiligst. Meinem aufrichtigsten Dank den beiden werthen Gatten füge nur noch hinzu die Versicherung, dass nächstens ein Paquet von hier, gleichfalls über Hamburg, abgehen werde, meine Theilnahme zu bezeugen und mein Andenken zu erneuern.

Mit den besten und treusten Wünschen mich empfehlend,

J. W. v. Goethe.

W., d. 17 May 1827.

[Translation.]

Let me hastily announce that your welcome packet, accompanied by a kind letter, sent from Edinburgh on the 15th of April, by way of Hamburg, reached me on the 15th of May, and found me in good health, busily employed for my friends. To my most sincere thanks to the dear husband and wife, I add only the information that a packet will speedily be despatched hence, also by way of Hamburg, in testimony of my sympathetic interest in you, and to recall me to your remembrance.

Commending myself to you, with best and truest wishes,

J. W. v. Goethe.

Weimar, 17*th May* 1827.

Carlyle, writing to his brother John on the 4th June, sends him a copy of this Letter, and says:

"To-day I had such a packet of letters all in a rush! A letter from Mrs. Montagu; and enclosed in the same frank a sublime note from Edward Irving, full of praise and thanks expressed in the most wondrous dialect; and last or rather first, for that was the paper we pounced on most eagerly, a dainty little letter from—Weimar! The good man has Knighted me too![1] Did you ever see so polite, true-hearted, altogether graceful a note? At the same time there is a naïve brevity in it which, in admiring, almost makes me laugh. Read and wonder.

And now we are all impatient to know what that *paquet* that is coming 'over Hamburg' will bring us. You shall know so soon as the new-made Knight or Baronet receives it."

V.—GOETHE to CARLYLE.[2]

[*20th July* 1827.]

In einem Schreiben vom 15 May,[3] welches ich mit der Post absendete und Sie hoffentlich zu rechter Zeit werden erhalten haben, vermeldete ich, wie viel Vergnügen mir Ihre Sendung

[1] Goethe's letter was addressed to "Sir" Thomas Carlyle.

[2] Portions of this Letter, with slight alterations, are printed in Goethe's Works; see *Life of Friedrich Schiller*, *Nachgelassene Werke* (Cotta, 1833), vi. 237; and *German Romance*, ibid. 261.

[3] See Letter IV., dated "17th" May.

gebracht. Sie fand mich auf dem Lande, wo ich sie mit mehrerer Ruhe betrachten und geniessen konnte. Gegenwärtig sehe ich mich in dem Stande, auch ein Packet an Sie abzuschicken mit dem Wunsche freundlicher Aufnahme.

Lassen Sie mich vorerst, mein Theuerster, von Ihrer Biographie Schillers das Beste sagen : sie ist merkwürdig, indem sie ein genaues Studium der Vorfälle seines Lebens beweist, so wie denn auch das Studium seiner Werke und eine innige Theilnahme an denselben daraus hervorgeht. Bewundernswürdig ist es wie Sie sich auf diese Weise eine genügende Einsicht in den Character und das hohe Verdienstliche dieses Mannes verschafft, so klar und so gehörig als es kaum aus der Ferne zu erwarten gewesen.

Hier bewahrheitet sich jedoch ein altes Wort : "der gute Wille hilft zu vollkommner Kenntniss." Denn gerade dass der Schott- länder den deutschen Mann mit Wohlwollen anerkennt, ihn verehrt und liebt, dadurch wird er dessen treffliche Eigenschaften am sichersten

gewahr, dadurch erhebt er sich zu einer Klarheit
zu der sogar Landsleute des Trefflichen in
früheren Tagen nicht gelangen konnten; denn
die Mitlebenden werden an vorzüglichen Menschen gar leicht irre; das Besondere der
Person stört sie, das laufende bewegliche
Leben verrückt ihre Standpunkte und hindert
das Kennen und Anerkennen eines solchen
Mannes.

Dieser aber war von so ausserordentlicher
Art, dass der Biograph die Idee eines vorzüglichen Mannes vor Augen halten und sie durch
individuelle Schicksale und Leistungen durchführen konnte, und sein Tagewerk dergestalt
vollbracht sah.

Die vor den *German Romance* mitgetheilten
Notizen über das Leben Musäus', Hoffmanns,
Richters, etc. kann man in ihrer Art gleichfalls
mit Beyfall aufnehmen; sie sind mit Sorgfalt
gesammelt, kürzlich dargestellt und geben von
eines jeden Autors individuellem Character
und der Einwirkung desselben auf seine
Schriften genugsame Vorkenntniss.

Durchaus beweist Herr Carlyle eine ruhige

klare Theilnahme an dem deutschen poetisch-
literarischen Beginnen; er giebt sich hin an
das eigenthümliche Bestreben der Nation, er
lässt den Einzelnen gelten, jeden an seiner
Stelle.

Sey mir nun erlaubt, allgemeine Betrachtungen hinzuzufügen, welche ich längst bey
mir im Stillen hege und die mir bey den
vorliegenden Arbeiten abermals frisch aufgeregt
worden :

Offenbar ist das Bestreben der besten
Dichter und ästhetischen Schriftsteller aller
Nationen schon seit geraumer Zeit auf das
allgemein Menschliche gerichtet. In jedem
Besondern, es sey nun historisch, mytholo-
gisch, fabelhaft, mehr oder weniger willkührlich
ersonnen, wird man durch Nationalität und
Persönlichkeit hindurch jenes Allgemeine immer
mehr durchleuchten und durchschimmern sehn.

Da nun auch im practischen Lebensgange
ein gleiches obwaltet und durch alles Irdisch-
Rohe, Wilde, Grausame, Falsche, Eigen-
nützige, Lügenhafte sich durchschlingt, und
überall einige Milde zu verbreiten trachtet, so

ist zwar nicht zu hoffen, dass ein allgemeiner
Friede dadurch sich einleite, aber doch dass
der unvermeidliche Streit nach und nach
lässlicher werde, der Krieg weniger grausam,
der Sieg weniger übermüthig.

Was nun in den Dichtungen aller Nationen
hierauf hindeutet und hinwirkt, dies ist es was
die Uebrigen sich anzueignen haben. Die
Besonderheiten einer jeden muss man kennen
lernen, um sie ihr zu lassen, um gerade dadurch
mit ihr zu verkehren; denn die Eigenheiten
einer Nation sind wie ihre Sprache und ihre
Münzsorten, sie erleichtern den Verkehr, ja sie
machen ihn erst vollkommen möglich.

Verzeihen Sie mir, mein Werthester, diese
vielleicht nicht ganz zusammenhängenden, noch
alsbald zu überschauenden Aeusserungen; sie
sind geschöpft aus dem Ocean der Betrachtungen, der um einen jeden Denkenden mit den
Jahren immer mehr anschwillt. Lassen Sie
mich noch Einiges hinzufügen, welches ich bey
einer andern Gelegenheit niederschrieb, das
sich jedoch hauptsächlich auf Ihr Geschäfft
unmittelbar beziehen lässt:

C

Eine wahrhaft allgemeine Duldung wird am sichersten erreicht, wenn man das Besondere der einzelnen Menschen und Völkerschaften auf sich beruhen lässt, bey der Ueberzeugung jedoch festhält, dass das wahrhaft Verdienstliche sich dadurch auszeichnet, dass es der ganzen Menschheit angehört. Zu einer solchen Vermittlung und wechselseitigen Anerkennung tragen die Deutschen seit langer Zeit schon bey.

Wer die deutsche Sprache versteht und studirt befindet sich auf dem Markte wo alle Nationen ihre Waaren anbieten, er spielt den Dolmetscher indem er sich selbst bereichert.

Und so ist jeder Uebersetzer anzusehen, dass er sich als Vermittler dieses allgemein geistigen Handels bemüht, und den Wechseltausch zu befördern sich zum Geschäfft macht. Denn, was man auch von der Unzulänglichkeit des Uebersetzens sagen mag, so ist und bleibt es doch eins der wichtigsten und würdigsten Geschäffte in dem allgemeinen Weltwesen.

Der Koran sagt: "Gott hat jedem Volke einen Propheten gegeben in seiner eignen Sprache." So ist jeder Uebersetzer ein Pro-

phet seinem Volke.   Luthers Bibelübersetzung
hat die grössten Wirkungen hervorgebracht,
wenn schon die Critik daran bis auf den heutigen
Tag immerfort bedingt und mäkelt.   Und was
ist denn das ganze ungeheure Geschäfft der
Bibelgesellschaft, als das Evangelium einem
jeden Volke in seiner eignen Sprache zu ver-
kündigen.

Hier lassen Sie mich schliessen, wo man ins
Unendliche fortfahren könnte, und erfreuen Sie
mich bald mit einiger Erwiederung, wodurch
ich Nachricht erhalte, dass gegenwärtige Sendung zu Ihnen gekommen ist.

Zum Schlusse lassen Sie mich denn auch
Ihre liebe Gattin begrüssen, für die ich einige
Kleinigkeiten, als Erwiederung ihrer anmuthi-
gen Gabe, beyzulegen mir die Freude mache.
Möge Ihnen ein glückliches Zusammenleben
viele Jahre bescheert seyn.

Nach allem diesen finde ich mich doch noch
angeregt, Einiges hinzuzufügen : Möge Herr
Carlyle alles Obige freundlich aufnehmen und
durch anhaltende Betrachtung in ein Gespräch
verwandeln, damit es ihm zu Muthe werde,

als wenn wir persönlich einander gegenüber
ständen.

Hab' ich ihm ja sogar noch für die Bemühung zu danken, die er an meine Arbeiten
gewendet hat, für den guten und wohlwollenden
Sinn mit dem er von meiner Persönlichkeit und
meinen Lebensereignissen zu sprechen geneigt
war. In dieser Ueberzeugung darf ich mich
denn auch zum Voraus freuen, dass künftighin,
wenn noch mehrere von meinen Arbeiten ihm
bekannt werden, besonders auch, wenn meine
Correspondenz mit Schillern erscheinen wird,
er weder von diesem Freunde noch von mir
seine Meinung ändern, sondern sie vielmehr
durch manches Besondere noch mehr bestätigt
finden wird.

Das Beste herzlich wünschend,

treu theilnehmend,

J. W. v. GOETHE.

WEIMAR, *d. 20 Jul. 1827.*

This letter was accompanied by the following
verses, as well as by a translation of the Scottish
Ballad "The Barring of the Door" (*Gutman und
Gutweib, Nachgelassene Werke*, vii. 84).

Matt und beschwerlich,	[Fainting and heavily,
Wandernd ermüdigt,	Weary with wandering,
Klimmt er gefährlich	In peril he climbs on
Nimmer befriedigt;	Never knowing content;
Felsen ersteigt er	Scaling the rocky heights
Wie es die Kraft erlaubt,	So as his strength permits,
Endlich erreicht er	At last he attains to
Gipfel und Bergeshaupt.	The peak and the mountain-top.
Hat er mühselig	Thus having painfully
Also den Tag vollbracht,	The day's task completed,
Nun wär' es thörig	Now were it foolishness
Hätt' er darauf noch Acht.	Still to pay heed to it.
Froh ist's unsäglich	'Tis joyous beyond words
Sitzendem hier,	In quiet to sit here,
Athmend behäglich	Reposing in gladness
An Geishirtens Thür.	By the door of the goatherd.
Speis' ich und trinke nun	Now do I eat and drink
Wie es vorhanden,	As it is offered me,
Sonne sie sinket nun	And the sun sinketh down
Allen den Landen;	Slowly o'er all the lands;
Schmeckt es heut Abend	Delights in this evening
Niemand wie mir,	No one as I do,
Sitzend mich labend	As I sit here refreshed
An Geishirtens Thür.[1]	By the door of the goatherd.]

[TRANSLATION.]

In a letter of 15th May, which I despatched by Post, and which I hope will have reached you

[1] Printed in the *Nachgelassene Werke*, vii. 82.

in due time, I informed you how much pleasure
your present had brought me.   It found me in
the country where I could examine and enjoy
it in greater quiet.   I am now, in my turn,
about to send you a packet, of which I request
your friendly acceptance.

Let me, first of all, my dear Sir, commend
most highly your Biography of Schiller.   It is
remarkable for the close study it shows of the
incidents of his life, whilst it also manifests a
sympathetic study of his works.   The accurate insight into the character and distinguished merit
of this man, which you have thus acquired is
really admirable, and so clear and just as was
hardly to have been expected from a foreigner.

In this an old saying is verified : " Love
helps to perfect knowledge."   For precisely
because the Scotchman regards the German
with kindliness, and honours and loves him,
does he recognise most surely his admirable
qualities, and thus he rises to a clearness of
view, to which even the great man's compatriots could not in earlier days attain.   For
their contemporaries very easily fall into error

concerning eminent men;—personal peculiarities
disturb them, the changeful current of life dis-
places their points of view, and hinders their
knowledge and recognition of such men.

Schiller, however, was of so exceptional a
nature, that his Biographer had but to keep before his eyes the ideal of a pre-eminent man, and
by maintaining it to the end, through individual
fortunes and actions, see his task fulfilled.

The notices of the lives of Musäus, Hoffman,
and Richter, prefixed to *German Romance*, are
also in their kind to be commended. They are
compiled with care, set forth concisely, and
give sufficient information concerning the individual character of each author, and of its
effect upon his writings.

Mr. Carlyle shows throughout a clear, calm
sympathy with the endeavours of poetic literature in Germany, and while he dwells on
what is specially characteristic of national
tendencies he gives due credit to each individual in his own place.

Let me add some general considerations,
which I have long cherished in silence, and

which have been stirred up afresh in me by the
present works.

It is obvious that the efforts of the best
poets and æsthetic writers of all nations have
now for some time been directed towards what
is universal in humanity.   In each special field,
whether in history, mythology, or fiction, more
or less arbitrarily conceived, one sees the traits
which are universal always more clearly revealed and illumining what is merely national
and personal.

Though something of the same sort prevails
now also in practical life, pervading all that
is earthy, crude, wild, cruel, false, selfish, and
treacherous, and striving to diffuse everywhere
some gentleness, we cannot indeed hope that
universal peace is being ushered in thereby,
but only that inevitable strife will be gradually
more restrained, war will become less cruel, and
victory less insolent.

Whatever in the poetry of any nation tends
to this and contributes to it, the others should
endeavour to appropriate.   The peculiarities
of each nation must be learned, and allowance

made for them, in order by these very means to hold intercourse with it; for the special characteristics of a nation are like its language and its currency: they facilitate intercourse, nay they first make it completely possible.

Pardon me, my dear Sir, for these remarks, which are perhaps not altogether coherent, nor to be comprehended at once; they are drawn from that ocean of meditations which, as years advance, swells and evermore deepens around every thinking person. Allow me to add yet something more, which I wrote on another occasion, but which may be immediately applied to your present pursuits:

A genuine, universal tolerance is most surely attained, if we do not quarrel with the peculiar characteristics of individual men and races, but only hold fast the conviction, that what is truly excellent is distinguished by its belonging to all mankind. To such intercourse and mutual recognition, the German people have long contributed.

Whoever understands and studies German finds himself in the market, where all nations

offer their wares ; he plays the interpreter, while
he enriches himself.

And thus every translator is to be regarded
as a middle-man in this universal spiritual commerce, and as making it his business to promote
this exchange : for say what we may of the insufficiency of translation, yet the work is and
will always be one of the weightiest and worthiest
affairs in the general concerns of the world.

The Koran says : " God has given to each
people a prophet in its own tongue !" Thus each
translator is a prophet to his people.   Luther's
translation of the Bible has produced the greatest
results, though criticism gives it qualified praise,
and picks faults in it, even to the present day.
What indeed is the whole enormous business
of the Bible Society, but to make known the
Gospel to all people in their own tongue ?

Here, though one might run on endlessly on
this topic, let me close.   Gratify me soon with
some reply, that I may know the present packet
has reached you.   In conclusion, permit me also
to greet your dear wife, for whom I give myself
the pleasure of adding some trifles in return for

her charming gift.   May a happy life together
be your portion for many years.

After all this I still find myself prompted to
add a word.   May Mr. Carlyle take in friendly
part what I have written above, and by continued musing convert it into a dialogue, so
that it may seem to him as if we stood face to
face in person.

I have indeed still to thank him for the pains
he has expended on my Works; for the good
and kindly feeling with which he has been
pleased to speak of me personally and of the
incidents of my life.   Assured of this feeling, I
venture to congratulate myself on the anticipa-
tion that hereafter, if other Works of mine
should become known to him, especially if my
Correspondence with Schiller should appear, he
will not change his opinion either of my friend
or of me, but rather by many particulars will
find it still further confirmed.

> With every cordial good wish,
> in faithful sympathy,
> J. W. v. GOETHE.

WEIMAR, 20*th July* 1827.

On the 11th August Carlyle wrote to his mother
that one day not long before,

" News came directly after breakfast that the packet from
Goethe had arrived in Leith !   Without delay I proceeded
thither ; found a little box carefully overlapped in waxcloth,
and directed to me.   After infinite wranglings and perplexed misdirected higglings I succeeded in rescuing the
precious packet from the fangs of the Custom-house sharks,
and in the afternoon it was safely deposited in our own
little parlour.   The daintiest *boxie* you ever saw ! so carefully packed, so neatly and tastefully contrived in everything.   There was a copy of Goëthe's poems in five beautiful little volumes '*for the valued marriage-pair Carlyle ;*'
two other little books for myself ; then two medals, one of
Goethe himself, and another of his father and mother ; and
lastly the prettiest wrought-iron necklace with a little figure
of the poet's face set in gold ' for my dear Spouse,' and a
most dashing pocket-book for me.   In the box containing
the necklace, and in each pocket of the pocket-book were
cards, each with a verse of poetry on it in the old master's
own hand ; all these I will translate to you by and by, as
well as the long letter which lay at the bottom of all, one
of the kindest and gravest epistles I ever read.   He praises
me for the *Life of Schiller* and the others ; asks me to send
him some account of ' my own previous history,' etc. etc. ;
in short it was all extremely graceful, affectionate and
patriarchal : you may conceive how much it pleased us.   I
believe a Ribbon with the order of the Garter would scarcely
have flattered either of us more."

On one of the cards in the pocket-book for
Carlyle was written :—

Herr Carlyle würde mir ein besonderes Vergnügen machen wenn er mir von seinem bisherigen Lebensgange einige Nachrichten geben wollte.

G.

W., d. 20 Jul. 1827.

Mr. Carlyle would do me a special favour if he would give me some particulars of his previous history.[1]

On another card :—

> Augenblicklich aufzuwarten
> Schicken Freunde solche Karten ;
> Diesmal aber heisst's nicht gern :
> Euer Freund ist weit und fern.[2]

GOETHE.

WEIMAR, d. 20 Jul. 1827.

> A friend sends up a card like this
> When instant visit he will pay ;
> But this time things are much amiss :
> Your friend, alas, is far away.

---

[1] Goethe writes to Zelter, 17th July 1827 : "Pray ask of the English literary friends in your neighbourhood, whether anything is known to them respecting Thomas Carlyle of Edinburgh, who, in a notable way, is doing much for German Literature." Zelter replies that he has not been able to learn anything on the subject.

[2] This and the verse which follows on the next page are printed in the *Nachgelassene Werke*, vii. 206, 207 ; and are both there inscribed "An Madame C. . . ."

And on the third card, enclosed in a box containing the necklace for Mrs. Carlyle [1] :—

> Wirst du in den Spiegel blicken
> Und vor deinen heitern Blicken
> Dich die ernste Zierde schmücken,
> Denke dass nichts besser schmückt,
> Als wenn man den Freund beglückt.[2]
>
> G.

W., d. 20 Jul. 1827.

VI.—CARLYLE to GOETHE.

EDINBURGH, 21 COMLEY BANK,
20th August 1827.

DEAR AND HONOURED SIR—I have now the
pleasure of signifying that your kind purpose
has been accomplished. Your note of the 17th
May reached us in two weeks, by the Post;
and the much-longed-for Packet, which it had
warned us to expect, has at length, duly forwarded and announced by Messrs. Parish and

---

[1] It is a black necklace of delicate wrought iron (such as
German ladies, having given up their jewels, were in the habit of
wearing after the battle of Jena); a pendant is attached to it, with
a head of Goethe cut in coloured glass, and with a gold setting.

[2] Carlyle has roughly translated the verse thus :—

> Wilt thou, at thy mirror, smiling place
> On a neck so light, so grave a toy,
> Think that nought so well the Wife can grace,
> As when wedded Wife brings Husband joy.

Co. of Hamburg, arrived here in safety, on the
ninth of this month.

If the best return for such gifts is the delight
they are enjoyed with, I may say that you are
not unrepaid ; for no Royal present could have
gratified us more. These books with their
Inscriptions,[1] the Autographs and tasteful ornaments, will be precious in other generations than
ours. Of the Necklace in particular I am bound
to mention that it is reposited among the most
valued jewels, and set apart " for great occasions " as an *ernste Zierde*, fit only to be worn
before Poets and intellectual men. Accept our
heartiest thanks for such friendly memorials of
a relation, which, faint as it is, we must always
regard as the most estimable of our life.

This little drawing-room may now be said
to be full of you. My translations from your
Works already stood, in fair binding, in the
Book-case, and portraits of you lay in port-

---

[1] The first volume of *Goethe's Werke* bears the inscription in
his own hand : " Dem werthen Ehpaare Carlisle [*sic*] für freundliche Theilnahme schönstens danckbar, Goethe. Weimar, May,
1827 ;" and *Kunst und Alterthum* (vol. vi., 1*st Heft*): "Herren
Carlisle zu freundlichem Andenken, Goethe " (same date).

folios; during our late absence in the country,
some good genius, to prepare a happy surprise
for us, had hung up, in the best framing and
light, a larger picture of you, which we understand to be the best resemblance : and now
your Medals lie on the mantelpiece ; your
books, in their silk paper covers, have displaced
even Tasso's *Gerusalemme ;* and from more
secret recesses your handwriting can be exhibited to favoured friends. It is thus that
good men may raise for themselves a little
sanctuary in houses and hearts that lie far
away. The tolerance, the kindness with which
you treat my labours in German literature, must
not mislead me into vanity ; but encourage me
to new effort in appropriating what is Beautiful
and True, wheresoever and howsoever it is to
be found. If "love" does indeed "help to
perfect knowledge," I may hope in time coming
to gain better insight both into Schiller and his
Friend ; for the love of such men lies deep in the
heart, and wedded to all that is worthy there.

For your ideas on the tendency of modern
poetry to promote a freer spiritual intercourse

among nations, I must also thank you: so far as I have yet seized their full import, they command my entire assent; nay, perhaps express for me much which I might otherwise have wanted words for. When I try to convert these written observations "into a Dialogue," it is as if one of the *Three* [1] were speaking: and speaking not *to* the world but *for* it, to me in particular. *Helena*, also, in that beautiful new edition of your poems, I have not failed to read; a bright mystic vision, with its Classic earnestness and Gothic splendour; but I must read it again and again before its whole manifold significance become clear to me. Could mere human prayers avail against an æsthetic necessity, Faust were surely made triumphant both over the Fiend and himself, and this by the readiest means; the one would go to Heaven, and the other back to his native Pit: for there is no tragic hero whom one pities more deeply than Faust.

You are kind enough to inquire about my bygone life. With what readiness could I speak to you of it, how often have I longed to

---

[1] The " Three Reverences," in Meister's *Travels*.

pour out the whole history before you! As it is, your Works have been a mirror to me; un-asked and unhoped-for, your wisdom has coun-selled me; and so peace and health of Soul have visited me from afar. For I was once an Unbeliever, not in Religion only, but in all the Mercy and Beauty of which it is the Symbol; storm-tossed in my own imaginations; a man divided from men; exasperated, wretched, driven almost to despair; so that Faust's wild *curse* seemed the only fit greeting for human life; and his passionate *Fluch vor allen der Geduld!*[1] was spoken from my very inmost heart. But now, thank Heaven, all this is altered: without change of external circumstances, solely by the new light which rose upon me, I attained to new thoughts, and a composure which I should once have considered as impossible. And now, under happier omens, though the bodily health which I lost in these struggles has never been and may never be restored to me, I look forward with cheer-fulness to a life spent in Literature, with such for-tune and such strength as may be granted me;

[1] *Faust*, Part I. Scene 4.

hoping little and fearing little from the world ; having learned that what I once called Happiness is not only not to be attained on Earth, but not even to be desired.   No wonder I should love the wise and worthy men by whose instructions so blessed a result has been brought about.   For these men, too, there can be no reward like that consciousness that in distant countries and times the hearts of their fellow-men will yearn towards them with gratitude and veneration, and those that are wandering in darkness turn towards them as to loadstars guiding into a secure home.

I shall still hope to hear from you, and again to write to you, and always acknowledge you as my Teacher and Benefactor.   May all good be long continued to you, for your own sake and that of Mankind !

With the truest reverence I subscribe myself, worthy Sir, your grateful Friend and Servant,

Thomas Carlyle.

[In Mrs. Carlyle's hand.]

My heartfelt thanks to the Poet for his graceful gift, which I prize more than a necklace of diamonds and kiss with truest regard.

J. W. Carlyle.

VII.—GOETHE to CARLYLE.

[*1st January* 1828.]

In diesen Tagen, mein Theuerster, geht
abermals eine Sendung über Hamburg; sie
enthält die zweite Lieferung meiner Werke,
worin Sie nichts Neues finden werden, der ich
aber die alte Gunst auf's Frische wieder zuzu-
wenden bitte.   Dabey liegen fünf Bände
Kunst und Alterthum, welche schwerlich
vollständig in Ihren Händen sind; auch das
1^e. Heft des sechsten Bandes.   In dieser
Zeitschrift, welche seit 1818 langsam vor-
schreitet, finden Sie manches was für Sie und
wohl auch für Ihre Nation interessant ist.   Das
Foreign Quarterly Review, wovon zwei Bände
in meinen Händen sind, wird solche Notizen
wohl aufnehmen.

In das Kästchen lege noch einige literarisch-
sittliche Bemerkungen, und füge nur die Anfrage wegen eines einzigen Punktes, der mich
besonders interessirt, hier bey; sie betrifft
Herrn Des Voeux; dessen Uebersetzung des

Tasso[1] nun auch wohl in Ihren Händen ist.
Er verwendete seinen hiesigen Aufenthalt
leidenschaftlich auf das Studium einer ihm
vorerst nicht geläufigen Sprache und auf ein
sorgfältiges Uebertragen gedachten Dramas.
Er machte mir durch eine gedruckte Copie seines
Manuscriptes die Bequemlichkeit, seine vorrück-
ende Arbeit nach und nach durchzusehen, wobey
ich freylich nichts wirken konnte, als zu beurtheilen ob die Uebersetzung, in so fern ich englisch lese, mit dem Sinn, den ich in meine Zeilen
zu legen gedachte, übereinstimmend zu finden
wäre. Und da will ich gern gestehen, dass,
nach einiger Uebereinkunft zu gewissen Abänd-
erungen, ich nichts mehr zu erinnern wusste was
mir für das Verständniss meines Werkes in einer
fremden Sprache wäre hinderlich gewesen. Nun
aber möcht' ich von Ihnen wissen, in wiefern
dieser Tasso als *Englisch* gelten kann. Sie werden mich höchlich verbinden, wenn Sie mich
hierüber aufklären und erleuchten ; denn eben
diese Bezüge vom Originale zur Uebersetzung
sind es ja, welche die Verhältnisse von Nation

[1] See *infra*, p. 87, *n.*

zu Nation am allerdeutlichsten aussprechen, und
die man zu Förderung der vor- und obwaltenden
allgemeinen Weltliteratur vorzüglich zu kennen
und zu beurtheilen hat.

An Ihre theure Gattin werden Sie mit
meinen schönsten Grüssen das Addressirte
gefällig abgeben.

Ferner habe ich sechs Medaillen beigelegt,
drei Weimarische, drei Genfer, wovon ich zwey
Herrn Walter Scott mit meinen verbindlichsten Grüssen einzuhändigen, die andern aber
an Wohlwollende zu vertheilen bitte.

Da ich die hier übrigen Seiten nicht leer
abschicken möchte, so füge noch einige vor-
läufige Betrachtungen über das *Foreign Quarterly Review* hier bey :

In diesem gleich vom Anfang solid und
würdig erscheinendem Werke finde ich mehrere
Aufsätze über deutsche Literatur : *Ernst
Schulze, Hoffmann* und unser *Theater;* ich
glaube darin den Edinburger Freund zu
erkennen, denn es wäre doch wunderbar, wenn
das alte Britannien ein paar Menächmen hervorgebracht haben sollte, welche gleich ruhig,

heiter, sinnig, sittig, gründlich und umsichtig,
klar und ausführlich, und was dergleichen gute
Eigenschaften sich noch mehr anschliessen, eine
fremde, geographisch-moralisch, und ästhetisch
abstehende, Mittellands-Cultur liebevoll darstel-
len könnten und möchten.   Auch die übrigen
Recensionen, in so fern ich sie gelesen habe,
finde ich auf einem soliden Vaterlandsgrunde
mit Einsicht, Umsicht und Mässigung geschrieben.   Und wenn ich z. B. Dupin's weltbürger-
liche Arbeiten sehr hoch schätze, so waren mir
doch die Bemerkungen des Referenten,[1] S. 496,
Vol. I. sehr willkommen.   Das Gleiche gilt von
Manchem was bey Gelegenheit der Religions-
händel in Schlesien geäussert wird.   In dem
nächsten Stücke von *Kunst und Alterthum*
denke ich mich über diese Berührungen aus
der Ferne freundlich zu erklären, und eine
solche wechselseitige Behandlung meinen ausländischen und innländischen Freunden bestens
zu empfehlen, indem ich das Testament Johan-
nis als das meinige schliesslich ausspreche und
als den Inhalt aller Weisheit einschärfe : *Kind-*

[1] See *infra*, p. 44, *n.*

lein liebt euch! wobey ich wohl hoffen darf,
dass dieses Wort meinen Zeitgenossen nicht so
seltsam vorkommen werde als den Schülern
des Evangelisten, die ganz andere höhere
Offenbarungen erwarteten.

Das Weitere mit der in diesen Tagen
abgehenden Sendung.

Treu verbunden,

J. W. v. Goethe.

Weimar, den 1 Januar 1828.

Können Sie mir vertrauen wer den Aufsatz :
State of German Literature im Edinburgh
Review, No. XCII., October 1827, geschrieben
hat ?   Hier glaubt man, es sey Herr Lockhart,
Herrn W. Scott's Schwiegersohn.   Ernst und
Wohlwollen sind gleich verehrungswerth.

[Translation.]

About this time, my very dear Sir, another
package goes to you, viâ Hamburg.   It contains the second Section of my Works,[1] in which

[1] An edition of all Goethe's writings designated as the "complete and final" one was commenced in 1827 and published

you will find nothing new, but on which I beg
you to bestow afresh the old favour.   There
are also five volumes of *Kunst und Alterthum*,
your copy of which is probably incomplete, as
well as the first part of vol. vi.   In this Journal,
which has proceeded slowly since 1818, you
will find many a thing of interest for yourself,
and also, it may be, for your country.   The
Foreign Quarterly Review, two volumes of
which are in my hands, will perhaps accept
notices concerning these matters.

I am also sending in the little box some
further remarks of an ethical-literary character;
and I only add on this occasion an inquiry on a
special point which particularly interests me.   It
concerns Mr. Des Voeux, whose Translation of
Tasso you probably now have.[1]   He employed
his stay here in the zealous study of a language
previously unfamiliar to him, and in carefully
translating the Drama referred to.   By means
of a printed copy of his manuscript he provided

in *Lieferungs*, Sections or *Deliveries*, of five volumes from half
year to half year, till its completion in 1831.   See Carlyle's
" Helena," *Miscellanies* (Library edition, 1869), vol. i. 172.

[1] See *infra*, p. 87, *n.*

me with an easy way of revising his work, by
degrees, as it advanced.   I could indeed contribute nothing to it except an opinion, so far as
my understanding of English allowed, whether
the translation expressed the meaning that I
intended to convey in my lines.   And I have
pleasure in stating that after certain changes
were agreed upon, I observed nothing further
which, in my opinion, was likely to interfere
with the understanding of my work in a foreign
tongue.   But now I wish to know from you
what may be the merit of this *Tasso* as an
English Translation ?   It will greatly oblige
me if you will inform and enlighten me as to
this, because it is precisely the bearing of an
original to a translation, which most clearly
indicates the relations of nation to nation, and
which one must especially know and estimate
for the furtherance of the prevailing, predominant and universal World-literature.

Will you be so good as to give your dear
wife, with my kindest regards, the parcel addressed to her ?

I send also six medals, three struck at
Weimar and three at Geneva, two of which
please present to Sir Walter Scott, with my
best regards, and as to the others, distribute
them to my well-wishers.

That I may not send the rest of this sheet
empty, I add some cursory remarks on the
Foreign Quarterly Review. In this work,
which from its very beginning seemed solid
and valuable, I find several essays on German
Literature ; on *Ernst Schulze, Hoffmann,* and
on our *Stage*. I think I discern in them my
Edinburgh friend, for it would be truly wonderful if old Britain should have produced a pair
of *Menæchmi,* alike able and ready to de-
scribe in a friendly and sympathetic spirit a
foreign Continental culture, remote geographi-
cally, morally, and æsthetically from their own,
in a tone at once calm and clear, with judgment,
just moral sentiment, thoroughness, fulness,
and such other like good qualities as might be
added to these. The other articles, so far as I
have read them, I find written on a solid basis
of national sentiment, with insight, breadth of

view and moderation. And though I value very highly, for example, Dupin's cosmopolitan works, yet the remarks of the Reviewer,[1] on p. 496, vol. i., were very welcome to me. The same is true of much of what is said in regard to religious affairs in Silesia. In the next number of *Kunst und Alterthum* I propose to make friendly mention of this contact from afar, and strongly to recommend to my friends, abroad and at home, such a reciprocal procedure ; accepting finally as my own, and enjoining as the essence of all wisdom, the Testament of St. John : *Little children, love one another !* and I may surely hope that this saying will not appear so strange to my contemporaries as it did to the disciples of the Evangelist, who were expecting far other and loftier revelations.

More with the parcel to be despatched in a day or two.

Your truly attached,

J. W. v. GOETHE.

WEIMAR, 1*st January* 1828.

---

[1] Dr. Ant. Todd Thomson, in a paper on *Les Forces Productives et Commerciales de la France*, par Dupin.

Can you tell me in confidence who wrote the article in the *Edinburgh Review*, No. XCII., October 1827, on the *State of German Literature?* Here, people believe it was Mr. Lockhart, Sir W. Scott's son-in-law. Its earnestness and good feeling are alike admirable.

The article was by Carlyle,—his second contribution to the *Edinburgh Review.* It is reprinted in his *Miscellanies* (iii. 191). The indirect and unintended compliment contained in this inquiry would naturally give Carlyle pleasure. He wrote to his brother, Dr. Carlyle, on the 7th March :—

"For the *Foreign Review* next November, I have also engaged to send in a long paper on Goethe's Character generally ; this of *Helena* being only a sort of introduction. Before I quit this subject of Reviews, I must quote you the following sentence written, *mit eigner hand,* by Goethe in a letter I had from him three weeks or four ago. He says : *Können Sie mir vertrauen wer den Aufsatz :* State of German Literature *im Edinburgh Review,* No. XCII. *geschrieben hat ? Hier glaubt man, es sey Herr Lockhart, Herrn W. Scott's Schwiegersohn. Ernst und Wohlwollen sind gleich verehrungswerth.* Good !—Goethe wrote on this occasion to say that another *box* was coming for us 'over Hamburg,' but the Leith men have never yet had a ship, and do not expect one for a week yet. It contains books ; and, stranger still, two medals which I am to give to Sir Walter

Scott in Goethe's name with *verbindlichsten Grüssen !*   This
will prove a curious introduction; I will tell you about it
when it happens.   No answer to the letter written about
St. Andrews, which must have met his at sea."

[Zur Brustnadel.]

Wenn der Freund, auf leichtem Grunde,
Heute dich als Mohr begrüsst,
Neid' ich ihm die sel'ge Stunde
Wo er deinen Blick geniesst.[1]

GOETHE.

WEIMAR, 1 Jan. 1828.

On a Breastpin.

When thy friend, in guise of Moor,
Greets thee now from background bright,
I envy him the happy hour
That brings him gladness in thy sight.

———

[1] Printed in the *Nachgelassene Werke*, vii. 194.   In the
centre of the card on which these lines are written, is pinned
a small brooch (a blackened-bronze medallion of Goethe's head,
on a polished steel background, with a gold setting).   For
another verse, sent with a bracelet, which ought to have been
inserted in this page, see *infra*, p. 151.

Den lieben treuen Edinburger Gatten
Zum Neuenjahre, 1828.

Wenn Phoebus Rosse sich zu schnell
In Dunst und Nebel stürzen,
Geselligkeit wird, blendend hell,
Die längste Nacht verkürzen.
Und wenn sich wieder auf zum Licht
Die Horen eilig drängen,
So wird ein liebend Frohgesicht
Den längsten Tag verlängen.[1]

GOETHE.

To the loyal and loving Pair, at Edinburgh,
For the New Year, 1828.

When Phœbus' steeds too quickly take
To dark and cloud their flight,
The lamp of love will surely make
Full short the longest night.
And when again towards the light
The Hours shall swiftly throng,
So will a face, full kind and bright,
The longest day prolong.

------

[1] This stanza is given in facsimile, by Düntzer, who says it was inscribed in an album, which Goethe presented to Madame von Mandelsloh. It is there dated "the shortest day, 1827." See also *Nachgelassene Werke*, vii. 217.

VIII.—GOETHE to CARLYLE.

Fortsetzung des mit der Post abgegangenen Briefes.

[*15th January* 1828.]

Sehen Sie Herrn Walter Scott, so sagen Sie ihm auf das Verbindlichste in meinem Namen Dank für den lieben heitern Brief, gerade in dem schönen Sinne geschrieben, dass der Mensch dem Menschen werth seyn müsse. So auch habe ich dessen Leben Napoleons erhalten, und solches in diesen Winterabenden und Nächten von Anfang bis zu Ende mit Aufmerksamkeit durchgelesen. Mir war höchst bedeutend zu sehen, wie sich der erste Erzähler des Jahrhunderts einem so ungemeinen Geschäft unterzieht und uns die überwichtigen Begebenheiten, deren Zeuge zu seyn wir gezwungen wurden, in ruhigem Zuge vorüberführt. Die Abtheilung durch Capitel in grosse zusammengehörige Massen giebt den verschlungenen Ereignissen die reinste Fasslichkeit, und so wird denn auch der Vortrag des Einzelnen auf das Unschätzbarste deutlich und anschaulich.

Ich las es im Original und da wirkte es ganz
eigentlich seiner Natur nach. Es ist ein patrio-
tischer Britte der spricht, der die Handlungen
des Feindes nicht wohl mit günstigen Augen
ansehen kann, der als ein rechtlicher Staats-
bürger zugleich mit den Unternehmungen der
Politik auch die Forderungen der Sittlichkeit
befriedigt wünscht, der den Gegner im frechen
Laufe des Glücks mit unseligen Folgen bedroht, und auch im bittersten Verfall ihn kaum
bedauern kann.

Und so war mir noch ausserdem das Werk
von der grössten Bedeutung, indem es mich
an das Miterlebte theils erinnerte, theils mir
manches Uebersehene neu vorführte, mich auf
einen unerwarteten Standpunkt versetzte, mir
zu erwägen gab was ich für abgeschlossen
hielt, und besonders auch mich befähigte die
Gegner dieses wichtigen Werkes, an denen es
nicht fehlen kann, zu beurtheilen und die Ein-
wendungen die sie von ihrer Seite vortragen,
zu würdigen. Sie sehen hieraus, dass zu Ende
des Jahrs keine höhere Gabe hätte zu mir
gelangen können. Es ist dieses Werk mir zu

E

einem goldnen Netz geworden, womit ich die Schattenbilder meines vergangenen Lebens [aus den[1]] letheischen Fluthen mit reichem Zuge heraufzufischen mich beschäftige.

Ungefähr dasselbe denke ich in dem nächsten Stücke von *Kunst und Alterthum* zu sagen, wo Sie auch einiges Heitere über Schillers [Leben] und *German Romance* finden werden. Melden Sie mir die Ankunft des Kästchens und sagen Sie mir dabey was Ihnen sonst zu Ihren Zwecken allenfalls wünschenswerth wäre; denn so schnell bewegen sich jetzt die Mittheilungen, dass mir wirklich die Anzeige von 30 deutschen Taschenbüchern für das Jahr 1828, im zweyten Bande des *Foreign Review* ein Lächeln abgewinnen musste.

Wenn nun Bücher und Zeitschriften gegenwärtig Nationen gleichsam auf der Eilpost verbinden, so tragen hiezu verständige Reisende nicht wenig bey. Herr Heavyside hat Sie besucht und uns von Ihren Um-und Zuständen das Angenehmste berichtet, so wie er denn auch

---

[1] MS., "meines."

von unserm Weimarischen Wesen es an Schilderung gewiss nicht fehlen liess. Als Führer der jungen Hopes hatte er in unserm, zwar beschränkten, aber doch innerlich reich ausgestatteten und bewegten Kreis, glückliche Jahre nützlich verlebt ; auch ist, wie ich höre, die Hopesche Familie mit der Bildung zufrieden, wozu die jungen Männer hier zu gelangen Gelegenheit fanden. Es kommt freylich vieles hier zusammen, Jünglingen, besonders Ihrer Nation vortheilhaft zu seyn ; der Doppelhof der regierenden und Erbgrossherzogl. Personen wo sie allgemein gut und mit Freysinnigkeit aufgenommen werden, nöthigt sie durch Auszeichnung zu einem feinen Anstand bey mannigfaltigen Vergnügungen. Die übrige gute Gesellschaft hält sie gleichmässig in heiterer Beschränkung, so dass alles Rohe, Unschickliche nach und nach beseitigt wird ; und wenn sie in dem Umgange mit unsern schönen und gebildeten Frauenzimmern Beschäftigung und Nahrung für Herz, Geist und Einbildungskraft finden, so werden sie abgehalten von allen den Ausschweifungen denen sich die Jugend mehr aus

langer Weile als aus Bedürfniss hingiebt.
Diese freye Dienstbarkeit ist vielleicht an
keinem andern Orte denkbar ; auch haben wir
das Vergnügen, dass dergleichen Männer die
es in Berlin und Dresden versuchten, gar bald
wieder hieher zurückgekehrt sind. Wie sich
denn auch eine lebhafte Correspondenz nach
Britannien unterhält, wodurch unsere Damen
wohl beweisen, dass die Gegenwart nicht aus-
drücklich nöthig ist, um einer wohlgegründeten
Neigung fortwährende Nahrung zu geben.
Endlich darf ich auch nicht unbemerkt lassen
dass vieljährige Freunde, wie z. B. gegenwärtig
Hr. Lawrence, von Zeit zu Zeit wiederkehren
und sich glücklich finden, den schönen Faden
früherer Verhältnisse ungesäumt wieder aufzu-
fassen. Herr Parry hat einen vieljährigen
Aufenthalt mit einer anständigen Heyrath
geschlossen.

Fortwirkender Theilnahme sich selbst, freund-
licher Aufnahme die Sendung lebhaft empfelend,

GOETHE.

WEIMAR, *d. 15 Jan. 1828.*

INHALT

der gegenwärtigen Sendung.

1. Zweyte Lieferung von Goethes Schriften, 6-10 Band incl.
2. Kunst und Alterth.   5 Bände, des 6 Bdes 1 Heft.
3. Vorwort zu Alexand. Manzonis poetischen Schriften.
4. Der 28e. August 1827 [*Dem Könige die Muse*].
5. Hermann und Dorothea, für Madame Carlyle.
6. Ingl. Almanach des Dames.
7. Auch ein Kästchen für dieselbe.
8. Ein Päckchen für Hn. Thomas Wolley, ein junger Mann der vergnügte und nützliche Tage bey uns verlebte und in gutem Andenken steht, sich gegenwärtig in Edinburg befinden soll.
9. Sechs bronze Medaillen.
10. Fortsetzung des Schreibens vom 15n. nebst einigen poetischen und sonstigen Beylagen im Couvert.

G.

Weimar, den 15 Januar 1828.

[Translation.]

Continuation of the Letter despatched by Post.

If you see Sir Walter Scott, pray offer him my warmest thanks for his valued and pleasant Letter, written frankly in the beautiful conviction that man must be precious to man. I have also received his Life of Napoleon; and

during these winter evenings and nights, I
have read it through attentively from beginning
to end.[1]   It was extremely significant to me to

[1] Eckermann, under date 25th July 1827, says, " Goethe,
the other day, received a Letter from Walter Scott, which gave
him great pleasure.   He showed it to me to-day, and as this
English handwriting seemed to him somewhat difficult to de-
cipher, he requested me to translate the Letter for him.   It
appears that Goethe had, in the first instance, written to the
renowned English Poet, and that this Letter is in answer to
his."   (These two Letters are printed in *Lockhart's Life of
Scott*, edition 1839, ix. 92-7.)   Eckermann, after quoting a
part of Scott's Letter, and after a few further remarks upon it,
proceeds : Goethe " took notice of the friendly and hearty
manner in which Walter Scott describes his domestic circle,
which, as an evidence of his brotherly trust in him, pleased
Goethe highly.—' I am now really eager,' he continued, ' to
see his *Life of Napoleon*, which he is sending me.   I hear
so much said against it, and with such passion, that I feel
sure, at the outset, it will be striking at any rate.'—I asked
him about Lockhart, and if he still recollected him.   ' Oh yes,
very well !' replied Goethe.   ' His personality made such a distinct impression that one would not forget it so soon.   He must
be, as I gather from English travellers, and from my Daughter-
in-law, a young man of whom good things in literature are to
be expected.—For the rest, I am almost surprised that Walter
Scott says nothing about Carlyle, who has such a special knowledge of German that he surely must be known to him.—In
Carlyle it is admirable how he, in his criticisms on our German
Writers, keeps before him the spiritual and moral essence as
the chief factor.   Carlyle is a moral force of great significance.
He has a great future before him, and indeed one can see no
end to all that he will do and effect by his influence.' "—
Gespräche mit Goethe.

see the first narrator of the century taking
upon himself so unusual a task, and bringing
before us in quiet succession the momentous
events which we ourselves had been compelled to witness. The division into chapters
of large homogeneous masses makes the in-
tricate course of affairs perfectly intelligible, and
the exposition of single incidents, of inestimable clearness and distinctness. I read it in
the original, and thus it produced its natural
effect. It is a patriotic Briton who speaks, who
cannot well view the acts of the enemy with
favourable eyes; who, as an upright citizen,
desires that even in political enterprises the
demands of morality should be satisfied, who
threatens his adversary in his audacious career
of good-luck with fatal consequences, and who
even in his most bitter downfall can scarcely
pity him.

The Work was further full of significance
to me, since, partly by recalling my own past
experiences, partly by bringing anew before
me many things I had overlooked, it placed
me on an unexpected standpoint, led me to

reconsider what I had taken as settled, and
especially, also, enabled me to be just to the
opponents, who cannot be wanting to so weighty
a work, and to estimate aright the objections
which from their side they may bring against it.
Thus you see, at the end of the year no more
precious gift could have reached me. To me
this Book has become a golden net, with which
I am busily hauling up, in an abundant draught,
out of the swelling Waters of Lethe, shadowy
images of my past life.

I think of saying something like this in the
next Part of *Kunst und Alterthum*, where also
you will find some pleasant things about *Schiller*
and *German Romance.* Let me know of the
arrival of the box ; and tell me at the same time
of anything that may be desirable to you in
your work, for communication is now so rapid,
that I could not but smile to see in the Second
Number of the *Foreign* [*Quarterly*] *Review* the
notice of thirty German " Pocket-Annuals "[1] for
the year 1828.

---

[1] " *Pocket-books*," Literary Almanacs, bearing analogy to
the " Annuals " then so popular in England.

While books and periodicals are at present, as it were, uniting nations by the mail-post, intelligent travellers contribute not a little to the same end. Mr. Heavyside has visited you, and has given us the pleasantest account of yourself and your surroundings; he will no doubt have given you a description of our mode of life here in Weimar. As tutor of the young Hopes he spent some profitable and pleasant years in our, contracted indeed, but intrinsically richly endowed and animated, circle. The Hope family, as I hear, are satisfied with the education which the young men have found an opportunity of acquiring in this place. There are indeed many advantages for young men here, especially for those of your country. The Double-Court of the reigning Grand Duke and the Hereditary Family, at which they are always kindly and generously received, constrains them, by this mark of distinction, to a refined demeanour at social entertainments of various kinds. The rest of our good society holds them, in like manner, under moderate and pleasant restraint, so that anything rude or un-

seemly in their bearing is gradually eliminated.
In association with our beautiful and cultivated
women they find interest and employment for
heart, mind and imagination, and are thus withheld from all those dissipations in which youth in-
dulges rather from ennui than from inclination.
This free bondage perhaps hardly exists anywhere else ; and we have satisfaction in finding
that men such as I speak of, who have tried life
in Berlin and Dresden, soon return to us.

Moreover an active correspondence is main-
tained with England, by which our ladies clearly
prove that actual presence is not absolutely
necessary to keep a well-founded esteem permanently alive. Finally, I must not omit to mention, that old friends, as, for instance, just now,
Mr. Lawrence, return from time to time, and are
happy in taking up at once the delightful threads
of earlier intercourse. Mr. Parry has concluded
a residence of many years with a good marriage.

Desiring for myself, a further communion
in thought and work, and for what I send, a
friendly reception,   GOETHE.

WEIMAR, 15*th January* 1828.

CONTENTS OF THE PRESENT PARCEL.

1. Second Section of Goethe's Writings, 6th-10th volumes.
2. *Kunst und Alterthum*, five volumes, and first part of the sixth.
3. Preface tô the Poetical Works of Alessandro Manzoni.
4. The 28th August 1827.[1]
5. For Mrs. Carlyle, *Hermann and Dorothea*,
6. Almanac des Dames,
7. And also a little box for her.
8. A little parcel for Mr. Thomas Wolley, a young man who pleased us and spent profitable days with us, and who is held in kind remembrance; he is probably at present in Edinburgh.
9. Six bronze medals.
10. Sequel to the letter of the 15th, with some poetical and other enclosures in the envelope.

G.

WEIMAR, 15*th January* 1828.

A well-known letter of Thackeray's describing from the point of view of a young Englishman the society of Weimar at this very period, affords entertaining and curiously close confirmation of Goethe's account of it. Thackeray, writing in 1855, says:

" Five and twenty years ago, at least a score of young English lads used to live at Weimar for study, or sport, or society; all of which were to be had in the friendly little

---

[1] A little pamphlet entitled, " The Muses to their King" (see *Kunst und Alterthum*, 1827, vi., 1*st Heft*, 217).

Saxon capital. The Grand Duke and Duchess received us with the kindliest hospitality. The Court was splendid, but yet most pleasant and homely. We were invited in our turns to dinners, balls, and assemblies there. Such young men as had a right, appeared in uniforms, diplomatic and military. Some, I remember, invented gorgeous clothing : the kind old Hof-Marschall of those days, M. de Spiegel (who had two of the most lovely daughters eyes ever looked on), being in nowise difficult as to the admission of these young Englanders. Of the winter nights we used to charter sedan chairs, in which we were carried through the snow to those pleasant Court entertainments. I for my part had the good luck to purchase Schiller's sword, which formed a part of my court costume, and still hangs in my study, and puts me in mind of days of youth, the most kindly and de-lightful.

" We knew the whole society of the little city, and but that the young ladies, one and all, spoke admirable English, we surely might have learned the very best German. The society met constantly. The ladies of the Court had their evenings. The theatre was open twice or thrice in the week, where we assembled, a large family party. . . .

" In 1831, though he had retired from the world, Goethe would nevertheless kindly receive strangers. His daughter-in-law's tea-table was always spread for us. We passed hours after hours there, and night after night with the pleasantest talk and music. We read over endless novels and poems in French, English, and German. My delight in those days was to make caricatures for children. I was touched to find that they were remembered, and some even kept until the present time ; and very proud to be told, as a lad, that the great Goethe had looked at some of them.

"He remained in his private apartments, where only a very few privileged persons were admitted ; but he liked to know all that was happening, and interested himself about all strangers. . . . Of course I remember very well the perturbation of spirit with which, as a lad of nineteen, I received the long-expected intimation that the Herr Geheimrath would see me on such a morning. This notable audience took place in a little antechamber of his private apartments, covered all round with antique casts and bas-reliefs. He was habited in a long grey or drab redingot, with a white neckcloth and a red ribbon in his buttonhole. He kept his hands behind his back, just as in Rauch's statuette. His complexion was very bright, clear, and rosy. His eyes extraordinarily dark, piercing, and brilliant. I felt quite afraid before them, and recollect comparing them to the eyes of the hero of a certain romance called *Melmoth the Wanderer*, which used to alarm us boys thirty years ago ; eyes of an individual who had made a bargain with a certain Person, and at an extreme old age retained these eyes in all their awful splendour. I fancied Goethe must have been still more handsome as an old man than even in the days of his youth. His voice was very rich and sweet. He asked me questions about myself, which I answered as best I could. I recollect I was at first astonished, and then somewhat relieved, when I found he spoke French with not a good accent.

"*Vidi tantum.* I saw him but three times. Once walking in the garden of his house in the *Frauenplan ;* once going to step into his chariot on a sunshiny day, wearing a cap and a cloak with a red collar. He was caressing at the time a beautiful little golden-haired granddaughter, over whose sweet fair face the earth has long since closed too.

"Any of us who had books or magazines from England

sent them to him, and he examined them eagerly. *Fraser's Magazine* had lately come out, and I remember he was interested in those admirable outline portraits which appeared in its pages. But there was one, a very ghastly caricature of Mr. R[ogers], which, as Madame de Goethe told me, he shut up and put away from him angrily. 'They would make me look like that,' he said; though in truth I can fancy nothing more serene, majestic, and *healthy* looking than the grand old Goethe.

"Though his sun was setting, the sky round about was calm and bright, and that little Weimar illumined by it. In every one of those kind salons the talk was still of Art and Letters. The theatre, though possessing no very extraordinary actors, was still conducted with a noble intelligence and order. The actors read books, and were men of letters and gentlemen, holding a not unkindly relationship with the *Adel*. At Court the conversation was exceedingly friendly, simple, and polished. The Grand Duchess (the present Grand Duchess Dowager), a lady of very remarkable endowments, would kindly borrow our books from us, lend us her own, and graciously talk to us young men about our literary tastes and pursuits. In the respect paid by this Court to the Patriarch of letters, there was something ennobling, I think, alike to the subject and sovereign. With a five and twenty years' experience since those happy days of which I write, and an acquaintance with an immense variety of human kind, I think I have never seen a society more simple, charitable, courteous, gentlemanlike than that of the dear little Saxon city, where the good Schiller and the great Goethe lived and lie buried." [1]

---

[1] *Life and Works of Goethe*, by G. H. Lewes (London, 1855), ii. pp. 442-446.

IX.—CARLYLE to GOETHE.

EDINBURGH, 21 COMLEY BANK,
17th January 1828.

RESPECTED SIR—In addition to the valued marks of your regard already conferred on me, I have now to solicit a favour of a more practical, and as I may justly fear, of a more questionable nature. If the liberty I take is too great, let me hope that I shall find in your goodness an excuse.

I am at present a candidate for the Professorship of Moral Philosophy in our ancient Scottish University of St. Andrews; a situation of considerable emolument and respectability, in which certain of my friends flatter me that I might be useful to myself and others. The Electors to the Office are the Principal and actual Professors of the College; who promise in this instance, contrary indeed to their too frequent practice, to be guided solely by grounds of a public sort; preferring that applicant who shall, by reference perhaps to his previous literary performances, or by Testimonials from men of established note, approve himself the ablest.   The qualifications required, or at least expected, are not so much any profound scientific acquaintance with Philosophy properly so called, as a general character for intelligence, integrity, and literary attainment ; all proofs of talent and spiritual worth of any kind being more or less available.   To the Electors personally I am altogether a stranger.

Of my fitness for this, or any other office, it is indeed little that I can expect you to know. Nevertheless, if you have traced in me any sense for what is True and Good, and any symptom, however faint, that I may realise in my own literary life some fraction of what I love and reverence in that of my Instructors, you will not hesitate to say so ; and a word from you may go further than many words from another. There is also a second reason why I ask this favour of you : the wish to feel myself connected by still more and still kinder ties with a man to whom I must reckon it among the pleasures of my existence that I stand in any relation whatever.   For the rest, let me assure you that good or ill success in this canvass is little likely

to affect my equanimity unduly ; I have studied
and lived to little purpose, if I have not, at the
age of two-and-thirty, learned in some degree
"to seek for that consistency and sequence
within myself, which external events will for
ever refuse me." I need only add, on this subject, that the form of such a document as I
solicit is altogether unimportant ; that of a
general Certificate or Testimonial, not specially
addressed at all, being as common as any other.

The main purpose of my letter is thus
accomplished ; but I cannot conclude without
expressing my satisfaction at the good news
we continue to hear from Weimar, and the
interest which all of us feel in your present so
important avocations. By returning travellers
and Friends resident in Germany we often get
some tidings of you. A younger Brother of
mine, at present studying Medicine and Philosophy in München, has the honour of an
acquaintance with your correspondent, Dr.
Sulpiz Boisserée ;[1] through whose means I

---

[1] Dr. John A. Carlyle sent to his Brother extracts which Boisserée had allowed him to make from Goethe's Letters. These

have just learned that you proceed with unabated diligence in the correction of your Works:
and what especially contents me, that we are
soon to expect some further improvement, perhaps enlargement of the *Wanderjahre ;* and at
all events a Second Part of *Faust.*   In the
Wanderjahre, so choice a piece of composition
does it seem to me, I confess I see not well
what improvements are to be made : so beautiful, so soft, and gracefully expressive an
embodiment of all that is finest in the Philosophy of Art and Life, has almost assumed the
aspect of perfection in my thoughts ; every
word has meaning to me ; there are sentences
which I could write in letters of gold.   Enlargement, indeed, I could desire without limit : and
yet the work, as it stands, has the singular
character of a *completed fragment,* so lightly yet
so cunningly is it joined together, and then the
concluding chapter, with its *Bleibe nicht am
Boden haften,*[1] as it were, scatters us all into

contain high praise of Carlyle, especially of his *Life of Schiller*
and *German Romance ;* as well as an account of Goethe's
labours on the Second Part of Faust.

[1] Carlyle translates it: "Keep not standing fix'd and rooted."

infinite space; and leaves the work lying like some fair landscape of an unknown wondrous region, bounded on this side with bright clouds, or melting on that into the vacant azure! May I ask if there *is* any hope that these clouds will roll away, and show us the undiscovered country that lies beneath them? Of Faust I am taught to expect with confidence, not only a continuation but a completion, and share in the general curiosity of Europe to see what it is.

Will you pardon me for speaking so freely of what I know so slightly? I may well feel an interest in your labours such as few do. My wife unites with me, as in all honest things, so in this, in warmest regards to you and yours. Nay, your Ottilie[1] is not unknown to her; with the sharp sight of female criticism she had already detected a lady's hand in the tasteful arrangement of that Packet, not yet understanding to whom it might be due. Will Ottilie von Goethe accept the friendly and respectful compliments of Jane Welsh Carlyle, who hopes

---

[1] Madame von Goethe, wife of Goethe's only surviving son, August, who died in 1830. See *infra*, p. 247, *n.*

one day to know her better ? For it is among our
settled wishes, I might almost say projects, some
time to see Germany, and its Art and Artists,
and the man who more than any other has made
it dear and honourable to us.   We even paint
out to ourselves the too hollow day-dream of
spending next winter, or if this Election prosper,
the summer which will follow it, in Weimar !
Alas, that Space cannot be contracted nor Time
lengthened out, and so many must not meet,
whose meeting could have been desired ! Meanwhile we will continue hoping ; and pray that,
seen or unseen, all good may ever abide with you.

Trusting soon to have the honour of a letter,
I remain, Respected Sir, yours with affectionate reverence,   THOMAS CARLYLE.

X.—GOETHE to CARLYLE.

[14*th March* 1828.]

Wenn   Beykommendes   schon   vor   acht
Wochen Gewünschtes noch zu rechter Zeit
ankommt so soll es mich freuen.   Das lange
Aussenbleiben zu entschuldigen müsste ich viel

von verketteten Arbeiten und Anforderungen,
berichten und beschreiben und könnte Ihnen
doch keinen Begriff von allen den Obliegenheiten geben die sich durch so lange Jahre an
mir herangehäuft und sich noch täglich eher
vermehren als vermindern.

Ein Kästchen mannigfaltigen Inhalts, abgegangen von hier den 20 Januar d. J. von
Hamburg durch Vermittlung der Hn. Parish
den 1 Febr. wird längst in Ihren Händen und
ich hoffe gut aufgenommen seyn.

Geben Sie mi einige Nachricht deshalb, wie
auch ob Gegenwärtiges einigermassen gefruchtet.

Grüssen Sie mir Ihre liebe Gattinn von
mir und den Meinigen und erhalten mir Ihre
treuen Gesinnungen wie ich sie auch lebens-
länglich zu hegen gewiss nicht unterlasse.

Theilnehmend u. mitwirkend,

J. W. v. GOETHE.

WEIMAR, d. 14 März 1828.

[TRANSLATION.]

I shall be glad if the enclosed [Testimonial],
which you asked for more than eight weeks

ago, should yet arrive in good time.   To excuse
my prolonged delay I should be obliged to make
a long story of an unbroken chain of labours and
engagements, and, even then, I should give you
no idea of the multitude of duties that have
been heaped upon me these many years, and
which still day by day rather increase than
diminish.

A little box containing a variety of objects, which left here on the 20th of January,
and Hamburg on the 1st of February, forwarded thence by Messrs. Parish, must have
reached you long since, and I hope proved
welcome.

Let me have some news of it, and inform
me also whether my present enclosure prove
of any use.   Greet your dear wife from me and
mine, and maintain kind feelings towards me,
such as on my part I shall certainly not cease
to cherish for you so long as I live.

In fellowship, heart and hand,

J. W. v. GOETHE.

WEIMAR, 14*th March* 1828.

XI.—GOETHE'S Testimonial to CARLYLE.

[14*th March* 1828.]

Wahre Ueberzeugung geht vom Herzen aus, das Gemüth, der eigentliche Sitz des Gewissens, richtet über das Zulässige und Unzulässige weit sicherer als der Verstand, der gar manches einsehen und bestimmen wird ohne den rechten Punct zu treffen.

Ein wohlwollender auf sich selbst merkender Character, der sich selbst zu ehren, mit sich selbst in Frieden zu leben wünscht und doch so manche Unvollkommenheit die sein Inneres verwirrt empfinden muss, manchen Fehler zu bedauern hat, der die Person nach aussen compromittirt, wodurch er sich denn nach beyden Seiten hin beunruhigt und bestritten findet, wird sich von diesen Beschwernissen auf alle Weise zu befreyen suchen.

Sind nun aber diese Misshelligkeiten in treuer Beharrlichkeit durchgefochten, hat der Mensch erkannt, dass man sich von Leiden und Dulden nur durch ein Streben und Thun zu

erholen vermag, dass für den Mangel ein
Verdienst, für den Fehler ein Ersatz zu suchen
und zu finden sey, so fühlt er sich behaglich
als einen neuen Menschen.

Dann aber drängt ihn sogleich eine ange-
borene Güte auch anderen gleiche Mühe,
gleiche Beschwerden zu erleichtern, zu ersparen,
seine Mitlebenden über die innere Natur, über
die äussere Welt aufzuklären, zu zeigen woher
die Widersprüche kommen, wie sie zu vermeiden und auszugleichen sind. Dabey aber
gesteht er dass dem allen ungeachtet im Laufe
des Lebens sowohl Aeusseres als Inneres unablässig im Conflict befangen bleibe und wie
man sich deshalb rüsten müsse täglich solchen
Kampf wiederholt zu bestehen.

Wie sich nun ohne Anmassung behaupten
lässt dass die deutsche Literatur in diesem
humanen Bezug viel geleistet hat, dass durch
sie eine sittlich psychologische Richtung
durchgeht, nicht in ascetischer Aengstlichkeit,
sondern eine freye naturgemässe Bildung und
heitere Gesetzlichkeit einleitend, so habe ich
Herrn Carlyle's bewundernswürdig tiefes

Studium der deutschen Literatur mit Vergnügen zu beobachten gehabt und mit Antheil
bemerkt, wie er nicht allein das Schöne und
Menschliche, Gute und Grosse bey uns zu finden
gewusst, sondern auch von dem Seinigen,
reichlich herübergetragen und uns mit den
Schätzen seines Gemüthes begabt hat. Man
muss ihm ein klares Urtheil über unsere
ästhetisch sittlichen Schriftsteller zugestehen,
und zugleich eigene Ansichten, wodurch er an den
Tag giebt dass er auf einem originalen Grund
beruhe und aus sich selbst die Erfordernisse des
Guten und Schönen zu entwickeln das Vermögen habe.

In diesem Sinne darf ich ihn wohl für einen
Mann halten, der eine Lehrstelle der Moral
mit Einfalt und Reinheit, mit Wirkung und
Einfluss bekleiden werde, indem er nach eigen
gebildeter Denkweise, nach angebornen Fähig-
keiten und erworbenen Kenntnissen, die ihm
anvertraute Jugend über ihre wahrhaften
Pflichten erklären, Einleitung und Antrieb der
Gemüther zu sittlicher Thätigkeit sich zum
Augenmerk nehmen, und sie dadurch einer

religiösen Vollendung unablässig zuführen
werde.

Dem Vorstehenden darf man wohl nunmehr
einige Erfahrungsbetrachtungen hinzufügen.

Ueber das Princip woraus die Sittlichkeit
abzuleiten sey, hat man sich nie vollkommen
vereinigen können. Einige haben den Eigen-
nutz als Triebfeder aller sittlichen Handlungen
angenommen ; andere wollten den Trieb nach
Wohlbehagen, nach Glückseligkeit als einzig
wirksam finden ; wieder andere setzten das
apodiktische Pflichtgebot oben an, und keine
dieser Voraussetzungen konnte allgemein anerkannt werden, man musste es zuletzt am
gerathensten finden aus dem ganzen Complex
der gesunden menschlichen Natur das Sittliche
so wie das Schöne zu entwickeln.

In Deutschland hatten wir schon vor
sechzig Jahren das Beyspiel eines glücklichen
Gelingens der Art. Unser *Gellert*, welcher
keine Ansprüche machte ein Philosoph von
Fach zu seyn, aber als ein grundguter, sittlicher
und verständiger Mann durchaus anerkannt

werden musste, las in Leipzig unter dem
grössten Zulauf eine höchst reine, ruhige,
verständige und verständliche Sittenlehre mit
grossem Beyfall und mit dem besten Erfolg;
sie war den Bedürfnissen seiner Zeit gemäss
und wurde erst spät durch den Druck bekannt.

Die Meynungen eines Philosophen greifen
sehr oft nicht in die Zeit ein, aber ein verständiger wohlwollender Mann, frey von
vorgefassten Begriffen, umsichtig auf das was
eben seiner Zeit Noth thut, wird von seinen
Gefühlen, Erfahrungen und Kenntnissen gerade
dasjenige mittheilen was in der Epoche wo er
auftritt die Jugend sicher und folgerecht in das
geschäftige und thatfordernde Leben hinein-
führt.[1]

J. W. v. Goethe.

Weimar, den 14th März, 1828.

[Translation.]

True conviction proceeds from the heart;
the Soul, the real seat of the Conscience, judges

---

[1] MS., "hineingefuhrt."

concerning what may be permitted and what
may not be permitted far more surely than the
Understanding, which will see into and determine
many things without hitting the right mark.

A well-disposed and self-observant man,
wishing to respect himself and to live at peace
with himself, and yet conscious of many an
imperfection perplexing his inner life, and
grieved by many a fault compromising him in
the eyes of others, whereby he finds himself
disturbed and opposed from within and from
without, will seek by all methods to free himself from such impediments.

When once, however, he has fought his way
faithfully and perseveringly through these dis-
cordant elements, and has recognised that only
by striving and by doing can he vanquish his
sorrow and suffering, that for each defect a
merit, for each fault an amends must be sought
and found, then does he feel himself at peace,
as a new man.

But then, too, does an innate good impulse
at once impel him to lighten the burden for
others and to save them from like sufferings,

to enlighten his fellow-creatures as to their
inner nature, and the outer world, to show
them whence contradictions come in and how
they are to be avoided and reconciled. At the
same time, however, notwithstanding all this,
he must confess that in the course of life, the
outer and the inner remain in incessant conflict,
and that one must therefore daily arm himself
to maintain the ever-renewed struggle.

It may now without arrogance be asserted
that German Literature has effected much for
humanity in this respect, that a moral-psycho-
logical tendency pervades it, introducing not
ascetic timidity, but a free culture in accordance
with nature, and in cheerful obedience to law,
and therefore I have observed with pleasure
Mr. Carlyle's admirably profound study of this
literature, and I have noticed with sympathy
how he has not only been able to discover
the beautiful and human, the good and great
in us, but has also contributed what was his
own, and has endowed us with the treasures
of his genius. It must be granted that he has
a clear judgment as to our Æsthetic and Ethic

Writers, and, at the same time, his own way
of looking at them, which proves that he
rests on an original foundation and has the
power to develop in himself the essentials of
what is good and beautiful.

In this sense, I may well regard him as a
man who would fill a Chair of Moral Philosophy, with single-heartedness, with purity,
effect and influence ; enlightening the youth en-
trusted to him as to their real duties, in accordance with his disciplined thought, his natural
gifts and his acquired knowledge, aiming at
leading and urging their minds to moral activity,
and thereby steadily guiding them towards a
religious completeness.

One may now be permitted to add to the
above, some considerations based on experience.

In regard to the original principle of
morality, men have never been able completely to agree. Some have considered self-
interest as the mainspring of all moral action ;
others have been disposed to consider the

desire for ease and comfort, for happiness, as
alone effective ; others again have made the
apodictic law of duty supreme : but none of
these hypotheses having been able to gain
general acceptance, it was at last found most
advisable to deduce the development of Morals
as well as of Æsthetics out of the whole Complex of healthy human nature.

We already had in Germany, more than
sixty years ago, an example of a happy success of this kind.   Our Gellert, who made no
claim to be a Philosopher, but was universally regarded as a thoroughly good, moral
and sensible man, delivered at Leipzig before
the greatest audiences, a most pure, sensible
and intelligible Course of Lectures on Moral
Philosophy, with great acceptance, and with
the best success ; it was adapted to the needs
of his time, and did not become known through
the Press till later on.[1]

---

[1] " En 1758, il [Gellert] donna un cours de morale dont le
succès fut prodigieux : ce n'était point un traité philosophique de
morale, mais une suite de réflexions, bien enchaînées et bien
présentées, sur la nature et la destination de l'homme, sur
l'importance et la beauté de la vertu ; toute pédanterie scolas-

It often happens that the opinions of a
philosopher do not influence his own time ; but
a sensible, genial man, free from preconceived
ideas, looking about him for what his time
specially needs, will communicate from his feelings, experiences and knowledge, exactly what
is required, in his own epoch, to guide youth
surely and logically into practical and active
life.

J. W. v. GOETHE.

Carlyle writes to his Brother John, from Craigenputtock, 16th April 1828 :

" Goethe's certificate arrived while I was in the country :
mustard after dinner ; which these rough feeders shall not
so much as smell !   It also is a magnanimous Testimonial,
beautifully written, and may elsewhere avail me.   The old
Sage fills a whole sheet with his *Aeusserungen ;* of which not
quite one leaf belongs directly to me, the rest being as it
were *Erklärungsbetrachtungen.*   Many things are mentioned
*wodurch er an den Tag giebt, dass er auf einem originalen
Grund beruhe, und die Erfordernisse des Guten und Schönen
aus sich selbst zu entwickeln das Vermögen habe;* a praise
which *He*, could he appropriate it rightly, ought to value
more than any Professorship in these parts.   To-morrow I am

tique en était bannie : cette manière simple et sans pretention
de science était alors un phénomène ; aussi fut-elle universelle-
ment goûtée."—*Biog. Universelle.*   This course of Lectures
was published in 1770, the year after Gellert's death.

to write to the *Weimarischen ;* for his Box also has now come to hand; with its medals for Sir Walter, its Books and Letters and verses for me ; and beautiful trinkets,—a bracelet, and the prettiest breastpin,—for Jane.   Four other medals are here for distribution ; which I think of conferring severally on Jeffrey, Wilson, Lockhart, Wordsworth ; but have yet had time only for writing to Scott, who is at present in London.   To a certainty you must come round by Weimar as you return, and see this World's-wonder, and tell us on your sincerity what manner of man he is, for daily he grows more inexplicable to me.   One letter is written like an oracle, the next shall be too redolent of *twaddle.*   How is it that the Author of *Faust* and *Meister* can *tryste* himself with such characters, as ' Herr ——' (the simplest and stupidest man of his day, a Westmoreland Gerundgrinder and *Cleishbotham*) and ' Captain ——,' a little, wizened cleanly man, most musical, most melancholy ?   Is he greater than man ; or in his old days growing less than many men ?   The former to me is unexampled, the latter incredible.   Go see, and tell us truly.   He will receive you well.—For myself, unshaken in my former belief, though Jane rather wavers, I have written forty long pages on his *Helena*, which are already printed, and will be here in a few days ; and now must commence a still longer Essay on the Man himself."

XII.—Carlyle to Goethe.

Edinburgh, 21 Comley Bank,
18th April 1828.

Respected Sir—Your letter of the 1st January reached me in due course of Post ;

G

awakening the gladdest anticipations, which, however, there was little hope of soon seeing fulfilled ; for, owing to the state of the Elbe, our Hamburg Shippers seldom sail in winter ; and, in this case, no vessel was to be expected till the beginning of the present month. A second letter, enclosing the Certificate I had requested from you, found me, some ten days ago, in the country : and last week, after my return hither, the so long wished-for *Box* did at length actually arrive, with all its contents in perfect entireness and safety. It is now my duty and privilege to acknowledge so many favours, yet with regret that I have done and can do so little to deserve them. Our best thanks are heartily yours : and with this may all be understood that could not in many words be expressed ; for feelings of such a sort are at no time capable of being rightly translated into speech. To give glad hours to those that love us, though " over the sea " must be truest happiness ; and here surely it is yours.

To Sir Walter Scott, who is at present in London, I have already written ; announcing so

delightful a message ; and even transcribing for
him what you say of his *Life of Napoleon ;* a
friendly criticism which, from such a quarter,
must gratify him highly, contrasted as it is with
the frequent censure he has had to suffer on
this head, both from foreign and domestic
readers.   Already we have even a second *Life
of Napoleon,*[1] also by a man of talent, where an
altogether opposite spirit prevails ; and which,
if I may judge from appearances, must have
been considerably applauded.   Ere long, I
expect to see Sir Walter, and present him your
Medals in person.   I know not whether you are
aware that he too is a reader of German, nay,
that at the entrance of his literary life, he translated your *Götz von Berlichingen,* to which
circumstance many of his critics attribute no
small influence on his subsequent poetical procedure.   The other four Medals I shall also
endeavour, not rashly but worthily, to dispose
of.   One, I already think of bestowing on Mr.
Lockhart, Sir Walter Scott's son-in-law, whose
love of German literature, and debts to you in

[1] Hazlitt's *Life of Napoleon.*   4 vols., London, 1827.

particular, he has omitted no opportunity of acknowledging.

And here I must not forbear to mention that Mr. Lockhart certainly did *not write* that Essay on the " State of German Literature" in the *Edinburgh Review ;* as indeed he has never written aught in that Journal, and could not well write aught, being Editor of the *Quarterly Review*, a work directly opposed to it, and Organ of the Tory party, as that other is of the Whig or Liberal. If you have not already forgotten our dim notions on the " State of German Literature," it must gratify me much to say that they are in this instance due to myself. The Editor of the *Edinburgh Review*,[1] who himself wrote the critique on *Wilhelm Meister*, and many years ago admitted a worthless enough Paper on your *Dichtung und Wahrheit*, is thought hereby to have virtually recanted his confession of faith with regard to German Literature ; and great is the amazement and even consternation of many an "*old Stager*" over most of whom this man has long

[1] Jeffrey.

reigned with a soft, yet almost despotic sway. Let it not surprise you if I give one of your medals even to him; for he also is a "well-wisher," as one good man must always be to another, however distance and want of right knowledge may, for a time, have warped his perceptions, and caused him to assume a cold or even unfriendly aspect.

On the whole, our study and love of German Literature seem to be rapidly progressive: in my time, that is, within the last six years, I should almost say that the readers of your language have increased tenfold; and with the readers the admirers; for with all minds of any endowment, these two titles, in the present state of matters, are synonymous. In proof of this, moreover, we can now refer not to one, but to two Foreign Journals, published in London, and eagerly, if not always wisely, looking ‚towards Germany: the *Foreign Quarterly Review*, and the *Foreign Review*, with the last of which I, too, have formed some connection. No. I. contained a sketch of your unhappy *Zacharias Werner* from my

hand ; and here since I began writing has No.
II. arrived, with a long paper in it, from the
same unworthy quarter, on the Interlude *Helena*,
with the promise of a still longer one, by the
next opportunity, on your Works and character
in general !   Nor am I without hope that these
criticisms, set forth with the best light and convictions I had, may meet with a certain tolerance from you.   It is not altogether, yet it is
in some degree, with mind as with matter in
this respect : where the humblest pool, so it be
but at rest within itself, may reflect faithfully
the image even of the sun.   For the rest, there
must be more *Menæchmi* among us than was
supposed ; seeing no one of those three Papers,
mentioned in your letter, was by me, and no
two of them by the same person.   That Article
on *Hoffmann* was written by Sir Walter Scott,
the two others by young men of this City, one of
them Editor of the Work ;[1] the other (Schulze's
critic), a translator of *Wallenstein*, and my acquaintance.[2]   A worthless bookseller-dispute,

[1] Mr. William Fraser, Editor of the *Foreign Review*.
[2] Mr. George Moir ; see *infra*, p. 101, *n.*

now terminated, gave rise to this division into two *Reviews*, which therefore to a certain extent, at least in the eyes of their publishers, appear as rivals; though among the Editors and writers there seems to be no quarrel; and our English readers, deriving only benefit from this competition, view it with indifference or even satisfaction.

But I must not neglect to speak of Mr. Des Voeux's " Translation " of your *Tasso*,[1] concerning which you honour me by asking my opinion. Sorry am I to be forced unequivocally to call it trivial, nay altogether unworthy. No English reader can here obtain any image of that beautiful Drama, or, at best, such an image as the rugged, bald and meagre school versions of *Homer*, may give him of the *Iliad*.

More than once I had to turn to the original

---

[1] " *Torquato Tasso*, from the German of Goethe : with other German Poetry translated by Charles Des Voeux, Esq.," dedicated to Goethe (1 vol., Longman and Co., 1827). A second edition, revised and corrected, according to Des Voeux's wish, by Ottilie, appeared at Weimar in 1833. He died before the printing of this Weimar edition was completed.

even for the meaning; nay, in some instances
the Author himself seems not to have known
it; for, *ich soll* (p. 69) is rendered by *I will*,
thus expressing a *purpose* instead of an *obligation;* and (p. 78) *erreicht* is mistaken for
darreicht and translated, not *attains* but *pre-
sents;* to say nothing of *wacker*, everywhere translated by *valiant*, which means only *kühn;* and
klug by *shrewd* (properly: scharf, scharfsinnig);
Faun (p. 60) by fawn (*Rehkalb*, probably a
misprint), and (p. 77) *meine Hand! Schlag'ein!*
by *my hand to shake*, literally and properly:
hier ist meine Hand—zu schütteln! Instead of
general observations I once thought of drawing
your attention to some single passage; for example, to Antonio's truly graceful character of
Ariosto, in Act I., to show in detail how the
fine spirit has evaporated in the transfusion, and
nothing remains to us but such a *caput mortuum*
as "source of love or child of glory," "talent's
power," "spirit forms and yet in person;"
and worst of all "in *juggle* FORMED by sportive
Cupid," which indeed is a *ne plus ultra* both in
sense and expression.   But I have already

occupied you too long with such a matter, concerning which nothing but your request could have authorised me to say one word.   In short, this translation is like our common translations from the German works ; which no reader of that language ever willingly looks into ; passable, or at least only mildly condemnable, when they deal with   Kotzebues   and   Hoffmanns ;   but altogether *sacrilegious* when they fix on *Fausts* and *Tassos.*

The *Kunst und Alterthum*, already known to me in part, I purpose to read and study from beginning to end : much surely there will be, profitable to myself ; and perhaps, as you anticipate, through me " to my nation."   Neither shall I ever cease to value this your *Testimonial*, which I keep as a prouder document than any patent from the Heralds' College.   On some future occasion it may avail me ; though for the present it was too late, and yet indeed early enough, because not even this, or any other earthly proof of mere *merit*, could have made it terminate differently.

But enough for once ! I shall again and still

again hope to hear from so honoured a Friend;
being now and ever most heartily and gratefully yours,

T. CARLYLE.

P.S.—A Captain Skinner called here lately
with your card, and delighted us by singing
Kennst du das Land in a style which might
almost have done honour to the Meister's *Artist*
on the Lago Maggiore. My wife often plays it for
me on the Pianoforte. No. II. of the *Foreign
Review*, which arrived here to-day, will reach
you in Weimar, as I hope, in a few days after
this letter. Your next letter will find me, if
directed thus: Thomas Carlyle, Esq., of Craigenputtock, Dumfries, Scotland; for after Whitsuntide [1] (the 26th of May) we go to reside
permanently on that little property of ours,
among the Mountains, seventy miles to the
South of Edinburgh. The 74th Regiment
is not here at present: yet Mr. Wolley may
be found, if in it, elsewhere, and is already
written to.

[1] In Scotland, not a church festival but a term-day.

XIII.—Mrs. Carlyle to Goethe.

CRAIGENPUTTOCK, DUMFRIES,
10th June 1828.

RESPECTED SIR—The Bearer of this is Mr. May, a Merchant of Glasgow, and my esteemed acquaintance ; who, in passing through Weimar, wishes, as he says himself, to see with his own eyes " the first man of the age."   I embrace the opportunity of sending you by him, in my own and my Husband's name, the continued assurance of our affection and grateful regard ; and am ever, with the truest sentiments, your Scholar and Admirer,   JANE W. CARLYLE.

XIV.—GOETHE TO CARLYLE.

[*15th June* 1828.]

Ihr gehaltreicher Brief vom 18 April ist zur rechten Zeit bey mir angekommen und hat mich im Drange gar mannigfaltiger Umstände getroffen.   Ich erhole mich gegenwärtig einigermassen um die dritte Lieferung meiner Werke anzukündigen, der ich wie der vorigen eine

gute Aufnahme hoffen darf.   Das Neue, bisher
noch nicht gedruckte, sey Ihnen besonders
empfohlen.

Herr Skinner ist wieder_ bey uns und
berichtet viel Gutes und Freundliches von
Ihnen und Ihren Zuständen; freylich müssen
wir Sie nun, an einem andern Orte, so lange
in unbestimmteren Lokalitäten denken, bis ein
reisender Freund uns wieder durch genauere
Schilderung näher bringt.

Vier Hefte Ihrer zwey Zeitschriften die sich
mit fremdem Interesse beschäftigen liegen vor
mir, und ich muss wiederholen, dass vielleicht
noch nie der Fall eintrat, dass eine Nation um
die andere sich so genau umgethan, dass eine
Nation an der Andern [so] viel Theil genommen,
als jetzt die Schottische an der Deutschen.
Eine so genaue als liebevolle Aufmerksamkeit
setzt sich durchaus fort und fort, ja ich darf
sagen, dass ich gewisse Eigenheiten, vorüber-
gegangenen bedeutenden Menschen abgewon-
nen sehe, in dem Grade um mir gewissermassen Angst zu machen, solche Persönlich-
keiten, die mir im Leben gar manchen Verdruss

gebracht, möchten wieder auferstehen und ihr
leidiges Spiel von vorne beginnen. Dergleichen war der unselige *Werner*, dessen
frazzenhaftes Betragen, bey einem entschiedenen Talente mir viel Noth gemacht, indessen
ich ihn aufs treuste und freundlichste zu fördern
suchte.   Ich musste Ihren Aufsatz zuerst
weglegen, bis in der Folge die Bewunderung
Ihrer Einsicht in dieses seltsame Individuum
den Widerwillen besiegte den ich gegen die
Erinnerung selbst empfand.

Desto erfreulicher war mir Ihre Behandlung
der *Helena*.   Sie haben auch hier sich nach
eigner schöner Weise benommen und da zu
gleicher Zeit aus Paris und Moskau über dieses
so lang gehegte und gepflegte Werk mir zwey
Aufsätze zukamen, so sprach ich mich darüber
lakonisch folgendergestalt aus : Der Schotte
sucht das Werk zu durchdringen, der Fran-
zose es zu verstehen, und der Russe sich es
anzueignen. Unverabredet haben also diese
drey die sämmtlichen Kategorien der Theilnahme an einem ästhetischen Werke dargestellt ; wobey sich versteht dass diese drey

Arten nicht entschieden getrennt seyn können,
sondern immer eine jede die andern zu ihren
Zwecken zu Hülfe rufen wird. Da ich mich
aber in solche Betrachtungen nicht einlassen
darf, obgleich bey solchem Zusammenstellen gar
manches Erfreuliche und Nützliche zu sagen
wäre, so habe ich einen jungen Freund ersucht
sich darüber auszusprechen mit Rücksicht auf
die unter uns geführten Gespräche.

Es ist Dr. Eckermann, der sich bey uns
aufhält und den ich als Hausgenossen anzusehen habe. Er macht die hier studirenden
jungen Engländer mit der deutschen Literatur
auf eine sehr einsichtige Weise bekannt und
ich muss wünschen, dass er auch mit Ihnen in
ein Verhältniss trete. Er ist von meinen
Gesinnungen, von meiner Denkweise, vollkommen unterrichtet, redigirt und ordnet die
kleineren Aufsätze wie sie in meinen Werken
abgedruckt werden sollen und möchte wohl,
wenn diese noch weitaussichtige Arbeit zu
vollenden mir nicht erlaubt seyn sollte, alsdann
kräftig eintreten, weil er von meinen Inten-
tionen durchaus unterrichtet ist.

Die Uebersetzung des Wallensteins[1] hat auf
mich einen ganz eignen Eindruck gemacht, da
ich die ganze Zeit als Schiller daran arbeitete,
ihm nicht von der Seite kam, zuletzt, mit dem
Stück völlig bekannt, solches vereint mit ihm
auf das Theater brachte, allen Proben bey-
wohnte und dadurch mehr Quaal und Pein
erlebte als billig, die nachfolgenden Vorstel-
lungen nicht versäumen durfte um die schwie-
rige Darstellung immer höher zu steigern; so
lässt sichs denken, dass dieses herrliche Stück
mir zuletzt trivial, ja widerlich werden musste;
auch hab' ich es in zwanzig Jahren nicht gesehen
und nicht gelesen.　Nun aber da ich es uner-
wartet in Shakspear's Sprache wieder gewahr
werde, so tritt es auf einmal wie ein frischge-
firnisstes Bild in allen seinen Theilen wieder
vor mich, und ich ergötze mich daran wie vor
Alters und noch dazu auf eine ganz eigene
Weise.　Sagen Sie das dem Uebersetzer
grüssend, nicht weniger auch, dass die Vorrede,
die eben auch in dem reintheilnehmenden
Sinn geschrieben ist, mir wohlgethan habe,

[1] See *infra*, p. 101, *n.*

nennen Sie mir ihn auch, damit aus dem Chor
der Philo-Germanen er als eine einzelne Person
hervortrete.

Hier aber tritt eine neue, vielleicht kaum
empfundene, vielleicht nie ausgesprochene
Bemerkung hervor: dass der Uebersetzer
nicht nur für seine Nation allein arbeitet,
sondern auch für die aus deren Sprache er
das Werk herübergenommen. Denn der Fall
kommt öfter vor als man denkt, dass eine
Nation Saft und Kraft aus einem Werke
aussaugt und in ihr eigenes inneres Leben
dergestalt aufnimmt, dass sie daran keine
weitere Freude haben, sich daraus keine
Nahrung weiter zueignen kann. Vorzüglich
begegnet dies den Deutschen, die gar zu
schnell alles was ihnen geboten wird, verarbeiten
und, indem sie es durch mancherley Wieder-
holungen umgestalten, es gewissermassen ver-
nichten. Deshalb denn sehr heilsam ist, wenn
ihnen das Eigne durch eine wohlgerathene
Uebersetzung späterhin wieder als frisch belebt
erscheint.

Beyliegenden Brief erhalte von dem guten

Eckermann, mit welchem ich Sie, wie schon
gesagt, in Verbindung wünsche. Er wird jede
Anfrage die Sie an ihn ergehen lassen gern
beantworten und kann Sie mit dem neusten
unserer Literatur, in sofern es Ihnen nützt und
frommt, nach Verlangen bekannt machen.

Treu theilnehmend,

J. W. v. Goethe.

Weimar, den 15 Juni 1828.

Leider überrascht uns beym Schluss dieses
Schreibens die traurige Nachricht vom Ableben
unsres vortrefflichen Fürsten des Grossherzogs
von Sachsen-Weimar-Eisenach welcher am
14. Juni auf einer Rückreise von Berlin nahe
bey Torgau das Zeitliche verliess. Ich eile
Gegenwärtiges abzusenden. Mit den Büchern
kommt noch manches zu Bemerkende.

Mit den schönsten Grüssen von mir und
Ottilien an ihre liebe Gattin, mit dem Wunsche
zu hören, dass Sie in Ihrer neuen Wohnung
glücklich eingerichtet seyen, fernere Mittheilung mir vorbehaltend,

[Goethe.]

H

[TRANSLATION.]

Your richly filled letter of the 18th of April
reached me in due time, and found me in the
midst of many pressing affairs. I am now to
some extent resting in order to announce the
third Section of my Works, which I venture to
hope will be no less welcome to you than the
preceding. Let me specially commend to you
the new, hitherto unprinted matter.

Mr. Skinner is again with us, and gives us
good and pleasant news of you and of your
surroundings. To be sure, we must now think
of you in another scene, in localities which must
be more dim to us, till some friendly traveller
brings us nearer to one another again by a
more minute description.

Four numbers of your two Journals, which
are devoted to foreign interests, are lying before me, and I must repeat that never before
perhaps did one nation take such pains to understand another, and show so much sympathy with
another, as Scotland now does in respect to

Germany.　Careful study, no less exact than kindly, continues to be manifested everywhere; and indeed I may say that I see certain characteristics of men whose significance belongs to the past, portrayed with such distinctness as almost to alarm me lest the very persons themselves, who in their lifetime occasioned me much annoyance, should come to life again, and begin anew their sorry sport.　For instance, the unlucky Werner, whose absurd conduct, combined with decided talent, gave me great trouble, whilst I was endeavouring to help him in a truly friendly spirit.　I had at first to put aside your essay about him, till afterwards my admiration of your insight into his strange character overcame the repugnance I felt at being reminded of him.

All the more pleasing to me was your treatment of *Helena.*　Here, too, you have quitted yourself in your own beautiful way, and since I received at the same time from Paris and Moscow two reviews of this long-fostered and cherished work, I expressed myself laconically in regard to them, as follows: The Scot seeks

to penetrate the work, the Frenchman to understand it, and the Russian to appropriate it.
These three have thus, without preconcerted
intention, represented all the categories of interest that may be taken in a work of art.   Of
course I do not mean that these three kinds can
be entirely separated, for each must always call
in the aid of the others.   However, not per-
mitting myself to enter into considerations of
this sort, though as to such comparisons, many
a pleasant and profitable thing might be said,
I have asked a young friend to write to you on
the subject, bearing in mind the conversations
which he and I have had regarding it.

This is Dr. Eckermann, who is living near
us, and whom I have come to regard as one of
the family.   In a very intelligent way he makes
young Englishmen, studying here, acquainted
with German literature, and I cannot but wish
that he may enter into relations with you also.
He is thoroughly acquainted with my sentiments and ways of thinking, edits and arranges
my smaller Pieces as they are being printed in
my Works, and may indeed, if it should not be

permitted me to finish this far-reaching task,
step in effectively, he being completely informed
as to my intentions.

The translation of *Wallenstein* [1] has made
a quite peculiar impression upon me. During
all the time that Schiller was at work upon it
I never left his side, until at length, being
perfectly familiar with the play, I together
with him put it upon the stage, attended all
rehearsals, and in doing so endured more
vexation and chagrin than was reasonable, and
then had to be present at the successive performances, in order to bring the difficult repre-
sentation nearer and nearer to perfection. Thus
it is easy to conceive that this masterly work
could not but at length become to me trivial,
nay, repulsive. And so I have not seen or read
it for twenty years. But now that it unex-
pectedly comes before me again, in Shakespeare's tongue, it reappears to me all at once,

[1] The translation of *Wallenstein* (Edinburgh, 1827), see
infra, p. 122, was by George Moir, afterwards Professor of
Rhetoric in Edinburgh University (died 1870).—Compare
with this Letter, Article *Wallenstein, Nachgelassene Werke*,
vi. 265.

in all its parts, like a freshly varnished picture, and I delight in it not only as of old, but also in a way quite peculiar. Say this, with my compliments, to the translator, also that the preface, which was written with the same completely sympathetic feeling, has given me much pleasure. And pray tell me his name, in order that he may stand out, from among the chorus of Philo-Germans, as a distinct individual.

And here occurs to me a new observation, perhaps scarcely thought of, perhaps never before expressed, that the translator works not alone for his own nation, but likewise for the one from whose language he has taken the work. For it happens oftener than one is apt to suppose, that a nation sucks out the sap and strength of a work, and absorbs it into its own inner life, so as to have no further pleasure in it, and to draw no more nourishment from it. This is especially the case with the German people, who consume far too quickly whatever is offered them, and while transforming it by various reworkings, they in a sense annihilate it. Therefore it is very salutary if what was their own, should, after a time, by means of a successful translation, re-appear to them, endowed with fresh life.

The enclosed letter comes from the good Eckermann, with whom, as I have already said, I would have you in communication. He will gladly answer any inquiry you may address to him, and can, so far as it may be of use or benefit to you, keep you informed, whenever you desire it, as to our most recent literature.

With faithful sympathy,

J. W. v. GOETHE.

WEIMAR, 15*th June* 1828.

Alas! as I close this letter, there comes upon us the sad news of the decease of our excellent Prince, the Grand Duke of Sachs-Weimar-Eisenach, who left this world of Time on the 14th of June, near Torgau, as he was returning from Berlin.[1] I hasten to despatch this. With the books will come various things I had to say further.

With kindest regards from me and Ottilie

---

[1] Eckermann, under date 15th June 1828, gives an account of Goethe's emotion when he heard of the death of this much-loved friend.

to your dear wife, and with the wish to hear
that you are happily settled in your new home,
reserving further intelligence,   [GOETHE.]

XV.—ECKERMANN to CARLYLE.

WEIMAR, d. 15*n. Juni* 1828.

Ihre fortgesetzten Bestrebungen und Ver-
dienste um die deutsche Literatur, mein theurer
und hochgeschätzter Herr Carlyle, haben schon
längst in mir den Wunsch entstehen lassen, eine
Gelegenheit zu finden meine Gesinnungen der
Zuneigung und Hochachtung gegen Sie auszusprechen, und es macht mich besonders glücklich, dass Se. Excellenz von Goethe mich jetzt
dazu auffordern.

Ganz frisch leben Sie in unserem Andenken
durch ihre Beurtheilung der Helena, wie uns
solche No. II. des *Foreign Review* überbracht
hat ; und ich kann nicht umhin zu sagen, dass
ich nicht leicht über einen literarischen Gegenstand grössere Freude empfunden habe als
eben bey Lesung dieser Beurtheilung und der
besonders trefflichen Uebersetzung.

Ein geistreicher Artikel im französischen
Globe war das Erste was von Bedeutung über
die Helena erschien ; sodann folgte das Urtheil
eines jungen russischen Dichters zu Moskau,
welches man gleichfalls sehr zu schätzen hatte.
Sie Selbst nun gehen weiter, sowohl durch
höheren Ernst als tiefere Gründlichkeit, woraus
denn ein klares und weiteres Detail entstanden,
während jene nur im Allgemeinen geblieben
sind.

Man könnte verlockt werden Ihrer Darstellung im Einzelnen zu folgen und sich mit
Ihnen schrittweise darüber zu besprechen,
wenn dieses nicht über die Gränzen eines
Briefes hinausgínge. Ich behalte mir daher
vor meine Ansichten über die Helena und
ihre Französischen, Russischen und Englischen
Beurtheiler, mit Einflechtung dessen was über
diesen wichtigen Gegenstand in Gesprächen
mit Goethe vorgekommen, in einer besonderen
Schrift niederzulegen und Ihnen zukommen zu
lassen, während ich jetzt nur flüchtig sage was
mir zunächst am Herzen liegt.

Ihre Uebersetzung, die mit dem Original in

Rhythmus und Treue des Ausdruckes völlig
gleichen Schritt geht, hat mir zuerst die Ueberzeugung gegeben, dass es möglich sey den
Faust in einer fremden Sprache vollkommen
wiederzugeben. Es erfordert dieses freylich das
tiefste Verständniss des Originals, verbunden
mit nicht geringen eigenen poetischen Kräften
und technischen Gewandheiten; aber Ihre
mitgetheilten Proben der Helena beweisen,
dass Sie alle diese Erfordernisse in hohem
Grade besitzen, indem Sie sowohl in der alt-
griechischen wie in der romantischen Gesin-
nungs- und verschiedenen poetischen Form-
Weise, sich gleich bewundernswürdig zu finden
und zu schicken gewusst. Ich hoffe Sie haben
die Helena ganz übersetzt, und werden auch so
mit der Fortsetzung des neuen Faust thun,
sowie auch der alte Theil, den Sie so gut
verstanden, sicher keinen besseren Uebersetzer
finden wird als eben Sie. Durch den Versuch
des Lord Leveson Gower hat England von
dem gedachten deutschen Werk einen höchst
unvollkommenen Begriff und es wäre zu
wünschen, dass diesem Mangel durch eine *gute*

Uebersetzung, wie sie von Ihnen zu erwarten
wäre, abgeholfen würde.

Vieles, was ich Ihnen noch in Bezug auf
Goethe zu sagen hätte, unterdrücke ich für
heute. Sie werden in Ihren Studien fortgehen
und England wird es Ihnen zu danken haben.
Wer einmal von Seinem Geiste ergriffen worden,
kommt nicht wieder los und so brauche ich
Ihnen nichts weiter zu sagen.

Herr Fraser in London, der die Güte gehabt
mir das *Foreign Review* und allerliebste Bijou
durch Hrn. Black zu übersenden, schreibt mir
von einer kleinen Reise die er zu Ihnen zu
machen im Begriff sey. Ich bitte um einen
Gruss wenn Sie ihn sehen oder ihm schreiben
sollten.

Ich hoffe bald von Ihnen direct zu hören wie
Sie Sich auf Ihrem neuen Landsitz eingerichtet
haben. Ihrer liebenswürdigen Gemalin, von
der ich oft gehört, sende ich meine besten
Grüsse und Wünsche.

Ganz der Ihrige,

ECKERMANN.

[TRANSLATION.]

WEIMAR, 15*th June* 1828.

Your continued efforts and services in behalf
of German Literature, my dear and much honoured Mr. Carlyle, led me long since to desire
an opportunity of expressing to you my feelings
of goodwill and respect, and it gives me special
pleasure that his Excellency von Goethe now
calls on me to do so.

You live much in our thoughts at this
moment, through your criticism of *Helena*,
which the second number of the *Foreign Review* has brought to us, and I cannot refrain
from saying, that I have seldom experienced
greater pleasure in any literary matter than in
reading this critique and your singularly excellent translations.

A clever article in the French *Globe* was
the first one of importance that appeared concerning *Helena*. Then followed the judgment
of a young Russian poet at Moscow, in which
also there was much of value. But you go

further, with deeper earnestness, as well as greater thoroughness of treatment, which results in clear and ample detail, while the others have dealt only in generalities. One might be tempted to follow your exposition in its particulars, and to discuss them with you step by step, would not this far exceed the limits of a letter. I intend therefore to write out in a special essay my opinions in regard to *Helena* and its French, Russian, and English critics, interweaving with them what has passed on this important subject in my conversations with Goethe, and to send it to you, meanwhile only saying hastily what I have most at heart.

Your translation, which keeps perfect step with the original in rhythm and fidelity of expression, has for the first time convinced me that it may be possible to render *Faust* perfectly in a foreign language. This certainly demands the deepest understanding of the original, with no small poetic power, and technical dexterity of one's own, but the portions of *Helena* which you give prove that you possess all these requisites in a high degree, for

you have succeeded marvellously in accommo-
dating and adapting yourself alike to the ancient
Greek and to the Romantic model of thought,
and to their characteristic poetic forms.   I
hope you have translated the whole of *Helena*
and will proceed to do the like with the re-
mainder of the new *Faust;* the old part, too,
which you so well understand, can, I am sure,
find no better translator than yourself.   Lord
Leveson-Gower's attempt has given England
a most imperfect conception of the German
work, and it is greatly to be desired that this
want should be supplied by a *good* translation,
such as might be expected from you.

Much that I had to say to you in respect to
Goethe, I suppress for to-day.   You will go on
prospering in your studies, and England will
owe you gratitude for them.   Whoever is once
taken possession of by *his* spirit, never escapes
from it, and therefore I need here say nothing
further.

Mr. Fraser, of London, who had the goodness to send me, by Mr. Black, the *Foreign
Review* and the charming *Bijou*, writes me of a

little journey he is intending to make to you.
Please give him my compliments when you see
or write to him.

I hope soon to hear direct from you how
you have settled yourself in your new home
in the country. To your amiable lady, of
whom I have often heard, I send my best
regards and wishes.

Truly yours,

ECKERMANN.

XVI.—GOETHE to CARLYLE.

(Fortsetzung des vorigen Briefs.)

Ottilie grüsst Madame Carlyle zum aller-
schönsten ; sie und ihre Schwester haben eine
Stickerey angefangen, welche mit diesem Transport fortgehen sollte. Diese freundliche Arbeit
durch nothwendige Badereisen und nun durch
das traurigste Ereigniss unterbrochen, soll, hoff'
ich, obgleich später, in anmuthiger Vollendung
dort eintreffen.

Der dritten Lieferung meiner Werke lege
auch das neuste Stück von Kunst und Alter-

thum bey ; Sie werden daraus ersehen, dass
wir Deutsche gleichfalls im Fall sind uns mit
fremden Literaturen zu beschäftigen. Wie
durch Schnellposten und Dampfschiffe rücken
auch durch Tages, Wochen und Monats-Schrif-
ten die Nationen mehr an einander und ich
werde, so lang es mir vergönnt ist, meine
Aufmerksamkeit besonders auch auf diesen
wechselseitigen Austausch zu wenden haben.
Doch hierüber möchte in der Folge noch
manches zu besprechen seyn ; Ihre Bemü-
hungen kommen zeitig genug zu uns, den
unsrigen sind auch schnellere Wege gebahnt ;
lassen Sie uns der eröffneten Communikation
immer freyer gebrauchen, besonders geben Sie
mir zunächst einen hinlänglichen Begriff von
Ihrem gegenwärtigen Aufenthalt, ich finde
Dumfries ein wenig über den 55n. Grad
am Fluss Nith unfern dessen Ausmündung in
das Meer ; wohnen Sie in dieser Stadt oder in
der Nähe ? und auf welchem Wege erhalten
Sie meine Pakete da Sie am westlichen Meere
gelegen sind, wahrscheinlich noch über Leith
und dann zu Lande ? Doch wie es auch sey,

lassen Sie bald von Sich hören in Erwiederung des Gegenwärtigen.   Grüssen Sie Ihre
liebe Frau.   Ich lege diesmal wenigstens einige
Noten für sie bey.

Gleichzeitig mit dem, den 18 Juni von
hier mit der Post abgegangenen Schreiben.
Abgesendet von Schloss Dornburg an der
Saale; mit Bitte alles an mich abgehende nach
Weimar zu addressiren.

G.

[TRANSLATION.]

(Continuation of the preceding letter.)

Ottilie sends most cordial greetings to Mrs.
Carlyle; she and her sister have begun a
piece of embroidery which should have gone
with this despatch.   This friendly work, interrupted by necessary journeys to some Baths,
and now by the saddest event, will I hope come
to her, though later, in graceful completeness.

I add to the third Section of my Works the
last number of *Kunst und Alterthum.*   You will
see from it that we Germans are likewise occupy-

I

ing ourselves with foreign Literature. By mail-
coaches and steam-packets, as well as by daily,
weekly and monthly periodicals, the nations
are drawing nearer to one another, and I shall,
so long as it is permitted me, have to turn my
attention to this mutual exchange also. On this
point, however, we may yet have many things
to say. Your labours come in good time to
us ; for ours, too, quicker means of conveyance
are prepared. Let us make use of this open
intercourse more and more freely ; especially do
you soon give me a clear idea of your present
abode. I find Dumfries a little above the 55th
degree of latitude, on the river Nith, near its
mouth. Do you live in this town or in its
neighbourhood ; and how do you get my
packages ? Since you are situated near the
western coast, probably still through Leith,
and then by land ? But however it may be,
let me soon hear from you in reply to this
letter. Greet your dear wife from me. This
time I am at least sending some pieces of
Music for her.

This, of the same date as the letter posted

on the 18th of June, is despatched from Castle
Dornburg on the Saale ; but please address
everything for me to Weimar.

G.

XVII.—GOETHE to CARLYLE.

[*8th August* 1828.]

Den traurigsten Fall der uns betraf, dass
wir unsern unschätzbaren Fürsten verloren,
habe schon früher gemeldet und ist Ihnen auf
jeden Fall durch die Zeitungen bekannt geworden. Ich lege eine kurze wohlgerathene
Schrift zu seinem Gedächtniss bey, woraus Sie
den allgemeinen Verlust beurtheilen, zugleich
aber auch näher an meinem Zustande Theil
nehmen werden, wie ich mich, nach einem mehr
als funfzigjährigen Zusammenleben, bey einer
solchen Entbehrung finden muss. Manches
was ich hinzufügen wollte unterbleibt für diesmal ; indessen ist es Bedürfniss alle meine
übrigen Lebens-Verhältnisse emsig fortzusetzen, weil ich nur darin eine Existenz finden
kann wenn ich, in Betrachtung dessen was er
gethan und geleistet, auf dem Wege fortgehe

den er eingeleitet und angedeutet hat.   Leben
Sie recht wohl und lassen bald von sich hören.

And so for ever
GOETHE.

SCHLOSS DORNBURG, den 8n. August 1828.

[TRANSLATION.]

The most sad calamity that has befallen us,
the loss of our inestimable Prince, I have
already announced, and, in any case, it has
become known to you through the newspapers.
I enclose a short well-written Piece in memory
of him, which will enable you to judge of the
general loss, and at the same time to sympathise more deeply with me, in the condition
in which, after more than fifty years of life
together, I am left by the loss.   Much that I
wished to add must be left unsaid for this time.
Meanwhile it is a necessity diligently to maintain all my remaining connections with life, for
I can find an existence only in contemplating
what he did and brought about, and in going
forward on the path which he has opened up
and indicated.

Fare you well, and let me hear from you soon.

"And so for ever,"

GOETHE.

CASTLE DORNBURG, *8th August* 1828.

XVIII.—CARLYLE to GOETHE.

CRAIGENPUTTOCK, DUMFRIES,
25th September 1828.

DEAR AND HONOURED SIR—A pleasing duty, which has long lain before me, need not now be put off any longer. Both your Packets are at length in my hands; the Post-letter, enclosing Dr. Eckermann's, has been here since the end of June; the Book-Parcel, by way of Hamburg and Leith, since last night; when our servant, due notice from Messrs. Parish's Agent being given, brought it up with him from Dumfries. All was in perfect safety, Books, Music, Manuscript; and certainly a singular and most welcome appearance in this our remote home, where, it would still seem, we are not *toto divisi orbe*, but in kind relation with what we reckon highest and best there. Herr Zelter's melodies

are to be proved to-night on the Pianoforte;
and *The Poet*, as Vogel has drawn him, will
look down on us, while we listen, with a friendly
monition that if Yesterday and To-day have been
spent in wise activity, we "may also hope for a
Morrow which shall not be less happy." [1]   In a
few hours, too, I purpose to enjoy this Second
Part of *Faust ;* and explore what further novelty
these estimable volumes contain.

One dainty little article I already notice in
the *Kunst und Alterthum :* your translation of
our ancient Scottish "Schwank" as Hans
Sachs would call it, *Get up and bar the door !*

---

[1] The engraving after Vogel, which was sent to Carlyle by
his brother John from Munich, has beneath it this Verse in
lithographed facsimile of Goethe's handwriting (see *Zahme
Xenien, Werke*, iv. 337):

> Liegt dir Gestern klar und offen,
> Wirkst du Heute kräftig frey ;
> Kannst auch auf ein Morgen hoffen
> Das nicht minder glücklich sey.
>
>   GOETHE.

WEIMAR, 7 *November* 1825.

Carlyle translates it thus (see *Miscellanies*, ii. p. 313):

> Know'st thou Yesterday, its aim and reason ;
> Work'st thou well To-day, for worthy things?
> Calmly wait the Morrow's hidden season,
> Need'st not fear what hap soe'er it brings.

The manuscript version I have often read ;[1] and not without a smile that I should hear, in a strange tongue, the old rough rhymes of my childhood so faithfully rendered back by the Author of *Mignon* and *Iphigenie.* As you are curious in Popular Poetry, I might mention that Scotland is very rich in such things ; old, quaint, rugged songs and verses written with a sly humour, a sly meaning, which still, as we think, characterises the national mind. Some of these pieces have even Royal Authors : there is *The Wife of Auchtermuchty*, a far homelier piece than yours, and of a similar character, which one of our Jameses is said to have written ; as another of them did undoubtedly compose our *Christ's Kirk on the Green*, a fragment full of a still more genial humour. But of all this at some other time.

For the present, I should thank you again, had I words, for this new testimony of your friendliness. Doubtless it does seem wonderful to us that you and yours, occupied with so many great concerns in which the whole world

---

[1] Sent by Goethe in a previous letter. See *supra*, p. 20.

is interested, should find any time to take
thought of us who live so far out of your
sphere and can have so little influence, recipro-
cally, on aught that pertains to you. But such
is the nature of this strangely complected
universe, that *all* men are linked together, and
the greatest will come into connection with the
least. Neither, though it is a fine tie, do I
reckon it a weak one, that unites me to you.
When I look back on my past life, it seems as
if you, a man of foreign speech, whom I have
never seen, and, alas, shall perhaps never see,
had been my chief Benefactor; nay, I may
say the only real Benefactor I ever met with;
inasmuch as wisdom is the *only* real good,
the only blessing which cannot be perverted,
which blesses both him that gives and him
that takes. In trying bereavements, when old
friends are snatched away from you, it must
be a consolation to think that neither in this
age, nor in any other can you ever be left *alone*;
but that wherever men seek Truth, spiritual
Clearness and Beauty, there *you* have brothers
and children. I pray Heaven that you may

long, long be spared to see good and do good
in this world : without you, existing Literature,
even that of Germany, so far as I can discern
it, were but a poor matter ; and without one
man, whom other men might judge clearly and
yet view with any true reverence.   Nevertheless the good seed that is sown cannot be
trodden down, or altogether choked with tares ;
and surely it is the highest of all privileges to
sow this seed, to have sown it : nay, it is
privilege enough if we have hands to reap it,
and eyes to see it growing !

But I must refrain myself here ; one small
sheet will not hold everything ; and I have
business matters to speak of.   Sir Walter Scott
has received your *Medals* several months ago,
not through me directly, for he had not returned
to Edinburgh when I left it ; but through Mr.
Jeffrey, our grand " British Critic," to whom,
as I learn, Sir Walter expressed himself
properly sensible of such an honour "from
one of his Masters in Art."   The other medals
have all been distributed, except one, which
I still hesitate whether to send to Mr. Lockhart,

or to Mr. Taylor of Norwich, who is at present
publishing *Specimens of German Poetry*, is a
man of learning, and long ago gave a version
of your *Iphigenie* which, on report, I understand to be of a superior sort.   Further, at
your request, I must mention that the Translator of *Wallenstein* is George Moir, a young
Edinburgh advocate, who cultivates Literature
in conjunction with Jurisprudence, and promises
to do well in both, being a person of clear faculty,
and though young, without any marked deficiency or redundancy either in talent or temper.
He is a man of very small bodily stature ; from
which cause, perhaps in part, I used to regard
him rather with a sort of fondness than of
pure equal friendship : he seemed to me a
little polished crystal, nearly colourless for the
present, but in which, at some hour, the Sun
might come to be refracted and reflected in
a fine play of tints.—As to the *Foreign Review*,
you may by this time have seen a long Paper
entitled, " Goethe," which appears in No. III.,
and for which I can only ask your pardon,
knowing too well that it is a poor enough

affair.   A far poorer one on *Heyne* is to come
out shortly in No. IV., after which I know not
what, or whether anything from me, is to
follow ; though Jean Paul, Novalis, Tieck, nay,
Lessing and Klopstock are all still lying before
me.   The only thing of any moment I have
written since I came hither is an Essay on
Burns, for the next number of the *Edinburgh
Review,* which, I suppose, will be published
in a few weeks.   Perhaps you have never
heard of this *Burns,* and yet he was a man of
the most decisive genius ; but born in the rank
of a Peasant, and miserably wasted away by
the complexities of his strange situation ; so
that all he effected was comparatively a trifle,
and he died before middle age.   We English,
especially we Scotch, love Burns more than
any other Poet we have had for centuries.
It has often struck me to remark that he was
born a few months only before Schiller, in the
year 1759 ; and that neither of these two men,
of whom I reckon Burns perhaps naturally even
the greater, ever heard the other's name ; but
that they shone as stars in opposite hemispheres,

the little Atmosphere of the Earth intercepting
their mutual light.

You inquire with such affection touching
our present abode and employments, that I
must say some words on that subject, while
I have still space.   Dumfries is a pretty town,
of some 15,000 inhabitants ; the Commercial
and Judicial Metropolis of a considerable
district on the Scottish border.   Our dwelling-
place is not in it, but fifteen miles (two hours'
riding) to the north-west of it, among the
Granite Mountains and black moors which
stretch westward through Galloway almost to
the Irish Sea.   This is, as it were, a green oasis
in that desert of heath and rock ; a piece of
ploughed and partially sheltered and orna-
mented ground, where corn ripens and trees
yield umbrage, though encircled on all hands
by moorfowl and only the hardiest breeds of
sheep.   Here, by dint of great endeavour we
have pargetted and garnished for ourselves
a clean substantial dwelling ; and settled down
in defect of any Professional or other Official
appointment, to cultivate Literature, on our

own resources, by way of occupation, and roses
and garden shrubs, and if possible health and
a peaceable temper of mind to forward it.
The roses are indeed still mostly to plant ; but
they already blossom in Hope ; and we have
two swift horses, which, with the mountain air,
are better than all physicians for sick nerves.
That exercise, which I am very fond of, is
almost my sole amusement ; for this is one of
the most solitary spots in Britain, being six
miles from *any* individual of the formally
visiting class.   It might have suited Rousseau
almost as well as his Island of St. Pierre ;
indeed I find that most of my city friends
impute to me a motive similar to his in coming
hither, and predict no good from it.   But I
came hither purely for this one reason : that
I might not have to write for bread, might
not be tempted to tell lies for money.   This
space of Earth is our own, and we can live in
it and write and think as seems best to us,
though Zoilus himself should become king of
letters.   And as to its solitude, a mail-coach
will any day transport us to Edinburgh, which

is our British Weimar.   Nay, even at this
time, I have a whole horse-load of French,
German, American, English Reviews and
Journals, were they of any worth, encumbering
the tables of my little library.   Moreover,
from any of our heights I can discern a Hill, a
day's journey to the eastward, where Agricola
with his Romans has left a camp ; at the foot
of which I was born, where my Father and
Mother are still living to love me.[1]   Time,
therefore, must be left to try : but if I sink into
folly, myself and not my situation will be to
blame.   Nevertheless I have many doubts
about my future literary activity ; on all which,
how gladly would I take *your* counsel !   Surely,
you will write to me again, and ere long ; that
I may still feel myself united to you.   Our
best prayers for all good to you and yours are
ever with you !   Farewell !   T. CARLYLE.

Jane unites with me in affectionate respects
to your Ottilie, whom, in many a day-dream,
she and I still hope to see and know in her

[1] Burnswark.

Father's circle. A Brother of mine will perhaps see you in winter or spring on his way from München.[1]

Dr. Eckermann's friendly and very flattering Letter deserved a speedier reply, and shall not long want a reply, though now a late one. He is known to me by his writings and by report, as an able and amiable man ; for whose acquaintance I should heartily thank you. Meanwhile be pleased to assure him of my regard, and purpose to express it directly. Many avocations must till now be my excuse.—

Leith is still a safe place of transit for German Packages. We are but eighty miles from it ; and the Messrs. Parish seem to be the most courteous of *Expeditors*.

XIX.—GOETHE to CARLYLE.

[*25th June* 1829.]

Käme so oft ein Anklang zu Ihnen hinüber als wir an Sie denken und von Ihnen sprechen : so würden Sie gar oft einen freundlichen Besuch

---

[1] Dr. Carlyle, to his regret, could not go to Weimar.

bey sich empfinden, dem Sie am traulichen Feuer
wohl gerne Gehör gäben, wenn Sie der Schnee
zwischen Felsen und Matten einklemmt.   Auch
wir, obgleich zwischen kreuzenden Landstrassen
gelegen, haben uns diesen Winter durch tiefen
Schnee manchmal bedrängt gefunden.

Indem ich nun aber eine schriftliche Unterhaltung von meiner *Fireside* zu der Ihrigen
wende, will ich damit anfangen dass ich der
lieben Dame Versicherung gebe: Ihr freundliches Schreiben sey uns, wie der Ueber-
bringer, sehr willkommen gewesen; er ist, wie
er wohl schon gemeldet haben wird, freundlichst aufgenommen und alsobald in gute, sogar
landsmännische Gesellschaft eingeführt worden.
Uns war es dabey besonders ein angenehmes
Gefühl, dass in der Folge jemand persönlich
den weit entfernten Freunden zunächst von
unsern Zuständen unmittelbare Nachricht geben
würde.   Desto schmerzlicher war uns das Ableben des guten Skinner, welcher, nach seiner
Rückkehr, uns von den Schottischen Freunden
angenehme Nachricht gegeben hatte, und bald
darauf hier sein Grab finden musste.

Von vielen und mannigfaltigen Obliegenheiten belastet, diktire Gegenwärtiges an einem
stillen Abend, veranlasst durch die vierte Lieferung meiner Werke, die ich, nach einiger Ueber-
legung, zurückzuhalten und erst mit der folgen-
den zu senden Willens bin; denn es ist nichts
Neues darin. Erhalten Sie solche später, so
werden Sie vielleicht veranlasst, das Aeltere
wieder anzusehen und sich in Einem und dem
Andern, nach dem inzwischen verlaufenem Zeit-
raum wieder zu bespiegeln. Ich für meinen
Theil finde darin eine besondere Prüfung
meiner selbst, wenn ich ein vor geraumer Zeit
gelesenes Werk wieder vor mich stelle, oder vielmehr davor hintrete; da ich denn zu bemerken
habe, dass es wohl an seinem Platze geblieben
ist, dass ich aber dagegen eine andere Stellung
angenommen habe, sie sey näher, ferner oder
irgend von einer andern Seite.

Nun aber werden Sie freundlichst einem
Wunsche nachsehen, den ich meinen entfernten
Freunden vorzulegen pflege. Ich mag nämlich,
wenn ich dieselben in Gedanken besuche, meine
Einbildungskraft nicht gern ins Leere schwär-

K

men lassen; ich erbitte mir daher eine Zeichnung,
eine Skizze ihrer Wohnung und deren Umgebung.   Dieses Ansinnen lass' ich nunmehr
auch an Sie gelangen.

So lange Sie in Edinburgh wohnten traut'
ich mir nicht Sie aufzusuchen ; denn wie hätte
ich hoffen können, in dieser übereinander
gethürmten, zwar oft abgebildeten, mir aber
doch immer räthselhaften Stadt, einen stillen
Freund aufzusuchen ; aber seit Ihrer Verän-
derung hab' ich mir das Thal, worin [der Nith][1]
fliesst, und das an dessen linken Ufer liegende
Dumfries, möglichst vergegenwärtigt.   Nach
Ihrer Beschreibung vermuthe ich Ihre Wohnung
auf dem rechten Ufer, da Sie denn freylich
von den herandringenden Granitklippen Ihres
Ostens ziemlich mögen eingeschränkt seyn.
[Durch] die Beschauung der Specialcharten, wie
ich sie erhalten konnte, durft' ich mir wohl, als
alterfahrner Geolog, einen allgemeinen Begriff
von diesem Zustande machen ; allein das
Eigenthümliche lässt sich auf solche Weise
nicht erreichen.   Deshalb ersuch' ich Sie um

[1] Space left blank in MS. evidently for "der Nith."

eine Zeichnung von Ihrer Wohnung, mit ihrer
Umgebung nach dem Gebirge zu ; eine andere
mit der Ansicht aus Ihren Fenstern, nach
dem Thal und Flusse so wie nach Dumfries
hin. Vielleicht zeichnen Sie selbst, oder Ihre
hochgebildete Gattin, ein Paar solche Blättchen;
vielleicht besucht Sie ein Bekannter, der die
Gefälligkeit hat dergleichen zu entwerfen ; denn
es ist nur von einer Skizze die Rede, wozu das
Talent, wie man sieht [vorzugs ?][1] -weis in Britannien allgemein verbreitet ist.

Ihren Landsmann Burns, der, wenn er
noch lebte, nunmehr Ihr Nachbar seyn würde,
kenn' ich so weit um ihn zu schätzen ; die
Erwähnung desselben in Ihrem Briefe veranlasst mich seine Gedichte wieder vorzunehmen,
vor allem die Geschichte seines Lebens wieder
durchzulesen, welche freylich wie die Geschichte
manches schönen Talents, höchst unerfreulich
ist.

Die poetische Gabe ist mit der Gabe das
Leben einzuleiten, und irgend einen Zustand
zu bestätigen, gar selten verbunden.

[1] Part of word torn by the seal.

An seinen Gedichten hab' ich einen freyen
Geist erkannt, der den Augenblick kräftig
anzufassen und ihm zugleich eine heitere Seite
abzugewinnen weiss.   Leider konnt' ich dies
nur von wenigen Stücken abnehmen, denn der
Schottische Dialect macht uns andere sogleich
irre, und zu einer Aufklärung über das Einzelne
fehlt uns Zeit u. Gelegenheit.

Vorstehendes liegt mit mehrern andern
Blättern, werthesten Freunden zugedacht, unter
meinen Expediendis, kommt aber spät zur
Absendung; diesmal meldets ein Kästchen an,
welches mit der vierten und fünften Lieferung
meiner Werke zunächst an Sie abgeht.   Möge
Gegenwärtiges, so wie das Nachkommende,
Sie und Ihre theure Gattin in gutem Zustande antreffen und Sie uns bald hievon
Nachricht geben.   Alles grüsst, meine Frau-
enzimmer legen jener Sendung etwas heiteres
bey.

Treu gedenckend,

J. W. v. GOETHE.

WEIMAR, d. 25 Juni 1829.

[TRANSLATION.]

Were an echo to reach you as often as we think and speak of you, you would very often be aware of a friendly presence to whom you would gladly give audience at your kindly fireside, when the snow is driving over rocks and fields. Even we, although situated between cross roads, have found ourselves this winter frequently impeded by deep snow. But now, since I am addressing a written conversation from my " fireside " to yours, let me begin it by assuring your dear lady that her friendly letter was very welcome to us, as well as its bearer. He has been, as indeed he will already have told you, received in the most friendly way, and introduced at once into good society, and even into that of compatriots. It was also specially pleasant to us to feel that, in days to come, some one would give to our far-distant friends direct and personal news of us and of our surroundings. And this makes still sadder to us the decease of good

Skinner, who on his return had given us
pleasant news of our Scotch friends, and soon
after, was to find his grave here.

Wearied with my manifold onerous duties, I
am dictating this on a quiet evening, prompted
to do so by the Fourth Section of my Works,
which, however, after some deliberation, I am of
a mind to keep back, and to send only with the
following Section, for there is nothing new in
it. When you receive it by and by, you will
perhaps be induced to look again at the older
pieces, and reflect yourself anew in one and
another, after the intervening period of time.
For my part I find it a special test of myself,
when I again set before me a book read long
ago, or rather put myself before it, for I cannot but observe that it, indeed, has remained
in its place, while I, on the other hand, have
taken up a different position towards it, perhaps
nearer, or farther from it, or even on another
side.

And now I pray you indulge me in a wish I
am wont to express to distant friends. When
I visit them in my thoughts, I do not like to

let my imagination wander in space. I therefore beg for myself a drawing, a sketch of their
dwelling, and its surroundings. And so I am
now addressing a like request to you.

As long as you were living in Edinburgh
I did not venture to seek you out, for how
could I hope, in that becastled town (which,
spite of many descriptions, always perplexes
me), to find out a quiet friend. But since
your change of abode I have figured to myself
as far as possible the Valley through which [the
Nith] flows, with Dumfries lying on its left bank.
From your description I suppose your dwelling
to be on the right bank, for you certainly would
be much hemmed in by the close-approach-
ing granite cliffs on the east. The inspection
of such local maps as I could obtain gives
me, an old hand at geology, some general
notion of the environment, but the precise
locality cannot be got at in this way. Therefore I ask of you a drawing of your house,
with its immediate surroundings towards the
mountains, and another of the view from your
windows towards the valley and the river, in

the direction of Dumfries.   Perhaps you or
your accomplished wife will make these two
drawings, or perhaps an acquaintance may visit
you, who will have the kindness to make them ;
for it is only a question of sketching, ability in
which, as one sees, [especially] in Great Britain,
is very general.

With your countryman Burns, who if he
were still living would be your neighbour, I
am sufficiently acquainted to prize him.   The
mention of him in your letter leads me to take
up his poems again, and especially to read once
more the story of his life, which truly, like
the history of many a fair genius, is extremely
sad.

The poetic gift is indeed seldom united with
the gift of managing life, and making good any
adequate position.

In his poems I have recognised a free
spirit, capable of grasping the moment with
vigour, and winning gladness from it.   To my
regret I could gather this from a few pieces
only, for the Scotch dialect makes most of his
poems perplexing to us, and both time and

opportunity are wanting for the explanation of them in detail.[1]

What precedes has been lying, with several other sheets intended for dear friends, among

[1] Eckermann, under date 25th April 1827, reports Goethe as saying : " Take Burns for example. Wherein lies the cause of his greatness, except that the old songs of his forefathers were still living in the mouths of his people, that they were, so to speak, sung to him in his cradle, that as a boy he grew up amongst them, and the high excellence of these models so dwelt in him, that he had in them a living basis on which he could proceed. And further, wherein is he great, except that his own songs at once found receptive ears amongst his people ; they were re-echoed by the reapers and binders in the fields, and he was greeted with them by his boon companions in the alehouse. No wonder that something should come of it !

" How poor in comparison do things seem with us in Germany ! For how many of our old, not less significant songs were alive in the hearts of the people, even when I was a youth ? Herder and those who followed after him had to begin, first of all, to collect them ; to drag them from oblivion ; then they were at least to be had in libraries. And later, what songs have not Burger and Voss composed ! Who can say that they are less valuable or less national than those of the excellent Burns ! And yet which of them has become living so that the people can re-echo them ? They have been written and published, and they stand in Libraries and take the common fate of German poets. Then of my own songs, which of them is living ? One and another is perhaps now and then sung by a pretty girl at the piano, but among the common people all is silence. With what feelings must I look back upon the time when Italian fishermen sang to me fragments of *Tasso.*"— *Gespräche mit Goethe.*

my *Expediendis*, and has been, indeed, too long delayed. I now announce to you the speedy despatch of a small box containing the Fourth and Fifth Sections of my Works. May this letter, as well as what follows it, find all well with you and your dear wife, and may you soon give us news of it. All greet you; the ladies of my household are about to add something pleasant to what I send.

With faithful remembrance,

J. W. v. GOETHE.

WEIMAR, 25*th June* 1829.

" I well remember," wrote Carlyle forty years later, " one beautiful summer evening [in 1829] as I lounged out of doors smoking my evening pipe, silent in the great silence, the woods and hilltops all gilt with the flaming splendour of a summer sun just about to set,—there came a rustle and. a sound of hoofs into the little bending avenue on my left (sun was behind the House and me), and the minute after Brother John and Margaret, direct from Scotsbrig, fresh and handsome on their little horses, ambled up, one of the gladdest sights and surprises to me. John had found a Letter from Goethe for me at the Post-Office, Dumfries; this, having sent them indoors, I read in my old posture and place ; pure white the fine big sheet itself, still purer the nobler meaning, all in it as if mutely pointing to Eternity,—Letter *fit* to be read in such a place and time."

XX.—ECKERMANN to CARLYLE.

WEIMAR, *d. 2n. Juli* 1829.

MEIN THEURER HERR UND FREUND—Ihr werther Brief vom 9ten[1] Decbr. v. J. hat mir viele Freude gemacht und wenn ich ihn erst jetzt beantworte so geschieht es weil ich auf eine allgemeine Sendung von Goethe gewartet habe, die nun abgeht begleitet von den besten Wünschen unseres Herzens.

Sie leben sehr in unserem Andenken, mit Ihren Studien und häuslichem Leben, und ich denke Sie mir oft bald reitend auf die Berge, bald im Garten beschäftigt, und bald mit Ihrer theuren Gattin, Servantes [*sic*] lesend, und Goethe.

Der Artikel im *Foreign Review* III. über Goethe, hat in Deutschland grosses Interesse gehabt. Die Stücke No. IV. und V. sind nicht zu unseren Augen gekommen und wir haben bis jetzt nicht gelesen was Sie über die neuesten deutschen Theater-Dichter mitgetheilt.[2]

Ich höre von Goethe, dass er Ihnen jetzt

---

[1] May be " 7ten," has been altered, and is not clear.

[2] See *infra*, p. 142 *n.*

die Briefe von ihm und Schiller sendet, und die
neue Ausgabe der Wanderjahre. Beydes muss
für Sie von ausserordentlichem Interesse seyn.
Die Briefe von Schiller werden Ihnen über die
fortschreitende Bildung dieses bedeutenden
Mannes, sowie über sein innigstes Verhältniss
zu Goethe die merkwürdigsten Aufschlüsse
geben ; und da Sie bereits durch Ihr " Leben
von Schiller " so bewundernswürdig einge-
drungen sind, so möchte wohl niemand von diesen
Briefen einen grösseren Gewinn haben, als eben
Sie. Mir ist Schiller nie so liebenswürdig erschienen als in diesen Briefen, die immer der reine
Erguss des Moments sind, und ohne alle Absicht
das treuste Bild von dem erhabenen Character
des Verfassers geben. Goethe erscheint durch
und durch klar entschieden und vollendet, wie wir
ihn immer gekannt haben. Ich bin gewiss dass
Ihnen diese Correspondenz zu einer zweiten
Auflage Ihres Lebens von Schiller die trefflichsten Materialien liefert.

Dass Ihr Leben von Schiller jetzt ins Deutsche
übersetzt wird, ist Ihnen wohl keine neue Nachricht.

Ich könnte Ihnen Vieles über die Wanderjahre sagen; doch die herrlichen Bändchen
liegen nun vor Ihnen, reizend genug um mit
wiederholter Liebe gelesen zu werden und klar
genug um sich selber auszusprechen. Die
hinzugekommenen neuen Schätze womit das
Ganze bereichert worden, sollen Ihnen hoffentlich zu einer baldigen Uebersetzung neue Lust
geben. Das Alte ist fast alles geblieben, nur
ist es hier in einer anderen Ordnung. Haben
Sie den Muth Ihren Band in Stücke zu schlagen,
und baldigst das ganze Werk neu aufzubauen,
so wird Ihre Nation es Ihnen hoffentlich Dank
wissen. Mir ist wenigstens in keiner Literatur
ein Roman bekannt, der an Geist so reich und
an den trefflichsten Tendenzen und Maximen so
umfassend wäre. Wenn Sie an Herrn Fraser[1]
schreiben, so bitte ich ihm die besten Grüsse
von mir zu sagen.

Goethe geniesst des herrlichsten Wohlseyns
und wenn man sein frisches Gesicht, sein strah-
lendes Auge und seinen leichten Gang sieht, und
wenn man an seinem Geist und den lebendigen

[1] See *supra*, p. 86 *n.*

Worten seines Mundes noch nicht die Spur von
irgend einer Alterschwäche zu bemerken hat,
so giebt uns diess die freudige Hoffnung, dass
er noch viele Jahre unter uns bleiben und wirken
werde.

Ich werde mich freuen bald wieder einige
Zeilen Ihres Andenkens zu sehen. Ich bitte
um die herzlichsten Empfehlungen an Ihre
theure Gemalin und beharre in den treuesten
Gesinnungen,

der Ihrige,

ECKERMANN.

[TRANSLATION.]

WEIMAR, 2d *July* 1829.

MY DEAR SIR AND FRIEND — Your valued
letter of the 9th December last gave me much
pleasure, and if I am only now answering it, it
is because I was waiting until Goethe should
be sending a variety of things, which now go
to you, accompanied by the best wishes of our
hearts.

You are much in our thoughts, with your
studies and your domestic life; and I often

think of you as now riding on the hills, now
occupied in your garden, or reading Cervantes
and Goethe with your dear lady.

The article on Goethe in the *Foreign Review*
(No. III.) has excited great interest in Germany. Nos. IV. and V. have not reached us ;
nor have we yet read your article on the most
recent German Playwrights.[1]

I hear from Goethe that he is now sending
you his *Correspondence with Schiller* and the
new edition of the *Wanderjahre.* They will
both be of extraordinary interest to you.
Schiller's Letters will bring vividly before you
the progressive stages of this remarkable man's
development, as well as his most intimate relations with Goethe. And as you have, through
your *Life of Schiller,* worked your way into
this subject so admirably, there is probably no
one who could derive greater profit from these
Letters than you. To me Schiller never appeared so lovable as he does in these Letters,

---

[1] For the article on *Goethe* (1828), see Carlyle's *Miscellanies,*
vol. i. p. 233. For *German Playwrights* (No. VI. of the *Foreign
Review*), see *ibid.* vol. ii. p. 117.

which are always the genuine effusion of the moment, and give, without at all intending it, the truest picture of the author's character. Goethe appears throughout, as we have known him, serenely decisive and complete. I am sure that this Correspondence will furnish you with the most admirable material for a second Edition of your *Life of Schiller.*

That this Life is being translated into German will, I suppose, be no news to you.

I could say a great deal about the *Wander-jahre ;* but the noble little volumes are now before you, charming enough to be read with renewed love, and clear enough to be allowed to speak for themselves. The newly added treasures with which the whole work is en-riched will, I hope, give you a new desire to translate them soon. Almost everything that was already there, remains ; but is arranged in a different order. If you had the courage to pull your volume to pieces and, on this new basis, to reconstruct the whole work without loss of time, one might hope that your country would be grateful to you. I, for my part, am acquainted with no novel in any literature so full of genius or so rich in the noblest precepts and maxims.

If you are writing to Mr. Fraser,[1] please give him my kind regards.

Goethe enjoys most excellent health ; and when one looks at his ruddy complexion, his radiant eye, and observes his light step, when moreover one can detect in his mind and in the living words from his lips, no trace of any of the weaknesses of old age, we have the joyful hope that he may still live and work amongst us for many years to come.

I shall be glad to see some lines from you soon again, in token of your remembrance. I beg you to present my cordial greetings to your dear lady ; and I remain,

Most faithfully yours,

ECKERMANN.

XXI.—GOETHE to CARLYLE.

[*6th July* 1829.]

Mein Schreiben vom 25 Juni wird nunmehr schon längst in Ihren Händen seyn. Die

---

[1] See *supra*, p. 86 *n.*

angekündigte Sendung geht erst jetzt ab;
diese Verspätung aber giebt mir glücklicherweise Gelegenheit von meinem Briefwechsel
mit Schiller die ersten Theile beyzulegen; Sie
werden darin zwey Freunde gewahr werden,
welche, von den verschiedensten Seiten
ausgehend, sich wechselseitig zu finden und
sich aneinander zu bilden suchen. Es wird
Ihnen diese Sammlung von mehr als einer
Seite bedeutend seyn, besonders da Sie auch
Ihre eigenen Lebensjahre, auf welcher Stufe
des Wachsthums und der Bildung Sie ge-
standen, an den Datums recapituliren können.

Auch einen Theil der Aushängebogen einer
Uebersetzung Ihres Lebens von Schiller liegt
bey. Ist es mir möglich, so sag' ich einige
Worte zur Einleitung; doch es sind meine
Tage so unverhältnissmässig überdrängt, als
dass ich alle meine Wünsche und Vorsätze
durchführen könnte.

Kommt Gegenwärtiges noch an vor dem
28. August, so bitte an demselben meinen
achtzigsten Geburtstag im Stillen zu feyern,
und mir zu den Tagen, die mir noch gegönnt

seyn sollten, eine verhältnissmässige Gabe von
Kräften eifrig zu erwünschen, auch von Zeit
zu Zeit erbitte mir von Ihren Zuständen und
Arbeiten einige Nachricht zu geben.

Auf dem Boden des Kästchens liegt eine
Gabe, von meinen Frauenzimmern freundlichst
gesendet ; diese Wandzierde soll Sie alle Tage
der Woche (sie wird französisch *Semainière*
genannt) und zwar zu mancher Stunde aufs
heiterste erinnern. Geniessen Sie mit Zufriedenheit der Ihnen gegönnten Ruhe und
Sammlung, dagegen mein Leben, äusserlich
zwar wenig bewegt, wenn es Ihnen als Vision
vor der Seele vorübergehen sollte, Ihnen als ein
wahrer Hexentumultkreis erscheinen müsste.

Ich erinnere mich nicht, ob ich Ihnen meine
Farbenlehre gesendet habe ; es ist ausser dem
Naturwissenschaftlichen doch so manches Allgemeine und Menschliche darin das Ihnen zusagen
müsste. Besitzen Sie dieses Werk nicht, so sende
es allernächst ; bitte um Nachricht darüber.

Und so fort an !

GOETHE.

WEIMAR, den 6 Juli 1829.

EIN GLEICHNISS.

Jüngst pflückt' ich einen Wiesenstraus
Trug ihn gedankenvoll nach Haus ;
Da hatten von der warmen Hand
Die Kronen sich alle zur Erde gewandt.
Ich setzte sie in frisches Glas ;
Und welch ein Wunder war mir das !
Die Köpfchen hoben sich empor,
Die Blätterstengel im grünen Flor ;
Und allzusammen so gesund
Als stünden sie noch auf Muttergrund.

So war mir's als ich wundersam
Mein Lied in fremder Sprache vernahm.[1]

[TRANSLATION.]

My communication of the 25th of June
will long ere this have come to hand. The
parcel announced in it is only now being despatched ; this delay, however, is fortunate, since
it gives me the opportunity of sending also
the first parts of my Correspondence with
Schiller. In it you will discern two friends,
who, setting out from altogether different
sides, seek to come to a reciprocal understand-

---

[1] Printed in the *Nachgelassene Werke*, vi. 150.

ing, and to elevate and instruct each other. This collection will be interesting to you on more sides than one ; but particularly because it will enable you to review the course of your own life, and to compare by the dates what your own stage of growth and culture was at a like age.

A part of the final proof-sheets of a translation of your *Life of Schiller* is also enclosed. If possible, I shall say some words by way of introduction ; but my days are so very much interrupted and obstructed that I cannot carry out all my wishes and intentions.

If this present letter should reach you before the 28th of August I beg you on that date quietly to keep my eightieth birthday, and earnestly to wish for me that in the days which may still be granted to me, a measure of strength may be given in proportion. I pray you also to give me news from time to time as to how you are situated and as to your work.

At the bottom of the little box there is lying a gift sent by the ladies of my family, with the friendliest feelings. This wall-ornament (called

in French a *semainière*) is to remind you pleas-
antly of us every day of the week, and indeed
at many an hour of the day. Contentedly enjoy
the composure and consistency which have been
granted to you ; my life, though indeed there is
little outward agitation in it, must appear, if a
vision of it should ever cross your mind, a veritable witches' circle of tumult in comparison.

I do not remember whether I have sent you
my *Farbenlehre*. Besides what relates to Natural
Philosophy, there is so much of general and
human interest in it that it cannot fail to please
you.   If you do not possess this work, I will
send it next time.   Pray inform me as to this.

And so for ever !

GOETHE.

WEIMAR, *6th July* 1829.

A COMPARISON.

Lately I gathered a nosegay in the fields, and musing
bore it home ; but held in my warm hand, the blossoms
had all drooped earthward.   I put them into fresh water,
and what a wonder did I then behold !   The little heads
lifted themselves up, so, too, the leafy stalks in their verdant
beauty ; and they were all as fresh as if still in their mother
earth.

The same feeling was mine when I wondering listened to my song in a foreign tongue.

———

[Zum Armband.]

Dies fessle deine rechte Hand
Die du dem Freund vertrauet;
Auch dencke dess der fern im Land
Nach Euch mit Liebe schauet.[1]

G.

With the Bracelet.

Clasp this around thy fair right hand
Which now the favour'd friend rewards;
Bethink thee, too, in foreign land
Of him who you with love regards.

———

Edle deutsche Häuslichkeit
Ueber's Meer gesendet,
Wo sich still in Thätigkeit
Häuslich Glück vollendet.[2]

Noble German housewif'ry
Across the sea is brought,
Where in peaceful industry
Household joy is wrought.

---

[1] *Nachgelassene Werke,* vii. 194. The bracelet is of various-coloured polished pebbles, bound together with gold. These lines ought to have been given on p. 46.

[2] *Nachgelassene Werke,* vii. 208.

XXII.—CARLYLE to GOETHE.

CRAIGENPUTTOCK, DUMFRIES,
3*d November* 1829.

DEAR AND HONOURED SIR—I must no longer
postpone acknowledging these welcome messages from Weimar : your Letter, which reached
us early in September ; and the Packet therein
announced, which duly followed it, about four
weeks ago. Both, with all their much-valued
contents, arrived in perfect safety and entireness ; giving curious proof of the complete
arrangements for transport in these times,
whereby the most delicate article can penetrate
through unknown nations, tumultuous cities,
and over wild seas, from the heart of the Continent, even into these deserts ; and what is
stranger still, how a voice of affection from
the mind we honour most in this age can con-
vey itself into minds that lie, in every sense, so
far divided from it. Six years ago, I should
have reckoned the possibility of a Letter, of a
Present from Goethe to *me*, little less wondrous

and dreamlike than from Shakespeare or
Homer. Yet so it is : the man to whom I
owe more than to any other—namely, some
measure of spiritual Light and Freedom—is no
longer a mere "airy tongue" to me, but a
Living Man, with feelings which, in many
kindest ways, reply and correspond to my own!
Let me pray only that it may long continue ;
and if the Scholar cannot meet with his
Teacher, face to face, in this world, may some
higher perennial meeting, amid inconceivable
environments, be appointed them in another !

But, descending from these lofty possibilities,
accept my best gratitude for your friendly feelings, so often and gracefully manifested towards
me, which, in this prose Earth, were precious,
coming even from the commonest man. To
you, our best return is to profit more and more
by the good you have done us, to appropriate
and practise more and more that high wisdom
which we, with the whole world, have to learn
from you.

My wife bids me say that she intends to read
your entire Works this winter ; so that, any

evening, when the candles are lit, you can fancy
a fair Friend assiduously studying you "far over
the sea;" one little light and living point, amid
the boundless Solitude and Night. She finished
the *Wahlverwandtschaften* very lately, with
high admiration, and a sorrow for poor Ottilie,
which, she admits, expressed itself in "streams
of tears." Shallow censurers of the morality
of the work, who are not altogether wanting
here, she withstands with true female zeal.

To your own living Ottilie, she requests me,
however, to present her best thanks for that
beautiful gift : it hangs in our drawing-room,
admired by all for its workmanship, and to us
far more precious for the hand and the household of which it is an hourly memorial. The
fair Artist, as I understand, is ere long to be
thanked more specially, and in due form, by
the receiver herself.

With my own share of the packet I feel not
less contented. Especially glad was I to find my
old favourite the *Wanderjahre* so considerably
enlarged : the new portions of the Book it was
my very first business to read, and I can already

discover no little matter for reflection in that
wonderful *Makarie*, and the many other exten-
sions, and new tendencies which that most
beautiful of all fragments has hereby acquired.
The *Briefwechsel*[1] I have also read ; and must
soon read again ; purposing to make it the
handle for an essay on Schiller in the *Foreign
Review.*   I particularly admired the honourable relation that displays itself between Schiller
and his Friend ; the frankness in mutual giving
and receiving ; the noble effort on both sides :
a reverence for foreign excellence is finely
united with a modest self-dependence in
Schiller, whose simple, high, earnest nature
again comes into clear light in this Correspondence.   The Proof-sheets of the Translation from
my poor *Life of Schiller* affected me with
various feelings ; among which, regret at the
essential triviality of the Original was nowise
wanting.   I wrote the little book honestly
enough, yet under too much constraint : it has
not the free flow of a book, but the cold,
buckram character of a College-exercise.   The

[1] *Correspondence between Goethe and Schiller.*

Translation, with two or three very unimportant mistakes of meaning, seems excellently done; far better than such a work deserved.

The *Farbenlehre*, which you are so good as offer me, I have never seen and shall thankfully accept and study, having long had a curiosity after it.   Natural Philosophy, Optics among the other branches, was for many years my favourite, or rather my exclusive pursuit; a circumstance which I must reckon of no little import, for good and evil, in my intellectual life. The mechanical style in which all these things are treated here, and in France, where my only teachers were, had already begun to sicken me; when other far more pressing investigations of a humane interest altogether detached me from Mathematics, whether pure or applied.[1]   I still

---

[1] Carlyle, in 1866, wrote :—" Perhaps it was mainly the accident that poor Leslie " (John Leslie, Professor of Mathematics in Edinburgh University), " alone of my Professors, had some genius in his business, and awoke a certain enthusiasm in me.   For several years, from 1813 onwards (perhaps seven in *all*), ' Geometry ' shone before me as undoubtedly the noblest of all sciences ; and I prosecuted it (or mathematics generally) in all my best hours and moods,—though far more pregnant inquiries were rising in me, and gradually *engrossing* me, *heart* as well as head.   So that, about 1820 or '21, I had entirely

remember that it was the desire to read *Werner's* Mineralogical Doctrines in the original, that first set me on studying German ; where truly I found a mine, far different from any of the Freyberg ones ! Nevertheless my love of Natural Science still subsists, or might easily be resuscitated ; and various hints, which I have now and then had, of your method in such inquiries give me hope of great satisfaction in studying it. The *Farbenlehre*, which I think is very imperfectly known, or rather altogether misknown, in England, will be a highly acceptable present.

This Letter is full of mere business details, and yet the most essential of these is still to come. A little packet, chiefly for your Ottilie, is getting ready,[1] and will be sent off one of

thrown mathematics aside ; and, except in one or two brief spurts, lasting perhaps a couple of days, and more or less of a morbid nature, have never in the least regarded it farther."

[1] It contained, among other things, a Scotch 'bonnet' made by Mrs. Carlyle, and accompanied by the following friendly but unmusical quatrain :

> Scotland prides her in the " Bonnet Blue "
> That it brooks no stain in Love or War :
> Be it, on Ottilie's head, a token true
> Of my Scottish love to kind Weimar !

CRAIGENPUTTOCK, 14*th December* 1829.

these days : it is also to contain the Sketches of our house and neighbourhood, such as you required ; and will come most probably by the Messrs. Parish of Hamburg, whose courtesy and punctuality in such matters I have often admired.   I might mention also that Herr Herbig, Bookseller in Leipzig, is Agent for the Publishers of the *Foreign Review* (Messrs. Black, Young and Young, 2 Tavistock Street, Covent Garden, London), through whom books would reach me, by quick steam conveyance, at all seasons of the year ; yet, in truth, I know not whether with equal security, or how your communication with Leipzig may stand.

In regard to my employments and manner of existence, literary and economic, I must not speak here.   I am still but an Essayist, and longing more than ever to be a Writer in a far better sense.   Meanwhile I do what I may ; and cannot complain of wanting audience, stolid as many of my little critics are and must be.   I have written on *Voltaire*, on *Novalis*, and was this day correcting proof-sheets of a paper on *Jean Paul*, for the *Foreign Review.*   I have some thoughts of writing a separate book on *Luther*, but whether this winter or not, is undecided.

I delayed, three weeks, writing this Letter, till a proposal (from some London booksellers) of my composing what they call a *History of German Literature*, were either finally agreed upon, or finally abandoned : but as yet neither of the two has happened.   In the event of my engaging with such a work, I mean to consult with Dr. Eckermann for help ; to whom, for his friendly Letter, I beg that my thanks and best regards may be offered.

All else I reserve till the Packet go.   We shall think of you daily, and ever with Love. May all good be with you !

I remain, your grateful Friend,

Thomas Carlyle.

XXIII.—Carlyle to Goethe.

Craigenputtock, Dumfries,
22d December 1829.

Respected Sir—The Packet, which I some time ago announced, at length sets out ; with

true wishes on our part that it may find you
happy and busy, and bring kind remembrances
of Friends that love you.   The *Sketches* of our
House and its environment are moderately
correct, and may serve the flattering purpose
you meant them for ; as it is not the beauty of
the Amulet, but its mere character as Amulet,
that gives it worth.   You will like the little
pictures no worse, when I inform you that they
are from the pencil of Mr. Moir, the Translator
of *Wallenstein,* who paid us a visit in Autumn,
and promises to see us again in Spring.   In
return for his workmanship, I presented him
with the last of those four *medals ;* to which
indeed, on other accounts, as a true admirer of
your works he had a good right.   He passed
through Weimar, last Summer ; but unluckily
at a time when you were absent : however,
he purposes to return ere long, and make
new sketches from the Rhine scenery ; and
hopes, next time, to have better fortune in
Weimar.

The portfolio is of my wife's manufacture,
who sends you among other love-tokens a lock

of her hair ; concerning which I am to say that, except to her Husband she never did the like to any man.   She begs, however, and hopes, that you will send her, in return, a lock of *your* hair ; which she will keep among her most precious possessions, and only leave, as a rich legacy, to the worthiest that comes after her.   For a heart that honestly loves you, I too hope that you will do so much.

The *Cowper's Poems* you are to accept from me as a New-year's gift, the value of which must lie chiefly in the intention of the giver. Cowper was the last of our Poets of the Old School ; a man of pure genius, but limited and ineffectual ; as indeed his bodily health was too feeble had there been no other deficiency.   He is still a great favourite, especially with the religious classes ; and bids fair to survive many a louder competitor for immortality.   As his merit, such as it is, appears to be genuine, it will to your eye readily disclose itself.

I have read the *Briefwechsel* a second time with no little satisfaction, and even to-day am sending off an Essay on Schiller, grounded on

M

that Work, for the *Foreign Review.*[1]   It will
gratify you to learn that a knowledge and
appreciation of Foreign, especially of German,
Literature, is spreading with increased rapidity
over all the domain of the English tongue ; so
that almost at the Antipodes, in New Holland
itself, the wise of your country are by this time
preaching their wisdom.   I have heard lately
that even in Oxford and Cambridge, our two
English Universities, which have all along been
regarded as the strongholds of Insular pride
and prejudice, there is a strange stir in this
matter.   Your Niebuhr has found an able translator in Cambridge ;[2] and in Oxford two or
three Germans already find employment as
teachers of their language ; the new light contained in which may well dazzle certain eyes.
Of the benefits that must in the end result from

---

[1] This Essay appeared in *Fraser's Magazine*, No. XIV.
(See Carlyle's *Miscellanies*, iii. 87.)

[2] *Two* able translators, Hare and Thirlwall, of Trinity
College, both personally known to Carlyle in after years.   It
will be remembered that Archdeacon Hare was, without in-
tending it, the cause of Carlyle's writing the *Life of Sterling*.
The translation of *Niebuhr's History of Rome*, by Hare and
Thirlwall, was published in 1828.

all this no man can be doubtful : let nations, like individuals, but know one another and mutual hatred will give place to mutual help-fulness ; and instead of natural enemies, as neighbouring countries are sometimes called, we shall all be natural friends.

That *Historical View of German Literature*, which I mentioned in my last letter, is now almost decided on ; and I hope in the course of next year to offer you a copy of some treatise on that subject. My knowledge, I feel too well, is limited enough ; but from a British writer, and by British readers, less will be ex-pected. Besides, it is the more recent, and comparatively a brief period that will chiefly interest us.

Were this " Historical View " once off my hands, I still purpose to try something infinitely greater ! Alas, alas ! the huge formless Chaos is here, but no creative voice to say, " Let there be Light," and make it into a world.

Some time ago we spent three weeks in Edinburgh ; warmly welcomed by old friends ; and looking not without interest on the current of many-coloured life, which here we may be said rather to listen to than to see.   I found the Literary men of that city still active in their vocation ; and to me undeservedly kind and courteous : nevertheless, the general tone of their speculation was such as to make me revisit my solitude, when the time came, with little regret.   The whole bent of British endeavour, both intellectual and practical, at this time, is towards Utility ; a creed which with you has happily had its day, but with us is now first rising into its full maturity.   Great controversies and misunderstandings on this matter, are to be expected among us at no distant period.

For the present, you are to figure your two Scottish Friends as embosom'd amid snow and " thick-ribbed ice ;" yet secured against grim winter by the glow of bright fires ; and often near you in imagination ; nay, often thinking the very thoughts which were once yours,—for a little red volume is seldom absent from our parlour.   By and by, we still trust to hear that all is well with you : the arrival of a Weimar letter ever makes a day of jubilee here.   May all good be with you and yours!

I remain, always your affectionate Friend and Servant,   THOMAS CARLYLE.

Were it convenient, we would beg some similar *Sketch* of your Mansion at Weimar;[1] concerning which I regularly question every Traveller, yet with too little effect.

To Dr. Eckermann I still owe a letter; which I mean ere long to pay, with increased advantage to myself.   Please to assure him of my continued regard.

XXIV.—CARLYLE to ECKERMANN.

CRAIGENPUTTOCK, DUMFRIES,
20th March 1830.

MY DEAR SIR—I have long owed myself the pleasure of writing to you, and might be a little puzzled to say why it had been so long.   Perhaps my chief reason was that a certain negotiation was in progress, touching some literary

---

[1] Goethe sent an engraving of his house to Carlyle.   See *infra*, Appendix II., p. 326.

work to be undertaken by me, on which I
wished to communicate with you; and so have
waited, impatiently enough, till in the slow
course of bibliopolic arrangements, I saw what
turn matters were to take. The business, I
believe, is now finally adjusted; indeed, in a
state of actual advance; so that on this, as on
all other topics, I can now address you without
embarrassment.

It is pity that Weimar lay so distant from
Scotland; with seas, and wide regions, to us
all waste and unpeopled, intervening. No spot
on this Globe is for me so significant at present;
as indeed it is but for their association with
human Worth and Effort that one City is nobler
than another, that all cities are not mere
stones and mortar. I can understand the long
journeys which Lovers of Wisdom were wont
to undertake in old days to see with their own
eyes some Teacher of Wisdom : all sights in
the Earth are poor and meaningless compared
with this. We still speculate here on a journey
to Weimar, and a winter's residence there; but
the way is long, the issue after all but a *luxury;*

then foolish little matters still detain us here : thus, though the spirit is willing, the flesh is weak. One still looks for a luckier time ; and many a pretty waking dream, though at last it prove but a phantasm, will for years be worth entertaining.

We long much to hear news of you : how your venerable Poet wears his green old age ; how his and your labours are prospering. Scarcely any German traveller finds his way hither ; so that, except public notices, we are left mostly to hope and guess. Often I look into Stieler's picture, and think the mild deep eyes ought to answer me. But they are only ink on paper, and do not.

About the 1st of last December we de- spatched a little box for Weimar, containing pencil-sketches of our House and environment, Books, and other trifles, among which, I believe, was something from my wife for Madame : but unluckily the frost set in directly after, the Elbe became unnavigable ; and the Edinburgh shippers gave little hope of the Packet leaving them till Spring. It was directed, as usual, to

the care of Messrs. Parish in Hamburg.   Pray
notify this to *Seiner Excellenz* unless happily it
be already in his hands.   Of our deep unabated
regard and love, I trust he needs no assurance.

I requested the Editor of the *Foreign Review*
to forward you some of my lucubrations, which
you said you had not seen ; nevertheless I am
afraid he has neglected it ; neither, I can warn
you, is the loss very great.   I was shocked to
learn that poor Müllner was dead : the very
post that brought me his version of my *Play-*
wrights in his *Mitternacht-Blatt,* conveyed also
those other tidings that the poor Jester was
now " quite chapfallen."   Alas, poor Yorick !
And why did *I* add another grain to his last
load of suffering, already too heavy for him [1]!—
Since then I have not cast one other glance
at your *Tartarus ;* but looked only at the
Elysium, which is far more profitable.

Of our English Literature at this moment,
the two chief features seem to be our increased

---

[1] In his article on *German Playwrights* (*Foreign Review*,
No. VI., 1829, see *Miscellanies*, vol. ii.), Carlyle had spoken with
some severity of Müllner's Plays and of his *Midnight Paper*.

and increasing attention to the Literature of neighbouring nations ; and the universal effort to render all sorts of knowledge *popular*, to accommodate our speculations, both in price and structure, to the largest possible number of readers.   In regard to that first peculiarity, you already know of our two *Foreign Reviews*, both of which affect to be prospering ; and now further we have a *Foreign Literary Gazette*,[1] published weekly in London, and which, though it is a mere steam-engine concern, managed by an utter *Dummkopf*, solely for lucre, appears to meet with sale, so great is the curiosity, so boundless is the ignorance of men : *dem Narrenkönig gehört die Welt*, at least all the temporalities thereof.   Our zeal for popularising, again, is to be seen on every side of us.   To say nothing of our *Societies for the Diffusion of useful Knowledge*, with their sixpenny treatises, really very meritorious, we have, I know not how many *Miscellanies*, *Family Libraries*, *Cabinet Cyclopædias*, and so forth ; and these not managed by any literary Gibeonites, but

---

[1] Edited by Mr. William Jerdan.

sometimes by the best men we have: Sir
Walter Scott, for instance, is publishing a
History of Scotland by one of these vehicles;
Thomas Moore is to write a History of Ireland
for the same work.   The other day, I may add,
there came a letter to me from a quite new
Brotherhood of that sort; earnestly requesting
a " Life of Goethe."   Knowing my correspondent[1] as a man of some weight and respectability in Literature, I have just answered him
that the making of Goethe known to England
was a task which any Englishman might be
proud of; but that, as for his Biography, the
only rational plan, as matters stood, was to
take what he had himself seen fit to impart on
the subject; and by proper commentary and
adaptation, above all, by a suitable version,
and not perversion, of what was to be translated, enable an Englishman to read it with
the eye of a German.   If anything come of this
proposal, and what, you shall by and by hear.

But it is more than time that I should say
a word about my *History of German Litera-*

---

[1] Mr. G. R. Gleig, on behalf of Dr. Lardner.

ture (if such can be the name of it), the task
above alluded to, and which also is to form
part of a joint-stock enterprise, the first of a
whole series of *Literary Histories*, French,
Italian, Spanish, English Literature being all
to be depicted in that "Cabinet Library" of
theirs. I am to have four volumes, and have
thought a good deal about the plan I am to
follow. The first volume is to be antiquarian,
I think; to treat of the *Nibelungenlied*, the
Minnesingers, Mastersingers, and so forth, and
may perhaps end with Hans Sachs. The
second will probably contain Luther and the
Reformation Satirists, with Opitz and his
school; down as far as Thomasius, Gottsched,
and the Swiss. The last two volumes must
be devoted to your modern, indeed recent
Literature, which is of all others the most
important to us. I need not say how much
any counsel of yours would oblige me in
regard to this matter, many parts of which
are still very dark to me. In particular, can
you mention any reasonable Book in which
the "New School" is exhibited; what was

its history, fairly stated, what its doctrines;
what in short was the *meaning* lying at the
bottom of that boundless hubbub, which so
often perplexes the stranger even yet with its
echoes in your Literature? Is Grüber's talk
(in his Wieland) about the *Xenienkrieg* to be
depended on, or is it mostly babble; and is
there any other work that will throw light on
that singular period? The *Briefwechsel*, two
volumes of which I have, is doubtless the
most authentic of all documents: but still my
understanding of it is far from sufficient. A
few words from you might perhaps save me
much groping; neither will you grudge that
trouble for me. Might I ask you to mention
what you think in general the most remarkable
epochs, and circumstances (*Momente*) of German Literature? Indeed nothing that you can
write on that subject will be otherwise than
welcome to me. But, alas! the sheet is done;
and I must so soon say *Lebewohl!* Pray do
not linger in writing; your news, too, will seem
highly important to us. Lastly, if it be not
troublesome: *use the Roman handwriting*;

the other is like a thick veil, requiring to be torn off first.

With best wishes, ever faithfully yours,

TH. CARLYLE.

Your German *Philister*, your Adelungs, Nicolais, etc. (of which sort we have plenty in England even now), and what figure their activity specially assumed, are also an object of great curiosity with me. We call them " Utilitarians" here, and they are mostly political, and " Radical," or republican.

My wife directs me to send her kind regards, and continued hope of one day seeing you. Pray employ me, if there is anything here in which I can serve you.

XXV.—GOETHE to CARLYLE.

[*13th April* 1830.]

Das werthe Schatzkästlein, nachdem es durch den strengsten Winter vom Continent lange abgehalten worden, ist endlich um die Hälfte März glücklich angelangt.

Um von seinem Gehalt zu sprechen, erwähne
zuerst der unschätzbaren Locke, die man wohl
mit dem theuren Haupte verbunden möchte
gesehen haben, die aber hier einzeln erblickt,
mich fast erschreckt hätte. Der Gegensatz
war zu auffallend; denn ich brauchte meinen
Schädel nicht zu berühren, um zu wissen dass
daselbst nur Stoppeln sich hervorthun; es war
nicht nöthig vor den Spiegel zu treten, um zu
erfahren dass eine lange Zeitreihe ihnen ein
missfarbiges Ansehen gegeben. Die Un-
möglichkeit der verlangten Erwiederung fiel
mir aufs Herz, und nöthigte mich zu Gedanken
deren man sich zu entschlagen pflegt. Am
Ende aber blieb mir doch nichts übrig als mich
an der Vorstellung zu begnügen: eine solche
Gabe sey dankbarlichst ohne Hoffnung irgend
einer genügenden Gegengift anzunehmen. Sie
soll auch heilig in der ihrer würdigen Brieftasche
aufbewahrt bleiben, und nur das Liebenswür-
digste ihr zugesellt werden.

Der Schottische elegante Turban hat, wie
ich versichern darf, zu manchem Vergnüg-
lichen Gelegenheit gegeben. Seit vielen Jahren

werden wir von den Einwohnern der drey
Königreiche besucht, welche gern einige Zeit
lang bey uns verweilen und guter Gesellschaft
geniessen mögen. Hierunter befinden sich
zwar weniger Schotten, doch kann es nicht
fehlen dass nicht noch das Andenken an einen
solchen Landsmann sich in einem schönen
Herzen so lebendig finde, um die National-
Prachtmütze, die Distel mit eingeschlossen, als
einen wünschenswerthesten Schmuck anzusehen,
und die gütige Senderin hätte sich gewiss gefreut
das lieblichste Gesicht von der Welt darunter
hervorgucken zu sehen. Ottilie aber dankt zum
allerverbindlichsten, und wird, sobald unsre
Trauertage vorüber sind, damit glorreich auf-
zutreten nicht ermangeln.

Lassen Sie mich nun eine nächste Gegen-
sendung ankündigen, welche zum Juni als der
günstigsten Jahreszeit sich wohl wird zusammen
gefunden haben. Sie erhalten :

1. Das Exemplar Ihres übersetzten Schillers, geschmückt mit den Bildern Ihrer länd-
lichen Wohnung, begleitet von einigen Bogen in
meiner Art, wodurch ich zugleich dem Büchlein

offnen Eingang zu verschaffen, besonders aber
die Communikation beyder Länder und Literaturen lebhafter zu erregen trachte. Ich wünsche
dass diese nach Kenntniss des Publicums ange-
wendeten Mittel Ihnen nicht missfallen, auch
der Gebrauch, den ich von Stellen unsrer
Correspondenz gemacht, nicht als Indiskretion
möge gedeutet werden. Wenn ich mich in
jüngeren Jahren vor dergleichen Mittheilungen
durchaus gehütet, so ziemt es dem höheren
Alter auch solche Wege nicht zu verschmähen.
Die günstige Aufnahme des Schillerischen
Briefwechsels gab mir eigentlich hiezu Anlass
und Muth.   Ferner finden Sie beygelegt :

2. Die vier noch fehlenden Bände ge-
dachter Briefe.   Mögen Sie Ihnen als Zauber-
wagen zu Diensten stehen, um sich in die
damalige Zeit in unsere Mitte zu versetzen, wo
es eine unbedingte Strebsamkeit galt, wo
niemand zu fordern dachte und nur zu verdienen
bemüht war.   Ich habe mir die vielen Jahre
her den Sinn, das Gefühl jener Tage zu erhalten gesucht und hoffe es soll mir fernerhin
gelingen.

3. Eine fünfte Sendung meiner Werke liegt sodann bey, worin sich wohl manches unterhaltende, unterrichtende, belehrende, brauchbar anzuwendende finden wird. Man gestehe zu dass es auch ideelle Utilitarier gebe, und es sollte mir sehr zur Freude gereichen wenn ich mich darunter zählen dürfte. Noch eine Lieferung, dann ist vorerst das beabsichtigte Ganze vollbracht, dessen Abschluss zu erleben ich mir kaum zu hoffen erlaubte. Nachträge giebt es noch hinreichend; meine Papiere sind in guter Ordnung.

4. Ein Exemplar meiner Farbenlehre und der dazu gehörigen Tafeln soll auch beygefügt werden; ich wünsche, dass Sie den zweyten, als den *historischen* Theil, zuerst lesen. Sie sehen da die Sache herankommen, stocken, sich aufklären, und wieder verdüstern. Sodann aber ein Bestreben nach neuem Lichte ohne allgemeinen Erfolg. Alsdann würde die erste Hälfte des ersten Theils, als die *didactische* Abtheilung eine allgemeine Vorstellung geben wie ich die Sache angegriffen wünsche. Frey lich ist ohne Anschauung der Experimente hier nicht durchzukommen; wie Sie es mit

der *polemischen* Abtheilung halten wollen und können, wird sich alsdann ergeben. Ist es mir möglich, so lege, besonders für Sie, ein einleitendes Wort bey.

5. Sagen Sie mir etwa zunächst wie Sie die deutsche Literatur bey den Ihrigen einleiten wollen ; ich eröffne Ihnen gern meine Gedanken über die Folge der Epochen. Man braucht nicht überall ausführlich zu seyn : gut aber ist's auf manches vorübergehende Interessante wenigstens hinzudeuten, um zu zeigen dass man es kennt. Dr. Eckermann macht mit meinem Sohn eine Reise gegen Süden und bedauert, nicht wie er gewünscht hatte, diesmal beyhülflich seyn zu können. Ich werde gern wie obgesagt seine Rolle vertreten. Diesen Sommer bleib' ich zu Hause und sehe bis Michael Geschäfte genug vor mir.

Gedenken Sie mit Ihrer lieben Gattin unsrer zum besten und empfangen wiederholten herzlichen Dank für die schöne Sendung.

Treu angehörig,

J. W. v. Goethe.

Weimar, den 13 Apr. 1830.

[Translation.]

[*13th April* 1830.]

The precious casket, after a long delay in reaching the Continent owing to the extreme severity of the winter, at last arrived safely about the middle of March.

As to its contents, I will mention first the incomparable lock of hair, which one would indeed have liked to see along with the dear head, but which, when it came to light by itself here, almost alarmed me. The contrast was too striking; for I did not need to touch my skull to become aware that only stubble was left there, nor was it necessary for me to go to the looking-glass to learn that a long flight of time had given it a discoloured look. The impossibility of making the desired return smote my heart; and forced thoughts upon me which one usually prefers to banish. In the end, however, nothing remained for me but to content myself with the reflection that such a gift was to be most thankfully received without hope of any adequate requital. For the rest it shall be kept sacred in the portfolio which is worthy of it, and only the most cherished objects shall bear it company.

The elegant Scotch *Bonnet*, I can assure you, has given much pleasure. For many years we have been visited by inhabitants of the Three Kingdoms, who like to remain with us for a time, and enjoy good society. Among these, indeed, there are comparatively few Scotchmen ; yet there cannot fail to be preserved in some fair heart here so lively an image of one of your countrymen that she must regard the splendid national head-dress, including the thistle, as a most pleasing ornament ; and the kind donor would certainly be delighted to see the most charming face in the world peering out from beneath it. Ottilie sends her most grateful thanks, and will not fail, as soon as our days of mourning are over,[1] to make a glorious appearance in it.

Let me now announce the despatch of another parcel in return, which will probably

---

[1] For the Dowager Grand Duchess (died February 1830).

be put together by June, as the most favourable
time of the year.   You will receive :—

1. A copy of the Translation of your *Schiller*,
embellished with the pictures of your country
dwelling and accompanied by a few pages of
my own, in which I endeavour to procure a
good reception for the little book, and especially to awaken a more lively intercourse between
the two Countries and their Literatures.   I
trust that you may not disapprove of the means
I have employed, in accordance with my knowledge of the public, and that you will not regard
the use I have made of some portions of our
correspondence as an indiscretion.   Although in
my earlier years I was at all times careful to
avoid publishing matters of the kind, it is fitting
that in my old age I should not despise even
such means.   What especially inclined and encouraged me towards this course was your
favourable reception of the Schiller *Correspondence*.   Further, you will find enclosed :

2. The four volumes, still wanting, of these
said Letters.   May they serve as a magic chariot
to transport you into our circle at that period

of frank and ingenuous striving, when no one thought of making claims, but only endeavoured to be deserving.   I have all these years sought to preserve in me the spirit and feeling of those days, and I trust that in the future, too, I may succeed in doing so.

3. A fifth instalment of my Works is also enclosed, in which may be found many a thing that is entertaining, improving, instructive and capable of practical application.   If you will admit that there may be idealist Utilitarians also, I should be very glad to be allowed to reckon myself as one of them.   One more Section and the intended whole will be complete, a con-summation which I scarcely allowed myself to hope I should live to see.   There will be no lack of addenda.   My papers are in good order.

4. A copy of my *Farbenlehre*, with the plates belonging to it, will accompany the other books.   I wish you would first read the second, that is, the *historical* part.   You see there the subject approaching, halting, becoming clear, and again growing dim ; then an attempt to obtain new light, without any general success.

After this the first half of the first part, that is, the *didactic*, would give you a general idea of the way in which I wish the matter to be apprehended. Unless, however, the experiments can be seen, this part cannot be fully understood. You will then see how you like the *polemic* portion, and what you can make of it. If possible, I will add, for your especial behoof, some introductory words.

5. Tell me before long how you propose to introduce German literature amongst your people, and I will gladly give you my thoughts on the sequence of its epochs. One does not need to enter into detail about every matter, but it is well at least to touch upon many a thing of transitory interest, to show that one is aware of it. Dr. Eckermann is making a journey southwards with my son, and regrets that he cannot be of use at present, as he had wished. I will gladly, as I have said, be his proxy. I am going to remain at home this summer, and I see before me plenty of work until Michaelmas.

I beg you and your dear wife to hold us in

kindliest remembrance, and to accept our repeated and cordial thanks for your beautiful
gifts.

With sincere attachment,

J. W. v. GOETHE.

WEIMAR, 13*th April* 1830.

XXVI.—CARLYLE to GOETHE.

CRAIGENPUTTOCK, DUMFRIES,
23*d May* 1830.

The Weimar letter, now as ever the most
welcome that could arrive here, reached us, in
due course, some two weeks ago.   We rejoice
to learn that you are still well and busy, still
gratified with our love for you, and still sending
over the Ocean a kind thought to us in our
remote home.   This fair relation and intercourse with what we have most cause to
venerate on Earth seems one of the strangest
things in our Life ; which, however, is all built
on wonder : *Ce que j'admire le plus c'est de* ME
VOIR ICI.

I know not whether I should mention the

sort of hope which has again arisen of our even
seeing you in person one day : that long-
cherished project of a visit to Germany now
assumes some faint shape of possibility ; in
which pilgrimage Weimar, the grand Sanctuary,
without which indeed *Deutschland* were but as
other Lands to us, would nowise be forgotten.
But it is better to check such Day-dreams than
encourage them ; the impediments and counter-
chances are so many, as Time, which brings
Roses,[1] brings also far other products.   Happy
it is, meanwhile, that whether we ever meet in
the body or not, we have already met you in
spirit, which union can never be parted, or
made of no effect.   Here in our Mountain
Solitude, you are often an inmate with us ; and
can whisper wise lessons and pleasant tales in
the ear of the Lady herself.   She spends many
an evening with you, and has done all winter,
greatly to her satisfaction.   One of her last
performances was the *Deutschen Ausgewan-
derten*, and that glorious *Mährchen*, a true
Universe of Imagination ; in regard to the

---

[1] *Die Zeit bringt Rosen*, is an old German proverb.

manifold, inexhaustible significance of which
(for the female eye guessed a significance under
it), I was oftener applied to for exposition than
I could give it; and at last, to quiet impor-
tunities, was obliged to promise that I would
some day write a commentary on it, as on one
of the deepest, most poetical things even
Goethe had ever written.[1] Nay, looking abroad,
I can further reflect with pleasure that thou-
sands of my countrymen, who had need enough
of such an acquaintance, are now also beginning
to know you: of late years, the voice of
Dulness, which was once loud enough on this
matter, has been growing feebler and feebler;
so that now, so far as I hear, it is altogether
silent, and quite a new tone has succeeded it.
On the whole, Britain and Germany will not
always remain strangers; but rather, like two
Sisters that have been long divided by distance
and evil tongues, will meet lovingly together,
and find that they are near of Kin.

---

[1] " The Tale " was translated, and, with a commentary,
published in *Fraser's Magazine*, No. XXXIII., 1832. See
Carlyle's *Miscellanies*, vol. iv., Appendix.

Since you are friendly enough to offer me help and countenance in my endeavours that way, let me lose no time in profiting thereby. In regard to that *History of German Literature*, I need not say, for it is plain by itself, that no word of yours can be other than valuable. Doubtless it were a high favour, could you impart to me any summary of that great subject, in the structure and historical sequence and coherence it has with you : your views, whether from my point of vision or not, whether contradictory of mine, or confirmatory, could not fail to be instructive.   For your guidance in this charitable service, perhaps my best method will be to explain, as clearly as I can here, what plan my Book specially follows, so far as it is yet written, or decidedly shaped in my thoughts.

Volume First, which was finished and sent to press a few days ago,[1] opens with some considerations on the great and growing importance of Literature ; the value of Literary commerce with other nations ; therefore of

---

[1] It was not printed.   See *infra*, pp. 207, 208.

Literary Histories, which forward this: then
some sketch of the method to be followed in a
Literary History of Germany, where so much
is yet altogether unknown to us, and only some
approximation to a *History* is possible for the
present.   Next comes a chapter on the old
Germans of Tacitus, the Northern Immigra-
tions (*Völkerwanderung*), and the primitive
national character of this People; the chief
features of which are Valour (*Tapferkeit*) and
meditative Depth; not forgetting, at the same
time, our own Saxon origin, and claims, by
general brotherhood and in virtue of so many
Hengists and Alfreds, to a share in that praise.
Then something of the German Traditions; of
their Language as the most indestructible of
Traditions, whereby Ulfilas and his Bible come
to be mentioned: further, of their ancient
Superstitions, and still existing *Volksmährchen*,
with a little specimen of them.   Then of long-
written Traditions; of the *Heldenbuch* and
Nibelungen Lied, with their old environment
of Fiction, looked at only from afar: especially
a long chapter on the *Nibelungen*, already an

object of curiosity here. The last chapter is
entitled the *Minnesingers*, and looks back
briefly to the time of Charlemagne and forward
to that of Rodolf von Hapsburg; endeavouring to delineate the chivalrous spirit of the
Swabian Era; and to show that here really
was a Poetic Period, though a feeble, simple
and *young* one; man being now for the first
time inspired with an Infinite Idea, having now
for the first time seen that he was a Man.—
This is all I have yet brought to paper, and I
fear it is worth little.

Next follows what I might denominate a
Didactic Period, wherein figure *Hugo von
Trimberg*, the author of *Reinecke Fuchs*, and
Sebastian Brandt: it reaches its culmination
and rises to a poetical degree under *Luther*
and *Hutten;* then again sinks, so far as
Literature is concerned, into Theological
Disputation, or mere Grammatical and Superficial Refinement, through many a *Thomasius*
and *Gottsched*, down to utter unbelief and
sensualism, when Poetry, except in accidental
tones, foreign in that age, has died away, and

become impossible. Of such accidental appearances I might reckon *Opitz* and his School the
principal ; in whose poetry, however, I can find
little inspiration ; at best some parallel to that
of our own Pope ; as *Hoffmannswaldau* and
Lohenstein, perhaps with far less talent,
resemble our Dryden. How this is to be
grouped into masses, and presented in full
light, I do not yet see clearly : however, I must
force it all into the second volume, and leaving
Bodmer and *Breitinger* to fight out their
quarrel with *Altvater Gottsched* as they may,
be prepared to begin my third volume with
Lessing and *Wieland.*

Lessing I could fancy as standing between
two Periods, an earnest Sceptic, struggling to
work himself into the Region of Spiritual Truth,
and often from some Pisgah-height obtain-
ing brave glimpses of that Promised Land.
Wieland, with many a Hagedorn, Rabener,
Gellert, co-operate, each in their degree ; and
so the march proceeds ; till under you and
Schiller, I should say, a Third grand Period had
evolved itself, as yet fairly developed in no

other Literature, but full of the richest pros-
pects for all : namely, a period of new
Spirituality and Belief; in the midst of old
Doubt and Denial; as it were, a new revela-
tion of Nature, and the Freedom and Infinitude
of Man, wherein Reverence is again rendered
compatible with Knowledge, and Art and
Religion are one. This is the Era which
chiefly concerns us of England, as of other
nations ; the rest being chiefly remembrance,
but this still present with us. How I am to
bring it out will require all consideration.
Though the most familiar to me of any other
department, I can yet see only that it will fill
my last two Volumes, and to good purpose, if I
can handle it well; but the divisions, and
subordination and co-ordination of such a
multiplicity of objects : *the Sorrows of Werther*
with the *Kraftmänner*, the Critical Philosophy,
the *Xenien* and what not, will occasion no little
difficulty ; or rather, in the long run, I shall be
obliged to stop where means fail, and so to
leave much unrepresented, and the rest combined in what order it can get into.

By this long description you will see how
matters stand with me, and where a helpful
word would most profit.   Innumerable questions I could ask ; for example, about the
Xenienkrieg, and your Nicolais and other
Utilitarians with their fortune among you ;
which sect, though under a British shape, is
at this day boisterous enough here ; whose
downfall, sure to come by and by, it were
pleasant to prophesy.   But perhaps some outline of your own General Scheme of German
Literary History, and the succession of its
epochs, would in the limits we are here confined to, prove most available.   It is almost
shameful to occupy your time with poor work
of mine : otherwise, as I said, no word that you
could speak on this matter could be useless.
We expect, not without impatience, that promised Packet, in which so many interesting
matters and kind memorials are to lie for us.
My wife unites with me in friendliest wishes to
you and yours.   May the Summer which is
now, after the wild snow-months, opening its
blossoms, even in these mountains, find you

happy, and leave you happy! Friends you will
have in many countries and in many centuries :
few men have been permitted to finish such a
task as yours.—Believe me ever, affectionately
your Scholar and Servant,

THOMAS CARLYLE.

XXVII.—GOETHE TO CARLYLE.

WEIMAR, *den 6 Juni* 1830.

Ihr werther Brief, mein Theuerster, vom
23 May, hat gerade nur 14 Tage gelaufen um
zu mir zu kommen, wodurch ich aufgeregt
werde alsobald zu antworten, weil ich hoffen
kann der meinige werde Sie an einem schönen
Junitage begrüssen. Es ist wirklich höchst
erfreulich dass die Einrichtungen unsrer gesit-
teten Welt, nach und nach, die Entfernung
zwischen Gleichgesinnten, Wohldenkenden ge-
schäftig vermindern, wogegen wir derselben
manches nachsehen können.

Zuvörderst also will ich aussprechen, dass an
dem Plane, wie Sie die Geschichte der deutschen
Literatur zu behandeln gedenken, nichts zu

O

erinnern ist, und dass ich nur hie und da
einige Lücken finde, auf die ich Ihre Aufmerksamkeit zu richten gedenke. Durchaus
aber werden Sie Sich überzeugen dass die
erste Edition eines solchen Werkes nur als
Concept zu betrachten ist, welches in den Fol-
genden immer mehr gereinigt und bereichert
hervortreten soll; Sie haben Ihr ganzes Leben
daran zu thun, und erfreuen Sich gewiss
eines entschiedenen Vortheils für Sich und
andere.

Zu Förderung dieses Ihres Zweckes, werde
ich die Absendung eines intentionirten Kästchens sogleich besorgen, welches die gute
Jahreszeit bald genug Ihnen zubringen wird.
Es enthält :

1. Vorlesungen über die Geschichte der
deutschen National-Literatur von Dr. Ludwig
Wachler, 2 Theile, 1818.

Dieses Werk schenkt' ich, als höchst brauchbar, im Jahre 1824 dem guten Dr. Eckermann ;
dieser, der so eben mit meinem Sohne nach
Süden gereist ist, lässt mir solches als eine
Gabe für Sie zurück, mit den besten Grüssen

und Segnungen.   Ich sende es, mit um so mehr Zufriedenheit, weil ich überzeugt bin dass Sie, diesem Faden folgend, nicht irren können.   Von dem meisten Einzelnen haben Sie Sich ja schon eigene Ueberzeugungen ausgebildet, mögen Sie über dieses und jenes nachfragen, so werde suchen treulich Antwort zu geben.

2. Ein höchst wichtiges Heftchen, unter dem Titel: Ueber Werden und Wirken der Literatur, zunächst auf Deutschlands Literatur unserer Zeit, von Dr. Ludwig *Wachler*, Breslau 1829.   Es giebt zu mancherley Betrachtungen Anlass wie derselbe Mann, nach 10 Jahren, sich wieder über Gegenstände kürzlich ausdrückt, deren Betrachtung er sein ganzes Leben gewidmet.   Durch obengemeldete zwey Bände werden Sie volkommen in den Stand gesetzt, das was er hier gewollt und ausgesprochen, aufzunehmen und zu benutzen.

3. Vier Bände meiner Correspondenz mit Schiller, und also das Ganze abgeschlossen. Dabey sey Ihnen völlig überlassen es, nach Ihrer reinen und wohl empfindenden Weise sich zuzueignen und den Freunden, die sich

hier unterhalten, noch immer näher zu treten.
In der Folge sende ich manches von der freundlichen und höchstsinnigen Aufnahme, welcher
diese Bände in Deutschland sich erfreuen; auch
wird Ihnen daraus zu Ihren Zwecken gar
manches deutlich werden.

4. Zwey Bände meiner Farbenlehre, mit
einem Hefte Tafeln.   Auch diese werden
Ihnen nicht ohne Frucht seyn.   Das Werk ist
gar zu sehr Fleisch von meinem Fleisch und
Bein von meinem Bein, als dass es Ihnen
nicht anmuthen sollte.   Sagen Sie mir einiges
darüber.   Das Allgemeine passt gewiss in
Ihre Denkweise, wünschten Sie wegen des
Besondern einige Aufklärung, so will ich
suchen sie zu geben.

5. Sie finden ferner in dem Kästchen den
Abschluss der Uebersetzung Ihres Leben
Schillers; die Herausgabe hat sich verzögert,
und ich wollte, dem Verleger so wie der Sache
zu Nutz, das Werklein eigens aufputzen; dem
Publicum hab ich es gewiss recht gemacht,
wenn Sie es nur verzeihen.

Das Titelkupfer stellt Ihre Wohnung dar in

der Nähe, die Titelvignette dasselbe [*sic*] in der
Ferne.   Nach den gesandten Zeichnungen,
wie ich hoffe, so gestochen dass es auch in
England nicht missfallen kann.   Aussen auf
dem Hefte sieht man vorn Schiller's Wohnung
in Weimar, auf der Rückseite ein Garten-
häuschen, das er sich selbst erbaute, um sich
von seiner Familie, von aller Welt zu trennen.
Wenn er sich daselbst befand, durfte Niemand
herantreten.   Es war auch kaum für einen
Schreibtisch Platz.   Sehr leicht gebaut, drohte
es in der Folge zu verfallen und ward
abgetragen; versteht sich nachdem er den
Garten weggegeben und nach Weimar gezo-
gen war.[1]

Nun aber wäre noch manches zu sagen von
einem Vorwort das ich dazu geschrieben, doch
wird es besser seyn Sie selbst, wenn Sie es
gelesen, empfinden und urtheilen zu lassen, ob
ich des Guten zu viel gethan, oder ob mir das
Zweckmässige gelungen sey.   In jedem Falle
war nöthig zu interessiren und aufzuregen.
Was weiter erfolgen kann, erwarten wir, was

[1] See *infra*, p. 204 *n*.

weiter zu thun ist, seh ich ziemlich schon
voraus.

Ihrer lieben Gattin das Allerfreundlichste!
Durch die übersendete Silhuette [*sic*] ist sie uns
schon viel näher getreten; so viel vermag der
genaue Schatten des edlen Wirklichen! Möge
Sie nun auch uns das Bildniss Ihres Gemahls
auf gleiche Weisse [*sic*] senden. Es freut mich
dass jenes famose Mährchen auch dort seine
Wirkung nicht verfehlt. Es ist ein Kunststück
das zum zweytenmale schwerlich gelingen würde.
Eine geregelte Einbildungskraft fordert un-
widerstehlich den Verstand auf, ihr etwas
Gesetzliches und Folgerechtes abzugewinnen,
womit er nie zu Stande kommt. Indessen
habe ich doch zwey Auslegungen, die ich
aufsuchen und, wo möglich, dem Kästchen
beylegen will.

Da ich nun, um *the single sheet* nicht zu
überschreiten, auch auf die äussere Seite des
Blatts gelangt bin, so will ich diesen Raum
noch benutzen um folgendes zu melden. Gleich
nach Abgang des ersten Kästchens, welcher
bald erfolgen soll, bereite sogleich ein neues

vor, in welchem Sie denn die Uebersetzung
Ihres Schillerischen Lebens und die siebente
Lieferung meiner Werke erhalten sollen, worin
enthalten sind 1. Tag-und Jahreshefte, Ergänz-
ung meiner sonstigen Bekenntnisse 2 Bände.
2. Recensionen und einiges Aeltere 1 Band.
3. Cellini 2 Bde. Was indessen noch zu
erinnern wäre, soll in dem Kästchen selbst
bemerkt werden.[1]   Mit dem Wunsch dass
Gegenwärtiges Sie in heitern Tagen und guter
Gesundheit treffen möge, schliesse ich mit
Versicherung treuster, unwandelbarer Theilnahme.

J. W. v. GOETHE.

Abgesandt, den 7 Juni 1830.

Eine unvergleichliche schwarze Haarlocke,
veranlasst mich noch ein Blättchen beyzulegen
und mit wahrhaftem Bedauern zu bemerken :
dass die verlangte Erwiederung leider unmög-
lich ist. Kurz und missfärbig, alles Schmuckes
entbehrend, muss das Alter sich begnügen wenn
sich dem Innern noch irgend eine Blüte aufthut,
indem die äussere verschwunden ist. Ich sinne

---

[1] See Appendix II. p. 324.

schon auf irgend ein Surrogat, ein solches zu
finden hat mir aber noch nicht glücken wollen.
Meine schönsten Grüsse der würdigen Gattin.

Möge das Kästchen glücklich angekommen seyn !

G.

[TRANSLATION.]

WEIMAR, *6th June* 1830.

Your valued letter, my dearest Sir, of the
23d of May, took only fourteen days in coming,
and this incites me to answer immediately,
since I can hope that mine may still greet you
on a lovely June day. It is certainly highly
gratifying that the distance between well disposed persons of a like turn of mind is being
steadily diminished, owing to the arrangements
of our civilised world, in return for which we
may excuse much that is amiss in it.

First of all I will declare that with respect to your proposed plan of treating the
History of German Literature there is no
alteration to be suggested, and that I only
find a few gaps here and there, to which
I mean to call your attention. You should,

however, be thoroughly convinced that the
first edition of such a book is to be considered only as a first sketch, which will be
enriched and made more correct in every successive edition. You have your whole life to
work at it, and may certainly rejoice in a positive
advantage from this to yourself and to others.

In furtherance of this object of yours, I will
immediately set about the despatching of a
parcel intended for you, which the favourable
time of the year will bring you soon enough.
It contains :

1. *Lectures on the History of German
National Literature,* by Dr. Ludwig Wachler,
2 parts, 1818.

This work I presented in 1824 as a most
useful one, to good Dr. Eckermann ;[1] he,
having now gone on a journey to the south
with my son, left it behind with me, as a

---

[1] On the inside of the cover of it is pasted a note, in
Eckermann's hand : "Ein mir sehr theures Geschenk von
Goethe. Sonntag Mittag d. 4 Januar 1824, aus seinen lieben
Händen empfangen." [A very precious gift from Goethe to
me. Received from his dear hands, Sunday, at midday, 4
January 1824.]

gift for you, with his kindest regards and good wishes. I send it with the greater satisfaction, because I am sure that in following this clew you cannot go wrong. You have indeed already formed your own convictions in regard to most particulars, but should you wish to inquire about any special matter, I will try to answer you faithfully.

2. A most important little tract, bearing the title *Ueber Werden und Wirken der Literatur* (Concerning the Growth and Influence of Literature), especially of the German Literature of our day, by Dr. Ludwig Wachler, Breslau, 1829. There is occasion for a variety of reflections on the way in which the same man, after an interval of ten years, again briefly expresses himself upon matters to the consideration of which he has devoted his whole life. By means of the above-mentioned two volumes you will be fully enabled to appreciate and to profit by the drift and substance of his later work.

3. Four Volumes of my Correspondence with Schiller, which complete the book. These I

simply hand over to you, that you may make
them your own, according to your usual clear
and sympathetic way, and may draw still nearer
to the friends who are here conversing together.
By and by I will send you many of the friendly
and exceedingly thoughtful notices which these
volumes have had the good fortune to call forth
in Germany; you will moreover get out of them
a great many hints, useful for your purpose.

4. Two volumes of my *Farbenlehre* with a
set of plates. These again will not be un-
profitable to you. The Work is indeed too
much flesh of my flesh and bone of my bone
not to create in you a friendly interest. Say
something to me about it. The general view
will certainly fall in with your way of thinking; should you wish an explanation on any
particular point, I will try and give it to
you.

5. Further you will find in the little box
the last sheets of the translation of your *Life of
Schiller*. The publication has been delayed,
and I wished to make the little work especially
pretty, for the sake of the publisher as well as

for its own.   I have certainly pleased the public ;
I only hope you will excuse it.

The frontispiece represents your house from
a near point of view, the vignette on the title-
page, the same from a distance,—I hope, so
engraved from the drawings which you sent, that
they cannot fail to please in England also.
Outside, on the front cover, is a view of Schiller's
house in Weimar ; and on the cover at the
back, a little Garden-house [at Jena] which he
himself built in order that he might with-
draw from his family and all the world.   When
he was there, no one was allowed to enter.
Besides there was scarcely room for a writing-
table in it.   It was so very slightly built that it
threatened afterwards to fall to ruin, and was
pulled down ; but this was after he had given
up the garden and moved to Weimar.[1]

There might still be much to say about a
preface I have written for it, but it will be better

---

[1] For a translation of Goethe's Introduction and Dedication
to the *Leben Schillers*, see *infra*, p. 299 (Appendix I.).   For
the views of Craigenputtock, of Schiller's house at Weimar
and of his Garden-house at Jena, see Carlyle's *Life of Schiller*
(Library edition, 1869), Appendix II.

to leave it to your own feelings, and when you
have read it, you will judge whether I have
overdone the matter, or have succeeded in doing
only what is suitable for the purpose.   In any
case it was necessary to excite interest and to
arouse attention.   We shall await what further
may ensue ; what is to be done further, I fore-
see tolerably well.

To your dear wife my most friendly greetings.   By means of the silhouette, she has come
much nearer to us ; such the power of the noble
original's veritable shadow !   May she now send
us such another portrait of her husband !   I am
glad that famous *Mährchen*, there also, does not
fail in its effect.   It is a piece of legerdemain
which would hardly succeed a second time.
A normal imagination irresistibly demands that
reason should extract from it something logical
and consistent, which reason never succeeds in
doing.   However, I possess two interpretations, which I will seek out, and if possible
send in the little box.

Since I have now, in order not to exceed " the
single sheet," reached the outside page, I shall

still make use of this space to communicate to you the following further information. Immediately upon the departure of the first little box, which will be very soon, I shall at once get ready another, in which you will receive the translation of your *Life of Schiller* and the seventh Section of my Works, which contains, 1. *Tag-und Jahres-hefte* (the completion of my former Confessions) in two volumes; 2. Reviews and some older Pieces, one volume; 3. *Cellini*, two volumes. What more may still be thought of shall be noted, and sent in the little box itself.[1]   In the hope that this letter may greet you in peaceful days and in good health, I conclude, with the assurance of my most faithful and unalterable sympathy,

J. W. v. Goethe.

(Sent *7th June* 1830.)

A peerless lock of black hair impels me to add still a little sheet, and with true regret to remark that the desired return is, alas, impossible. Short and discoloured and devoid of all charm, old age must be content if any flowers

[1] See Appendix II. p. 324.

at all will still blossom in the inner man when the outward bloom has vanished.   I am already seeking for some substitute, but have not yet been lucky enough to find one.   My warmest greetings to your esteemed wife.

I hope the little box has arrived safe!

G.

XXVIII.—CARLYLE to GOETHE.

CRAIGENPUTTOCK, DUMFRIES,
31st August 1830.

DEAR AND HONOURED SIR—A letter, which, as you expected, was welcomed by us on a bright June day; and some six weeks afterwards, a Packet containing Books and other Valuables, the whole of which arrived in perfect order,—are two new kindnesses on your part which still remain to be acknowledged.   This grateful duty I have delayed till now, as I wished, before writing, to have something definite to say about the bibliopolic fate of that *History of German Literature*, in which you are pleased to take an interest, and over the Publication of which an evil star had for some time,

though as yet with uncertain aspects, appeared
to rule.   That projected Series of Literary
Histories has fallen to the ground, no proper
hands, for most departments of it, having
showed themselves : in consequence the booksellers have grown languid ; the Editor,[1] a well-
meaning, but ineffectual person (late Editor of
the *Foreign Review*, which has now again
merged itself in the *Foreign Quarterly*), has
not only mourned by those streams of Babel,
but actually hung his harp on the willows, that
is to say, abandoned Literature altogether, and
is now struggling to be elected Member of
Parliament for some "rotten borough" in
Kent ; whereby the whole Literary-History
concern lies in a state of fatal stagnation.
After some correspondence and exertion, I
have succeeded in extricating my own poor
Manuscript from such ungainly neighbourhood,
with intent to reposit it quietly in my drawer,
where, according to all appearance, it may now
lie for an indefinite period.

Neither, now that the trouble of it is over,

[1] See *supra*, p. 86 *n.*

do I much regret this arrangement: the work
itself may profit by a keeping till the ninth
year; and for my own part, as my Name was
to have stood on the title-page, I cannot but
rejoice, so far as that goes, that my first professed appearance in Literature may now take
place under some less questionable character
than that of a Compiler; being ambitious, one
day, of far higher honours. It is true, as you
say somewhere, and it ought ever to be borne
in mind, that "an Artist in doing anything does
All:" nevertheless how few are Artists in this
sense; and till one knows that he *cannot* be a
Mason, why should he publicly hire himself as
Hodman!

For the rest, I am about finishing the
Book; at least, putting it into such a shape
that it can be published at any future period.
Within the space of a volume and half, I had
got down, in a continuous narrative, to the
Reformation: a hasty section would carry me
to Lessing's day; after which I had determined,
on maturer calculation of my means and aim,
to treat the rest in a fragmentary and rhapsodic

method ; singling out from the Mass, which is too vast and confused for me to shape into History, the main summits and figures, and dwelling largely on these as individual objects ; whereby, to an attentive reader, some imperfect yet not untrue image of the so chaotic whole might at length present itself. Separate Essays on various personages of that period, from the very highest down to a far lower grade, I have already written ; to which from time to time I purpose to add others : so that the work is left in a growing state ; and when concluded, and knit up by some general considerations, retrospective and prospective, will one day set before my countrymen a full view of all that I have thought or guessed on this to me so important subject. The present undertaking once fairly put to a side, as it now nearly is, I must forthwith betake me to something more congenial and original : except writing from the heart and if possible to the heart, Life has no other business for me, no other pleasure. When I look at the wonderful Chaos within me, full of natural Supernaturalism, and all manner of Antediluvian fragments; and how the Universe is daily growing more mysterious as well as more august, and the influences from without more heterogeneous and perplexing; I see not well what is to come of it all, and only conjecture from the violence of the fermentation that something strange may come. As you feel a fatherly concern in my spiritual progress, which you know well, for all true disciples of yours, to be the one thing needful, I lay these details before you with the less reluctance.

But now turning to more immediately practical matters, let me thank you heartily for that new Cargo of friendly memorials and useful implements which the Weimar Carriers and the Hamburg Shippers have transported hither. With your spacious, lordly Town-mansion we have made ourselves familiar; and look wistfully through the windows, as if we could see our Friend and Teacher sitting there. However, the little Garden-house with its domestic contraction and flowery privacy, is the scene we like best to figure you in, as you yourself

like best to occupy it.   As for the Books, I
have found *Wachler*, so kindly granted me by
Dr. Eckermann, a sound substantial help, in
whose spirit I warmly agree, in whose vigorous
summaries much knowledge is to be gathered.
The *Farbenlehre* I have already looked into
with satisfaction and curiosity ; and mean, this
winter, to master it, so far as possible, according
to the plan you recommend.   Should I attain
to any right understanding of the doctrine, it will
be a pleasing office to publish such insight here,
where vague contradictory reports are all that
circulate at present.   But chiefly I must thank
you for that noble *Briefwechsel* which does
"like a magic chariot" convey me into beloved
scenes, and seasons of the glorious Past, where
Friends ever dear to me, though distant, though
dead, speak audibly.   So pure and generous a
relation as yours with Schiller, founded on such
honest principles, tending towards such lofty
objects, and in its progress so pleasant, smooth
and helpful, is altogether unexampled in what
we Moderns call Literature ; it is a Friendship
worthy of Classical days, when men's hearts

had not yet become incapable of that feeling,
and Art was, what it ever should be, an inspired
function, and the Artist a Priest and Prophet.
The world is deeply your debtor, first for
having acted such a part with your Friend, and
now for having given us this imperishable
memorial of it, which will grow in value, as years
and generations are added to it. You will for-
give me also if I fancy that herein I have got a
new light upon your character ; and seen there,
in warm, beneficent activity, much that I only
surmised before. To Schiller, whose high and
true, yet solitary, pain-stricken, self-consuming
spirit is almost tragically apparent in these
letters, such a union must have been invaluable;
to you also it must have been a rare blessing,
for "infinite is the strength man lends to man."
I am to finish the last volume to-night, and shall
take leave of it with a mournful feeling, as of a
fine Poem, not written but acted, which had
been cut short by death. My wife, who par-
ticipates in these sentiments, bids me ask of
you, for her, a little scrap of Schiller's handwriting, if you can spare such, to be treasured

here along with your own, among the most precious things.

We look forward with impatience for that translated *Life of Schiller*, with its wondrous accompaniments ; especially that Introduction, in which you condescend to fear that some things you have said may be considered indiscreet! To me it can never be other than honourable to be in any such way associated with you, in sight of any man, or of all men. The last section of your Works we also long to see : and I am here requested to remind you, if possible without importunity, of that promised Interpretation of the *Mährchen*, which is still earnestly wanted by the female intellect. Neither am I to forget that new-made *Chaos*,[1] in which your Ottilie gracefully occupies herself : we smiled to see ourselves in print there ; and by a new opportunity, new contributions will not be wanting.

Some weeks ago I had a strange letter with certain strange Books from a Society in Paris, which calls itself *La Société Saint Simonienne*, and professes, among other wonderful things,

---

[1] See *infra*, p. 235 *n*.

now that Saint Simon is dead, to be instituting a new Religion in the world. Their address to me grounded itself on an Essay, entitled *Signs of the Times* which I had written for the *Edinburgh Review*, about a year ago, and which seemed to point me out as their man. If you have chanced to notice that Saint Simonian affair, which long turned on Political Economy, and but lately became Artistic and Religious, I could like much to hear your thoughts on it.— For the present I can enter on nothing further, though much remains to be said. I hope it will be my turn to write again, ere long; and that often through winter we shall hear good tidings of you, and send friendly greetings : best wishes we shall daily send. With loving regards, such as can belong to no other, I remain always your grateful Friend,   Thomas Carlyle.

XXIX.—Goethe to Carlyle.

[5*th October* 1830.]

Und so geht denn auch, mein Theuerster, abermals ein Kästchen an Sie ab, indessen

mein Brief vom 7. Juni und das Kästchen,
abgegangen den 13., wohl schon bey Ihnen
angekommen sind, und ich nun bald die Mel-
dung des Empfangs brieflich von Ihnen hoffen
darf.

Das Gegenwärtige, gleichfalls der Sorgfalt
Hn. Parish's überlassene, enthält denn endlich
das so lange vorbereitete und immer verspä-
tete *Leben Schillers*, in deutscher Uebersetzung.
Mögen Sie zufrieden seyn mit der Art wie ich
wünschte Sie und meine Berliner Freunde in
lebhaftem und fruchtbarem Verhältniss zu
sehen. In meinen Jahren muss es mir ange-
legen seyn, die vielen Bezüge, die sich bey
mir zusammenknüpften, sich anderwärts wieder
anknüpfen zu sehen, und zu beschleunigen was
der Gute wünscht und wünschen muss: eine
gewisse sittlich freysinnige Uebereinstimmung
durch die Welt, und wär' es auch nur im Stillen,
ja oft gehindert, zu verbreiten ; dergestalt damit
sich manches friedlich zurecht lege, um[1] nicht
erst zerstreut umhergetrieben und kaum ins
Gleiche, nach grossem Verlust, gesetzt zu wer-

[1] MS., "und."

den. Möge Ihnen gelingen, Ihrer Nation die
Vortheile der Deutschen bekannt zu machen, wie
wir uns immerfort thätig erweisen den unsrigen
die Vorzüge der Fremden zu verdeutlichen.

Da Sie Ihre Geschichte der deutschen Literatur nicht zu beeilen brauchen, so wird Ihnen,
zu weiterer Einsicht in dieselbe, das Werk von
Wachler höchst wichtig seyn. Was in diesem
Fach vorhanden ist, sehen Sie deutlich verzeich-
net; Ihr Geist, Ihr Gemüth wird Ihnen andeu-
ten um was zunächst von diesem allen Sie sich
umzuthun haben. Alsdann werden Sie finden
was Ihre Nation interessiren könnte, ausführlicher
oder kurzgefasster, wobey es denn immer doch
zu jeder Zeit und an jedem Orte darauf ankommt, dass etwas menschlich Wohlgesinntes
durchgeführt, überliefert, und wo möglich bestätigt werde. Die wilde Unterbrechung der
deutschen Bildung, besonders vom Anfang des
17. Jahrhunderts bis ins 18. hinein, wird Sie
betrüben. Wie sich ein Volk nach und nach
wieder hilft, ist aber desto merkwürdiger. Hiemit nun allen guten Geistern und Einflüssen
empfohlen.

Die Berliner Freunde haben meine Wid-
mung Ihres Schillerischen Lebens gar geneigt
aufgenommen und sind zu allen wechselseitigen
Mittheilungen erbötig. Sie haben mir ein Diplom
zugeschickt, worin sie Herrn Thomas Carlyle
zu Craigenputtock zum auswärtigen Ehrenmit-
glied ernennen. Dieses werthe Blatt, sende mit
dem nächsten Kästchen das wohl vor Winters
noch zu Ihnen kommt; es wird die letzte Lieferung meiner Werke enthalten, der ich noch
einiges Interessante hinzuzufügen hoffe.

Da die Briefpost nicht so wie der andere
Transport im Winter unterbrochen wird, so
lassen Sie mich von Zeit zu Zeit etwas von
Sich wissen, ehe wir wieder völlig einschneien,
wozu für diesen Winter, ob ich gleich nicht
gerne Witterung voraussage, abermals bedenkliche Aussichten sind.

Nach Abschluss dieses Blattes, das ich gleich
senden will, damit es dem Kästchen, welches
am 29. August an die Herren Parish abgegangen ist, nach oder voreile, grüsse ich beide
liebe Gatten zum schönsten.

Herr Carlyle wird, meinem Wunsch gemäss,

den werthen Berlinern ein freundlich Wörtchen
sagen.   Dem Gegenwärtigen lasse bald ein
anderes folgen.   Ein talentvoller junger Mann
und glücklicher Uebersetzer beschäftigt sich mit
Burns; ich bin darauf sehr verlangend.   Leben
Sie recht wohl, schreiben Sie bald, denn für mich
werden Tage und Wochen immer kostbarer.—

Und so denn, fort an !

GOETHE.

WEIMAR, d. 5 October 1830.

Abschrift, HITZIG to GOETHE.[1]

In der heutigen Sitzung der Gesellschaft für ausländische[2]
Literatur wurde Herr Thomas Carlyle von Craigenputtock
in Schottland durch einmüthigen Beschluss sämtlicher
anwesenden Mitglieder zum auswärtigen Mitgliede dieser
Gesellschaft ernannt.   Dieselbe hofft mit Zuversicht, dass
dieser ausgezeichnete Gelehrte, der von Goethe an ihn
ergehenden Einladung entsprechend, zur Beförderung ihrer
Zwecke, so weit sie auf die Kenntniss und Verbreitung der
Englischen Literatur in Deutschland, und der Deutschen in
Grossbrittanien gerichtet sind, gern die Hand bieten, und
so zur Erreichung des gemeinsamen Zieles allgemeiner
Bildung thätig mitwirken werde.

---

[1] For Goethe's Letter introducing Carlyle to the members
of this Society, see Appendix I. p. 299.

[2] MS., " vaterländische."

Hr. Carlyle wird hiervon durch Abschrift dieser Verhandlung in Kenntniss gesetzt.

So geschehen Berlin in der Versammlung vom 24n. Septbr. 1830.

Die Gesellschaft für ausländische Literatur.

HITZIG.

[TRANSLATION.]

Once more, my dearest Sir, a little box is going to you, and meantime, my letter of the 7th of June, and the box that was sent on the 13th have probably reached you some time since, and I may now soon hope to have a letter from you informing me of their arrival.

The present one (likewise committed to the care of Messrs. Parish) contains at last the *Life of Schiller* in the German translation, so long in getting ready, and always delayed. I hope you will be satisfied with the mode in which I wished to see you and my Berlin friends in active and fruitful communication. At my age I cannot but be anxious to see the many relations, which have woven themselves around me, knit up anew elsewhere, and to promote, were it only by private efforts, often impeded, what every good man desires, and must desire, the diffusion of a certain morally liberal harmony of sentiment throughout the world ; so that by this means many things may quietly adjust themselves, instead of being scattered hither and thither at first so as to make it almost impossible, after great loss, to set them right again. May you succeed in making your nation acquainted with the good points of the Germans, as we on our part are always active in bringing before our own people what is excellent in foreign nations.

As you do not need to hurry in your History of German Literature, Wachler's book will be of the greatest importance in giving you further insight into it. You will see clearly recorded what exists in this field, and your intelligence and genius will indicate to you, what you should first take up, in all these matters. Then you will find what will interest your countrymen, either in full or in brief, so that constantly at all epochs and in every place the result may be to exhibit, transmit, and if possible, establish something beneficial to mankind.

The barbarous interruption of German culture, especially from the beginning of the seventeenth century onwards into the eighteenth, will sadden you. The gradual recovery of a nation, however, is all the more striking. In this be all good spirits and influences now called to aid.

Our Berlin friends have accepted my dedication of your *Life of Schiller* very favourably, and are ready for all reciprocal communications. They have sent me a Diploma, in which they appoint Mr. Thomas Carlyle of Craigenputtock a foreign honorary member. This valuable document I will put into the next little box, which will probably reach you before the winter. It will contain the last Section of my Works, to which I hope to add something more that is interesting.

Since the letter post is not interrupted in winter like other means of transport, let me know something of you from time to time, before we are again completely snowed-in, in respect to which for this winter, though I do not like to predict the weather, there are once more unfavourable signs.

In ending this letter, which I will send off at once, that it may precede or directly follow the little box that went to Messrs. Parish on the 29th of August, I send my warmest regards to the dear Pair.

Mr. Carlyle will, in accordance with my wish, say a friendly word to the worthy Berliners. Another letter will soon follow this. A young man of much talent, and successful as a translator, is busy with Burns.[1] I take an eager interest in his work. Fare you right well; write soon, for days and weeks are becoming more and more precious to me.

And so then, onward!

GOETHE.

WEIMAR, *5th October* 1830.

Copy, HITZIG to GOETHE.

In to-day's meeting of the Society for Foreign Literature, Mr. Thomas Carlyle, of Craigenputtock, Scotland, was elected, by the unanimous vote of the members present, a Foreign Member of this Society. The Society confidently hopes that this distinguished scholar, in response to the invitation transmitted to him by Goethe, will readily give his assistance to the furtherance of its objects, so far as

---

[1] Philipp Kaufmann is the name of this young gentleman.

they are directed to the knowledge and diffusion of English literature in Germany, and of German in Great Britain, and thus actively unite in the effort to attain the common end of universal culture.

Mr. Carlyle is informed hereof by an extract from the minutes.

Done at Berlin, at the Meeting on the 24th of September 1830.

For the Society for Foreign Literature,

HITZIG.

XXX.—GOETHE to CARLYLE.

[*17th October* 1830.]

Mein letztes Schreiben vom 5. Octbr. wird indessen zu Ihnen, mein Theuerster, gelangt seyn, worin ich zugleich das Decret abschriftlich eingeschaltet habe, welche Sie zum auswärtigen Mitgliede der Gesellschaft für ausländische Literatur zu Berlin ernennt. Gegenwärtig theil' ich das Schreiben gleichfalls in Copia mit, wodurch jenes eingesendet ward. Ich freue mich dass Sie durch diese Vermittlung ein Verhältniss in Deutschland gewinnen das Ihnen in der Folge in manchen Fällen nützlich werden kann.

Wenn uns die Zeit mit dem Verluste älterer

Freunde bedroht, so müssen wir suchen uns
jüngeren anzuschliessen.   Von der Société
St. Simonienne bitte Sich fern zu halten.   Auch
hierüber gelegentlich das Nähere.

Treulichst,

J. W. v. GOETHE.

WEIMAR, d. 17 Octbr. 1830.

Abschrift, HITZIG to GOETHE.

*   *   *   *   *   *

Herrn Th. Carlyle, der das unschätzbare Glück geniesst,
seine literarische Thätigkeit durch Ihren Rath geleitet,
durch Ihre Mitwirkung gefördert, durch Ihre Freundschaft
erhöht und belebt zu sehen, und der dieser Gunst des
Geschicks so würdig ist, glaubten wir unsre hohe Achtung
und den Wunsch einer nähern Verbindung mit ihm am
deutlichsten dadurch zu beweisen, dass wir ihn einmüthig
zum auswärtigen Mitgliede unsrer Gesellschaft ernannten.
Nachdem Ew. Excellenz diese Verbindung eingeleitet, ja
durch die Aneignung seines unserm unvergänglichen Schiller
geweihten Werkes ihn gleichsam schon zu dem unsrigen
gemacht haben, dürfen wir hoffen, dass er unsrer Einladung
zur gemeinsamen Förderung des hohen Zweckes folgen
werde, und bitten Sie dieses unser lebhaftes Verlangen durch
Ihre gütige Vermittelung an ihn gelangen zu lassen.

Wir schliessen mit dem Wunsche, der für jeden edelge-
sinnten Deutschen zum Gebet wird, dass der Himmel dem
Vaterland Ihr Leben noch lange Jahre erhalten möge,

Q

dieses Leben, wovon jeder Moment ein befruchtender Keim ist zur Veredlung und Erhebung für Zeit und Nachwelt.

Beschlossen Berlin in der Versammlung vom 24. Septbr. 1830.

Die Gesellschaft für ausländische Literatur.

HITZIG.

[TRANSLATION.]

My last letter of the 5th of October, in which I inserted a copy of the vote, nominating you, my dearest Sir, a member of the Society of Foreign Literature at Berlin, will, I trust, have reached you. I now send you a copy of the letter in which that vote was transmitted to me. I am glad that by this means you have secured relations with Germany, which may hereafter in many cases be useful to you.

When time threatens us with the loss of older friends, we must seek to attach ourselves to younger ones. From the St. Simonian Society pray hold yourself aloof. More about this on another occasion.

Most faithfully,

J. W. v. GOETHE.

WEIMAR, 17th October 1830.

Copy, HITZIG *to* GOETHE.

[*24th September* 1830.]

*   *   *   *   *   *

As to Mr. Thomas Carlyle, who enjoys the inestimable good fortune of having his literary labours guided by your advice, furthered by your co-operation, and quickened and elevated by your friendship, and who so well deserves this favour of fate, we have unanimously chosen him a Foreign Member of our Society, believing that thereby we could best prove our high esteem for him and our desire for a closer relation with him. Since your Excellency has brought about this connection, nay more, has, through the adoption of his Work consecrated to our immortal Schiller, as it were, already made him one of us, we trust he will comply with our invitation to join us in the promotion of our high aim, and we beg of you to permit this, our sincere desire, to reach him through your kind mediation.

We conclude with the wish, which in every noble-minded German becomes a prayer, that Heaven will spare your life to our country for many years to come,—a life whose every moment is a fruitful seed of ennoblement and elevation for the present time and future ages.

Done at Berlin at the Meeting on the 24th of September 1830.

For the Society for Foreign Literature,   HITZIG.

XXXI.—CARLYLE to GOETHE.

CRAIGENPUTTOCK, DUMFRIES,
23d October 1830.

MY HONOURED FRIEND—From the first sentence of your otherwise most welcome Letter,

I draw the unpleasant apprehension that mine
of August last has failed to reach you.   The
like, it is true, never happened in our past correspondence : nevertheless to such accidents
we are ever liable ; at all events, this suspicion
of neglect, under which I may have fallen, is of
such a sort that I lose not a moment in remov-
ing it.   Did no letter for you, then, arrive in the
beginning of September announcing that your
Packet of the 13th June, and Letter of the 7th
had both happily come to hand ; and been
received with the old feelings of thankfulness
and gladness, which such expressions of your
regard must ever merit from us ? [1]   I will still
hope [it did] : for the Letter, of which unluckily
I have kept no memorandum, and cannot more
accurately specify the date, was without any
doubt despatched hence, and safely committed
to the Post-Office ; after which, so punctual are
the rules and arrangements of that Establish-
ment, there seems no probability of miscarriage
on this side the German shore ; except, indeed,
one of our Mail Ships had been wrecked ; of

---

[1] This is Letter XXVIII.   See *supra*, p. 207.

which in the Newspapers I observed no notice. If such hope, which I still cherish, prove well-founded, let the present Letter be considered as a conscientious supererogation : in all things touching my duties of gratitude towards you, I would willingly make assurance doubly sure. When the Packet, which we are now permitted shortly to expect, reaches us, I will write again. Meanwhile be pleased to entertain the conviction that our regard, our love for you is not susceptible of change or interruption ; that few days, none perhaps wherein I am well employed, pass over me in these solitudes, without affectionate remembrances and thoughts full of kindly veneration for the Friend who *fern im Lande* sometimes also thinks of us.

In this Letter are two prophetic allusions breathing a noble pathetic dignity, which nevertheless affect me with alarm and pain. Far distant be that day so mournful for us, and for millions ! It is true, I might ask myself what are you to me but a Voice ; and is not that Voice one of those that cannot die ? Will not also, when we are still more inaccessibly parted, the memory of past kindness abide, perennially sweet, with the survivor ?   Neither in any case do we sorrow as those that have no Hope.   He who has seen into the high meaning of " ENTSAGEN " cherishes even. here a still Faith in quite another Future than the vulgar devotee believes, or the vulgar sceptic denies. " God is Great," say the Orientals ; to which we add only, " God is good," as the beginning and end of all our Philosophy.   But let us look away from these solemnities, which, however, the wise man at no moment forgets : the blessed-ness of Life is not in living, but in working well ; and he to whom a Task, rarely exampled in the history of men, was given, and who has done it, and is still doing it, " looks both before and after " with calm eyes, though the dew of " natural tears " may gather there.   We will hope and pray that a life so precious may be lengthened, in peaceful activity, to the utmost term ; that long years of kind earthly brother-hood are still appointed us.

If my last Letter were not lost, it would con-vey to you in warm terms the admiration I felt

for the *Schillersche Briefwechsel,* which I was
then on the point of finishing. A singularly
kind chance brought two such men into neighbourhood : their relation, so full of generous
Helpfulness, and the highest Endeavour, is one
which, especially in these times, it does us good
to look upon ; to you especially, as the more
independent of the two, and by whom the sick,
retiring, almost monastic Schiller was still held
in some communion with the world, the lovers of
Genius will feel deeply indebted ; first for your
friendly ministerings to this noble man ; and
now for perpetuating this record of so rare a
union. In Schiller himself there is almost a
spirit-like abstraction and elevation ; yet a painful isolation, except from you, is also manifest :
we could figure him as some Prometheus : steal-
ing fire, indeed, from Heaven ; but to whom also
the Gods as punishment had sent chains and
a gnawing vulture. How different was his fate
from that of our own poor Burns, blest with an
equal talent, as high a spirit ; but smitten with
a far heavier curse, and to whom no guiding
Friend, warmly as his heart could love, and

still long for wisdom, was ever given! One such
as you might have saved him, and nothing else
could ; but only the vain, the idle, the dissipated
gathered round him ; he was alone among his
kind, and courage and patience at last failed
him, and he lost all that made him Man. He
was of Schiller's age ; in the second year of that
fair Weimar union, Burns perished miserably,
deserted and disgraced, in that same Dumfries,
where they have erected Mausoleums over him,
now that it is all unavailing, and would buy a
scrap of his handwriting, as if it were Bank-
paper ; such is the sad history which, in generation after generation, is too often repeated to us.

Having here come upon Burns, I will add
my heartiest wishes, not unmixed with considerable fears of a negative result, that your young
Translator may be successful with him. The
changeful, too fugitive expressiveness of his
diction is one great charm with Burns ; at all
times hard to seize by a Translator, and no
doubt doubly so, when hidden in the rough
guise of our Scottish provincial dialect. Besides his chief, indeed almost his only, true

Poetical writings are Songs, which are of all
the most unmanageable. Otherwise Burns is
only a *Volksdichter*, more notable for shrewd
sense, passionate attachment, and a certain
rustic humour than any higher qualities. I
shall be full of curiosity to see your countryman's version, the first, I believe, into any
foreign tongue : if he fail, beyond the due limits
of Poetical and Translatorial license, the highest
kindness we can do him here will be to forget
him; the whole British nation is passionately
attached to Burns; the very Inn-windows where
he chanced to scribble in idle hours, with his
versifying and often satirical Diamond, have all
been unglassed, and the scribbled panes sold into
distant quarters, there to be hung up in frames !
There is an infinite Dilettantism in the world ;
but also a certain universal Love for Spiritual
Light, and " Reverence for what is above us."

Quitting Burns, I must not omit to thank
you, were it even a second time, for *Wachler*,
whom I find, in my Historical Studies, a solid,
trustworthy and useful help. I mentioned last
time, that my German Literary History was,

so far as concerned Publication, standing in a state of abeyance, the original Bibliopolic Scheme, of which it formed part, having fallen to the ground. There is now another possibility of its being sent forth ; as a separate work ; which I shall like better. The negotiation is not in my hands : but perhaps before the next letter, I may have it in my power to communicate the issue. Meanwhile I have been engaged a little in other more ambitious enterprises : but whether the result may be a Book, or only a pair of Magazine Essays, I cannot yet predict ; but will mention in due time, if it prove worthy of mention.

The news from Berlin, full particulars of which, with so many other interesting things, I expect by your Packet, could not be other than gratifying. To Friends recommended by you my best services must be always due. One of these men, if the name *Hitzig* belongs to the Biographer of Hoffmann and Werner, is already favourably known to me.[1] A letter, according to your wish,

---

[1] Carlyle had spoken approvingly of Hitzig, in the *Life and Writings of Werner* (*Miscellanies*, i. p. 105).

with offer of heartiest co-operation in a work which I also reckon so important, shall not be wanting.

There is much more to be said, were not the unstretchable paper too near an end. For the *Farbenlehre* I shall afterwards thank you more at large. To your Ottilie express our kindest wishes every way ; hope also for prosperity in her Editorship of that fair *Chaos*[1] (like the grace-

---

[1] Eckermann says, under date 5th April 1830 :—"We came at length to speak of the ' *Chaos*,' which is a Weimar Periodical conducted by Madame von Goethe, in which not only the German ladies and gentlemen of this place take part, but also, more especially, the young English, French, and other Foreigners who are staying here ; so that nearly every number of it is a medley of almost every known European language. ' It is very pretty of my daughter,' said Goethe, ' and she ought to be commended and thanked for having established a journal which is in the highest degree original, and for having so stimulated the individual members of our community, that it should now have survived almost a twelvemonth. It is, indeed, but a dilettante pastime, and I know right well that nothing great or lasting will come of it ; still it is pretty, and it is to a certain extent a mirror of the intellectual standing of our present Weimar society. And then, too, which is the main thing, it gives our young ladies and gentlemen, who often don't know what to do with themselves, some occupation. And also it is an intellectual centre, which offers them opportunities for conversation and entertainment, and thus keeps them from mere inanity and hollow gossip. I read every page as it comes fresh from the press, and can say that

ful one of a Lady's portfolio), for which, among
these mountains, new materials, I believe, are
preparing.   Forget not your kind resolution of
soon writing again.   Through the winter you
shall duly hear of me : it is a deep snow, through
which Mail-guards will not either drive or ride ;
and now steam carries men and ships across the
water in all seasons.   My friendly regards to Dr.
Eckermann, if he is with you.   My wife joins
me in sincerest prayers that all good may be
with you.   God have you in His keeping!—I
am ever, your affectionate Friend and Servant,

THOMAS CARLYLE.

XXXII.—CARLYLE to GOETHE.

CRAIGENPUTTOCK, 15th November 1830.

MY HONOURED FRIEND—With the truest
pleasure we received your Letter of the 17th
October, some ten days ago, and, strangely
enough, **that** same evening, by another conveyance, arrived the long-looked-for Hamburg

in the whole I have seen nothing that was inept, and indeed
some things in it that were even very pretty.' "—*Gespräche
mit Goethe.*

Box, with all its precious contents in perfect order. Already, on the 23d of last Month, I had written to you, chiefly in regard to a former letter, which I then feared might have been lost: now, however, by a certain phrase, I discover that such fear was groundless ; that hitherto our messages pass safely, over rough seas and tumultuous lands, and do not once miss their road. Among the many wonders of modern society, such a benefit is not the least wonderful; and ought, indeed, as you once remarked, to make amends for much that we could wish otherwise. Not knowing the particular Address of our Berlin Friends, and thinking better, at all events, that you, who had planted the seed of that relation, should also witness its germinating, I have enclosed a few lines under this cover, and shall employ your kindness to forward them as you see fittest. I hope also that the footing you have procured me on the German soil will prove a lasting one, and pleasant to my neighbours : for me the remembrance of him to whom I owe it will render the connection doubly valuable.

Concerning the Box and its Books, I must first mention that wonderful *Life of Schiller*, with its proud Introduction,[1] fitter to have stood at the head of some Epic Poem of my writing than there.   That I should see myself, before all the world, set forth as the Friend of Goethe, is an honour of which, some few years ago, I could not, in my wildest flights, have dreamed ; of which I should still desire no better happiness than to feel myself worthy.   For the rest the book is nearly the most beautiful I have ever seen ; the Preface graceful and pertinent, as well as highly flattering : these House-pictures themselves seem more appropriate than I could have fancied.   On the whole, as one of our rhymers says : " 'Tis distance lends enchantment to the view "; had this Craigenputtock mansion stood among the Harz Mountains or the Vosges, this authentic image of it would have interested me as well as another.   But that our remote Scottish Home should stand here, faithfully represented by a German burin under *your* auspices, this is a fact which we shall

[1] See *supra*, p. 204 *n.*

never get to understand. The King's palace
of Holyrood was not dealt with so royally ; and
that our rough-cast Dwelling, with its humble
Sycamores and unfrequented hills, should have
such preferment ! We repeat often : a House,
like a Prophet, save in its own country, is not
without Honour.

For that matchless copy of your Poems,
the more precious for the memorable Day it
was inscribed on,[1] my wife, whose gratification is of the highest, requests a little space
here to thank you in her own words. The
last *Lieferung* I have already gone over ;
especially the *Tag-und Jahresheft*, in the like
of which I could read without limit.—Here,
however, let me mention an accident and
omission, which, as important to me, you
will gladly rectify : namely, *that the fore-last
Lieferung was not sent ; that from volume* 25

---

[1] *Goethe's Gedichte* (Cotta 1829), two volumes, in blue silk
cover, and with autograph inscription, " Der entfernten theuren
Freundin Jane W. Carlyle, mit freundlichstem Gruss, am 28
Aug. 1830, W. Goethe, Weimar." [" To my dear, far-distant
friend Jane W. Carlyle, with kindest greeting, on the 28th of
August, ' Goethe's Birthday,' 1830."]

to volume 31, *of that beautiful Edition, there is a blank.* Let me trust, also, that your task is not yet finished ; that from among your valuable Papers, copious Selections, and Completions of many sorts are yet in store for us. My room here is exhausted, otherwise there were innumerable things to say. In No. CIII. of the *Edinburgh Review* is a Criticism of *Lord L. Gower's Translations*, which, as wiping away a reproach from British Literature, I could not but welcome. The Critic, who, I learn, is a man of forty, "a scholar, politician, and philosopher," appears to understand nothing whatever of *Faust*, except that the Author is the first of contemporaneous minds, and that Lord Gower understands *less* than nothing of it. Even this, however, is something, and not long ago would have seemed surprising. I myself am sometimes meditating a Translation of *Faust*, for which the English world is getting more and more prepared. But of all this more at large by the next occasion. Might I beg for another word from you by your earliest convenience. The winter will not shut up our

thoughts, our wishes.   May all Good be ever
with you ; may your days long be preserved
in peace for the millions to whom they are
precious !

T. Carlyle.

[Postscript by Mrs. Carlyle.]

I have requested a vacant corner of my
Husband's sheet; that I might, in my own
person add a word of acknowledgment.   But
what my heart feels towards you finds no fit
utterance in *words;* and seeks some mode of
expression that were infinite : in action, rather
in high endeavour, would my love, my faith,
my deep sense of your goodness express itself ;
and then only, should these feelings become
worthy of their exalted object.   *Goethe's*
'*friend*,' '*dear* friend !' words more delightful than *great Queen* so named.   " I bear
a charmed heart"; the fairy-like gift on which
those words are written [1] shall be my talisman
to destroy unworthy influences.   Judge then
how I must value it !   In the most secret place

---

[1] See *supra*, p. 239 *n.*

R

of my house I scarcely think it sufficiently safe;
where I look at it from time to time with a
mingled feeling of pride and reverence. Accept my heartfelt thanks for this and so many
other tokens of your kindness; and still think
of me as your affectionate friend and faithful
disciple,   JANE W. CARLYLE.

XXXIII.—ECKERMANN to CARLYLE.

[6th December 1830.]

Mein theurer Herr und Freund!—Verzeihen
Sie dass ich mit einer Antwort auf Ihr letztes
werthes Schreiben bis jezt in Rückstand geblieben bin.   Ich erhielt es im April einen Tag vor
meiner Abreise nach Italien mit Herrn v. Goethe,
dem Sohn. Ich bin in voriger Woche von dieser
Reise   nach   Weimar   zurückgekehrt,   jedoch
allein, indem jener Freund, wie Sie vielleicht
auch aus den Zeitungen werden gesehen haben,
in Rom seine irdische Bahn beschlossen hat.
Seine   Familie   hat   diesen   Verlust   eines
geliebten Mitgliedes schmerzlich empfunden,

sich jedoch nach und nach in das Unabänder-
liche, Geschehene, ergeben, und sich nunmehr
ganz wieder dem Lebendigen und Thätigen
zugewendet. Besonders ist Goethe's hohes
Wirken keinen Tag unterbrochen worden, wie
man denn an Ihm überhaupt die Maxime zu
verehren hat, jedes unnütze Leiden durch nützliche Thätigkeit zu überwältigen.

Kaum war ich nun einige Tage wieder hier,
als Goethe in der Nacht von 25. auf den 26.
November mit einem heftigen Blutsturz
erwachte, so dass Sein Leben in Gefahr
schwebte und nur ein schneller Aderlass und
eine so kräftige Natur wie die Seinige Ihn
retten konnte. Sie mögen denken dass ganz
Weimar dadurch in grosse Aufregung und in
nicht geringe Sorge versetzt wurde. Am
zweyten Tage jedoch liess uns die beruhigende
Aussage seines trefflichen Arztes, des Hofrath
Vogel, schon wieder die beste Hoffnung
schöpfen und so ist denn Goethe von Tag
zu Tag seiner vollkommenen Genesung
entgegengeschritten, so dass Er jetzt schon
wieder auf, und in gewohnter Weise beschäftigt,

ist, wie wohl Er sich noch stille bey Sich hält und wie billig noch alle äussere Anregung vermeidet. Die Krankheit war also nicht zum Tode sondern zur Ehre Gottes, und wir schöpfen aus diesem glänzenden Sieg Seiner unvergleichlichen Natur die sicherste Hoffnung, Ihn nunmehr noch manches schöne Jahr in vollkommenen Kräften thätig voran zu sehen.

Vor allen freue ich mich nun auf die Vollendung des Faust woran jetzt so viel gethan, dass sie nicht ferner zu den Unmöglichkeiten zu rechnen ist. Ich freue mich dazu als zu einem Werk das an Umfang und inneren Reichthum nicht seines Gleichen haben wird, indem es nicht allein nach allen Verhältnissen der geistigen und sinnlichen Welt hinrührt, sondern auch die menschliche Brust mit allen ihren Leidenschaften und Thätigkeiten, mit ihren Richtungen auf das Wirkliche, so wie auf die imaginären Regionen des Glaubens und Aberglaubens vollkommen ausspricht, und zwar in allen denkbaren Formen und Versen der Poesie. Deutschland wird sich daran üben um es zu verstehen und vollkommen zu geniessen, und

die Nachbarnationen werden es ihren vorzüg-
lichsten Talenten danken, wenn sie dieses
Deutsche Product durch immer gelungenere
Versionen bey sich national machen.

Es steht mir zwar nicht zu Ihnen zu rathen,
wäre ich jedoch an Ihrer Stelle, so würde ich
sicher für meine Nation etwas dankbares unter-
nehmen, wenn ich die schönsten Mussestunden
einiger Jahre auf eine treue Uebersetzung des
Faust verwendete. Die Proben Ihrer *Helena*
haben zur Genüge gezeigt, dass Sie nicht allein
das deutsche Original vollkommen verstehen,
sondern auch Ihre eigene Sprache genugsam in
Ihrer Gewalt haben, um das Empfundene und
Verstandene anmuthig und geistreich wieder
auszudrücken. Die Uebersetzung des Lord L.
Gower mag denen genügen die das Original nicht
kennen, und man mag sie als Vorläufer eines Bes-
sern schätzen, allein genau besehen mag es ihm
gefehlt haben, beydes an Einsicht wie an Muth.

Man soll aber nie fragen ob eine Nation für
ein Werk reif[1] sey, bevor man wagen will es ihr

---

[1] Two words here, likely to be torn by the seal, are repeated in the margin in Goethe's hand.

zu bringen.   In solcher Erwartung hätte Goethe
noch lange Zeit haben mögen.   Die Nationen
aber reifen an kühnen Werken heran und man
soll ihnen daher das Beste nicht vorenthalten.

Ich hatte vor, Ihnen noch manches von
meiner Reise zu schreiben, ich wollte Ihnen
von manchem grossen Eindrucke erzählen den
ich gehabt, wie mich der Mont Blanc und
Monte Rosa so wie der Garda und Genfer See
in Bezug auf die Farbenlehre beschäftiget; auch
dass ich auf meiner Rückreise mich der Uebersetzung Ihres Lebens von Schiller erfreut;
allein es fehlt mir heute an Raum wie an Zeit;
und ich schliesse für diessmal, mit den herzlichsten Grüssen an Sie und Ihre Frau Gemalin,
und mit dem Wunsch recht bald wieder von
Ihnen zu hören.

Ihr treuer Freund,

ECKERMANN.

WEIMAR, d. 6. *Dcbr*. 1830.

[Postscript by Goethe in his own handwriting.]

Glücklicherweise kann ich eigenhändig hinzufügen dass ich lebe, und hoffen darf noch eine

Zeitlang in der Nähe meiner Geliebten zu ver-
weilen.   Gruss und Segen den theuern Gatten!
Ihre beyden Briefe sind angelangt, der nach
Berlin bestellt.

J. W. v. GOETHE.

WEIMAR, *d. 7. Dcbr. 1830.*

[TRANSLATION.]

MY DEAR SIR AND FRIEND!—Pardon me,
that my answer to your last valued letter
has been delayed until now.   I received it
in April, the day before setting out for Italy
with Herr von Goethe, the son.   I returned to
Weimar from this journey last week, but alone,
for that friend, as you perhaps have seen in the
newspapers, closed his earthly course in Rome.[1]

---

[1] Eckermann and August von Goethe set out on this journey
on the 22d of April 1830; but August, whose conduct had
made his absence from Weimar desirable even to his Father,
who was much attached to him, was soon galled by Eckermann's restraint, and, with Goethe's permission, the two travellers parted company at Genoa on the 12th of September;
August, after visits to Pompeii and to Naples, proceeded to
Rome, where a stroke of paralysis brought his life to a close on
the 27th of October 1830.   He was buried near the Pyramid
of Cestius; Thorwaldsen (out of respect for August's Father)

His family have keenly felt this loss of a beloved member, but they have gradually sub-
mitted to what has unalterably befallen, and
have now once more wholly turned back to the
living and their concerns.   Above all, Goethe's
high task was not interrupted for a single day ;
for on all occasions we have to revere in him
the principle of mastering useless sorrow by
useful activity.

I had returned, however, but a few days, when
on the night of the 25th-26th of November
Goethe awoke with so violent a hemorrhage of
the lungs, that his life was in danger, and was
only saved by a speedy blood-letting and by the
vigour of his constitution.   You may imagine
that all Weimar was thrown by this into a state
of great emotion and no little anxiety.   However, on the second day, the encouraging report
of his eminent physician, Hofrath Vogel, gave

designed and erected a monument to his memory.   Eckermann
did not return to Weimar until the 23d of November.   He
was most kindly received by Goethe, "who talked of many
things, only not a word of his son."—See *Düntzer's Life oj
Goethe*, translated by Thomas W. Lyster (2 vols., London,
1883), ii. pp. 416-421.

us the best hopes; and, from day to day, Goethe
has steadily advanced toward complete recovery, so that he is now again up and busy in
his usual ways, although he still remains quietly
at home, and avoids, as is desirable, all external
excitement.   Thus the illness was not fatal,
but for the glory of God; and from this striking victory of his incomparable constitution,
we derive the most confident hope that we
shall yet see him at work, and in complete
possession of his powers, for many fair years
to come.

Above all, I now look forward to the completion of *Faust*, of which so much is finished,
that it is no longer to be counted among the
impossibilities.   And I rejoice in the work as
one, which in compass and in richness of contents will not have its like, touching as it does
not only on all the relations of the spiritual and
intellectual world, but also giving complete expression to the human heart, with all its passions
and energies, with its dispositions for action,
as well as for the imaginary regions of belief and
superstition; and this too, in every conceivable

form and measure of poetry. Germany will try its strength on the work, in order to understand and fully enjoy it, and neighbouring nations will be grateful to their men of most distinguished talent, if by versions, ever more and more successful, they make this German product one of their own national possessions.

It is indeed not for me to offer advice, but if I were in your place, I should certainly undertake something for which my country would be grateful, by employing, for some years, my best leisure hours on a faithful translation of *Faust*. The specimens of your *Helena* have sufficiently shown, that you not only completely understand the German original, but have also your own language sufficiently at command to express in it the sentiment and meaning with grace and spirit. Lord L. Gower's translation may be sufficient for those who do not know the original, and may be valued as the forerunner of a better version, but, critically examined, it seems to be lacking alike in insight and in vigour.

But one should never ask if a Nation is

ready for a work, before one ventures to offer it.
Were that the case Goethe might still have had to
wait a long time.   Nations are indeed matured
by means of daring works, and therefore the
best ought not to be withheld from them.

I had intended to write to you many things
of my journey.   I wanted to tell you of the
many deep impressions I received ; how Mont
Blanc and Monte Rosa, as well as the Lakes of
Garda and Geneva, had occupied me in reference to the *Farbenlehre,* and also that on my
homeward journey I was cheered by the translation of your *Life of Schiller ;* but both time
and space fail me to-day, and I now conclude
with most cordial greetings to you and your
lady, and with the hope that I may soon hear
from you again.

Your faithful friend,

ECKERMANN.

WEIMAR, *6th December* 1830.

Happily I can add with my own hand that I
am alive, and may hope yet for a time to abide
with my loved ones.   Greetings and blessings

to the dear Pair.   Your two letters have arrived,
and the one for Berlin has been forwarded.

J. W. v. GOETHE.

WEIMAR, *7th December* 1830.

Carlyle, writing to his Mother on the 11th February 1831, told her of the receipt of the preceding
letter, and of his reply to it :—

"We had a letter from Goethe, or rather from Goethe's
secretary, with a short kind postscript from Goethe to tell
that he was 'still in the land of the living and beside his
loved ones.'   He has lost his only son (far from him,
travelling in Italy) ; and has had a violent fit of sickness
(a flux of blood), so that for two days his own life was
despaired of.   He bore his son's death like a hero; 'did
not cease from his labours for a single day.'   I have written
to him all that was kind : engaged among other things to
translate his Poem of *Faust*, which I reckoned would be a
gratification to him.   If my own *Book*[1] were out, I would
begin it with alacrity."

XXXIV.—CARLYLE to GOETHE.

CRAIGENPUTTOCK, DUMFRIES,
22d January 1831.

MY DEAR AND HONOURED FRIEND—I learn
with the truest sorrow, by Dr. Eckermann's

---

[1] *Sartor Resartus.*

Letter, and the Public Journals, what has befallen at Weimar ; that you have lost him who
was the most precious to you in this world ;
that your own life, threatened by violent disease,
has been in extreme danger.   My only consolation is that you yourself are still preserved
to us ; that you bore your heavy stroke with
the heroic wisdom we should have anticipated
of you.   It is a truth, which we are daily
taught in stern lessons, that here nothing has a
"continuing city ;" that man's life is as a
"vapour which quickly fleeth away."   Within
the bygone Twelvemonth I too have lost no
fewer than five of my near relatives : the last,
a Sister, peculiarly endeared to me by worth and
kind remembrances, whom I now seem to have
loved almost more than any other of my kindred.
"We shall go to them, they shall not return to
us."   Meantime, while Days are given us, let
us employ them : "Our Field is Time," what
we plant therein has to grow through Eternity ;
our Hope and Comfort is "to work while it is
called To-day."   And so : Forward ! Forward !

What Dr. Eckermann mentions of your being

busied with a *Continuation of Faust* could not be
other than great news for me. Pray tell him also
that his counsel and admonition about an English
version of *Faust* came in the right season ; that
I had already long been meditating such an enterprise, and had well nigh determined, before
much time elapsed, on attempting it. The British
World is daily getting readier for a true copy of
Faust : already we everywhere understand that
Faust is no theatrical spectacle, but a Poem ;
that they who know and can know nothing of
it, must also say nothing of it ; which, within
the last four years, is an immense advancement.
Lord L. Gower's Translation is now universally
admitted to be one of the worst, perhaps the
very worst, of such a work, ever accomplished
in Britain ; our Island, I think, owes you some
amends ; would that I were the man to pay it !
As I said, however, I have as good as determined to make the endeavour ere long.

In an early number of the *Edinburgh Review*,
perhaps in the next, there is to appear, as I
learn, a criticism of the *Briefwechsel*, involving
most probably a delineation and comparison of

the two great Correspondents. I must warn
all German Friends to expect but little : the
Critic, I apprehend, will be the same who
criticised *Faust* and Lord Gower in the last
Number of that Periodical :[1] an admiring Dilettantism, but no true insight or earnest criticism,
is to be looked for.—I too am again to speak
a word on that favourite subject, a word of
warning and direction, where the harvest is
great, and the reapers many and more zealous
than experienced. A certain William Taylor
of Norwich, the Translator of your *Iphigenie,*
has written what he calls a *Historic Survey of
German Poetry ;* the tendency of which you
may judge of sufficiently by this one fact, that
the longest Article but one is on August von
Kotzebue. Taylor is a man of real talent, but
a Polemical Sceptic only ; with no eye for
Poetry, who sees in the highest minds only
their relation to the Church Creed ; whose book,
therefore, as likely to mislead many, I have felt
called upon to contradict, and, by such artillery

[1] Mr. William Empson, Jeffrey's son-in-law, afterwards
editor of the *Edinburgh Review.* See *infra*, p. 282.

as I had, batter down into its original rubbish.
I fear you will not like the satirical style : the
more agreeable will some concluding speculations be on what I have named *World-Literature*, after you; and how Europe, in the
communion of these its chief writers, is again
to have a " Sacred College and Council of
Amphictyons," and become more and more one
universal Commonwealth.   This, it seems to
me, is one of the most cheering signs of the
future that are yet discernible.   Literature is
now nearly all in all to us ; not our speech
only, but our Worship and Lawgiving ; our
best Priest must henceforth be our Poet ; the
Vates will in future be practically all that he
ever was in theory,—or else *Nothing*, which
last consummation we cannot consent to admit.
The *Review of Taylor* is not to appear for some
months :[1] in the meanwhile, I am working at
another curious enterprise of my own, which is
yet too amorphous to be prophesied of.[2]

---

[1] It appeared in the *Edinburgh Review*, No. CV., 1831.
See *Miscellanies*, vol. iii., p. 283.

[2] *Sartor Resartus*.

Leaving now these Paper Speculations, let me descend a little to the solid Earth. We have a mild winter here, are busy and peaceable : often look into that Weimar House, and figure our Friend and Master there, and pray for all blessings on him. A little collection of Memorials, intended to cross the sea, is also gathering itself together : we anticipate that before the next 28th of August, at all events, it will have saluted you. I have already got nearly all my writings for the *Foreign Review ;* and will send them in the shape of *Aushängebogen*, since they are yet in no other. Learning from your *Tag-und Jahresheft* that you had no copy of the English *Iphigenie*, I sent to London to procure one ; hitherto without effect ; however, as the work stands entire in this *Taylor's Historic Survey*, I will study to send it in one or the other form. Some weeks ago we heard of a wandering Portrait-painter being at Dumfries, who took what were called admirable likenesses, in pencil, at two hours' sitting : whereupon we drove down, and set the Artist to work ; who unhappily produced, by way of Portrait for me,

a piece of beautiful pencilling, which had no
feature of mine about it; so that it cannot be
sent to Weimar, being worth nothing : however,
my wife has undertaken to copy and rectify it;
at all events, to clip you some profile of me.
Would that there were aught else we could do
for you in our Island ; had I but a true work of
my own writing to send!

The Saint Simonians in Paris have again
transmitted me a large mass of their performances : Expositions of their Doctrine; Pro-
clamations sent forth during the famous Three
Days ; many numbers of their weekly Journal.
They seem to me to be earnest, zealous, and
nowise ignorant men, but wandering in strange
paths.   I should say they have discovered and
laid to heart this momentous and now almost
forgotten truth, *Man is still Man;* and are
already beginning to make false applications of
it.[1]   I have every disposition to follow your
advice, and stand apart from them ; looking

---

[1] Carlyle, in *Sartor Resartus* (Book III., chapter xii.),
speaking of the Saint-Simonian Society, expresses the same
idea in almost the same words.

on their Society and its progress nevertheless as a true and remarkable Sign of the
Times.

In our own country, too, the political atmosphere grows turbid, and great things are
fermenting and will long ferment. To which
also I reckon that my proper relation is that
chiefly of Spectator : the world is heavily
struggling out into the new era; the struggle
has lasted centuries, and may yet last centuries :
let him who has seed-corn, or can borrow seed-
corn, cast it into these troubled Nile-waters,
where, in due season, it will be found after
many days. Some of our friends are high in
the new Ministry, especially the Edinburgh
Reviewer of *Meister*, a good man and bad
critic :[1] but the Sun and Seasons are the only
changes that visit the wilderness. *Mein Acker
ist die Zeit.*

Perhaps ere long a letter will come from
Weimar, to tell us that you are still well, and
nobly occupied. Meanwhile, know always that
we love you and reverence you. To your dear

[1] Jeffrey.

Ottilie speak peace, and from us, all that is kind and sympathising. "God is great, God is good."—I remain ever, your affectionate, grateful Friend,   Thomas Carlyle.

Please to return Dr. Eckermann my friendliest thanks, and encourage him to *repeat* his kind favour : I will surely reply to it.

XXXV.—Hitzig to Carlyle.

[*28th January* 1831.]

Ew. Wohlgeborn waren uns schon vor dem Erscheinen Ihrer Lebensbeschreibung unsers grossen Landmannes zu ehrenwerth bekannt, als dass letztere nicht in uns den Wunsch erregen sollen, mit Ihnen in nähere Beziehung zu treten. Dies zu bewirken schien uns die geeigneteste Weise, Sie zur Mitgliedschaft unserer anspruchlosen literarischen Verbrüderung einzuladen, und wir statten Ihnen unsern verbindlichsten Dank ab, dass Sie unsere freundliche Einladung eben so freundlich angenommen.

Dagegen fürchten wir, dass Ew. Wohlgeborn

in einem Irrthum sich befinden, wenn Sie der
Ansicht wären, dass unsere Gesellschaft eine
besondere Wirksamkeit *nach aussen* wünsche.
Ihr Hauptzweck besteht in dem Genuss
ausländischer Geisteswerke und in der
gewünschten Verbindung mit ausländischen
Dichtern und Aesthetikern, um sich solche
näher der Quelle zu verschaffen und eine
bewährtere Bekanntschaft mit dem reellen
Neuen, als durch die getrübtere der Journale
zu erlangen. Die Gesellschaft, noch zu jung,
besitzt bis jetzt keine Diplome und wünschte
auch, wenn diese einst ausgefertigt werden,
dass ihre Mitglieder davon keinen öffentlichen
Gebrauch machten. Der Deutsche lebt einmal
—auch nach 1831 [*sic*]—mehr für die Familie,
als für die Oeffentlichkeit, er trägt das Familien-
leben gern in die Literatur über, wo es sich
thun lässt. Ew. Wohlgeborn werden aus
diesen Gründen die Bitte entschuldigen, von
dem Titel eines Ehrenmitgliedes unserer Gesellschaft keinen öffentlichen Gebrauch zu machen,
indem er einen Schein des Anspruchs auf die
Gesellschaft werfen würde, den diese gern

vermiede.　Beifolgend theilen wir Ihnen vor-
läufig, nebst einer Anzeige Ihres Werks vom
Herrn Dr. Seidel, unsere Statuten, und ein
älteres Namensverzeichniss unserer Mitglieder,
deren Zahl sich seit der Zeit auf eine erfreuliche
Weise vermehrt hat, nach Ihrem Wunsche mit.
Der unsere ist, dass uns recht bald Gelegenheit
würde, wozu Sie uns Hoffnung gemacht, Sie
persönlich in unserer Mitte zu sehen.

Hochachtungsvoll,

Ew. Wohlgeborn,

ergebenste,

Die Gesellschaft für ausländische Literatur,

HITZIG.

BERLIN, beschlossen in der
Sitzung vom 28ten Januar 1831.

[TRANSLATION.]

Sir—You were already, before the appearance of your Biography of our great countryman,
too honourably known to us for this work to fail
in exciting in us the wish to enter into closer
relation with you.　The fittest means of accom-

plishing this was, it seemed to us, to invite you to become a Member of our unpretending Literary Brotherhood, and we offer you our most grateful thanks for having accepted, in so friendly a manner, our friendly invitation.

At the same time we fear that you, Sir, may have misapprehended us, if you have thought our view was to gain for our society any particular *outside* agency. Its chief aim consists in the enjoyment of foreign intellectual works, and in desiring a connection with foreign poets and æsthetic writers, for the sake of providing ourselves with this enjoyment nearer the source, and of securing more authentic information concerning what is really new than the dim medium of the Periodicals affords. The Society is still too young to issue Diplomas, and, if in future it should do so, it would desire its members to make no public use of them. It is the way of the German—even in 1831—to live more for the family than for the public, and he likes, where it is possible, to carry the habits of family life into Literature. You will therefore pardon the request, that you will make no public use of

the title of Honorary Member of our Society,
since it would tend to give to it an appearance
of pretension which it would gladly avoid.
Meanwhile, in accordance with your wish, we
enclose to you, together with a notice of your
Work by Dr. Seidel, our Rules, and an old
list of our Members, whose number has, since
that was made, increased in a very satisfactory
manner.   Our wish is, that we may very soon
have the opportunity, of which you give us the
hope, of seeing you in person among us.

With high respect,

Sir,

Your most obedient,

For the Society for Foreign Literature,

HITZIG.

BERLIN, done at the Meeting of
the 28th of January 1831.

XXXVI.—GOETHE to CARLYLE.

[*2d June* 1831.]

Bey eintretendem Frühling, welcher Sie
gewiss auch schon besucht haben wird, finde

ich gemüthlich Sie wieder zu begrüssen und zu
versichern dass wir diesen Winter an Sie, als
eingeschneite Freunde öfter gedacht haben.
Wenn ich sage wir, so ist es dass Ottilie mit
ihren Kindern, nachdem der Gatte, als Mittel-
person beliebt hat, in der ehemaligen Haupt-
stadt der Welt, zurückzubleiben, sich natürlich
und sittlicher Weise näher an mich anschliesst ;
da wir denn genugsam wechselseitiges Interesse
und daraus entspringende Unterhaltung finden,
und zwar mitunter so abgesondert von der
übrigen Welt, dass wir eine Art von Craigenputtock mitten in Weimar zu bilden im Falle
waren.

Gegenwärtiges, welches schnell genug bey
Ihnen ankommen wird, lasse vorausgehen, indem ich eine Ihnen bestimmte Sendung noch
zurückhalte.

Der Inhalt meiner letzten 5 Bände ist Ihnen
meist bekannt und was er für Sie Neues enthält,
wird Ihnen, später wie früher, einige Unterhaltung geben.   Es ist aber manches auf mich
und Schiller Bezügliches zeither hervorgetreten,
welches ich erst sammeln und ordnen möchte,

damit Sie auf einmal etwas Bedeutendes
erhielten.

Sogar möcht' ich eine Antwort auf gegenwärtigen Brief erwarten um von Ihnen zu
vernehmen ob Sie vielleicht auf einiges in
Deutschland erschienene von hieraus zu sen-
dende aufmerksam geworden, was Sie allenfalls
zu sehen wünschten. Das alles könnte zu
gleicher Zeit anlangen, denn wenn ich die gute
Jahrszeit vor mir sehe, so scheint mir, man
könne nichts verspäten.

Der gute Eckermann ist glücklich zurückgekehrt, heiter und in seiner Art wohlgemuth.
Sein zartes und zugleich lebhaftes, man möchte
sagen, leidenschaftliches Gefühl ist mir von
grossem Werth, indem ich ihm manches Unge-
druckte, bisher ungenutzt Ruhende vertraulich
mittheile, da er denn die schöne Gabe besitzt,
das Vorhandene, als genügsamer Leser, freundlich zu schätzen und doch auch wieder, nach
Gefühl und Geschmack zu Forderndes deutlich
auszusprechen weiss.

Vorstehendes war längst zur Absendung

bestimmt, blieb aber liegen bis ich das beysammen hätte, was doch auch werth wäre übers Meer sich zu Ihnen zu begeben.   Sie erhalten also:—

1. Vier Hefte *Neureutherischer Randzeichnungen*, zu meinen Parabeln und sonstigen Gedichten.   Schon vor Jahren wurde, in München, ein altes Gebetbuch entdeckt, wo der Text den geringsten Raum der Seite einnahm, die Ränder aber von Albrecht Dürer, auf die wundersamste Weise, mit Figuren und Zierrathen geschmückt waren.   Hievon wird genannter junger Mann entzündet, dass er, mit wundersamstem Geschick, Randzeichnungen zu vielen meiner Gedichte unternahm, und sie, mit anmuthig congruirenden Bildern commentirte. Wie diess geschehen muss man vor Augen blicken, weil es etwas Neues, Ungesehenes und deshalb nicht zu beschreiben ist.   Möge dieses reizende Heft unsern Eremiten der Grafschaft Dumfries oft wiederholt heitere Lebensaussichten gewähren.

2. Die letzte Sendung meiner Werke ; lassen Sie sich zu dem schon Bekannten freundlich

hinführen. Ich habe mit einer poetischen
Masse geschlossen, weil denn doch die Poesie
das glückliche Asyl der Menschheit bleiben
wird, indem sie sich zwischen den ersten düstern
Irrthum und den letzten verkühlenden Zweifel
mitten hineinsetzt, jenen in Klarheit zu führen
trachtet, diesen aber deutlich und theilnehmend
zu werden nöthigt, so werden nicht viele wirk-
samere Mittel gefunden werden um den Menschen in seinem Kreise löblich zu beschäftigen.

3. Die zwey Bändchen Schiller *redivivus*
werden Ihnen Freude machen; sie regen manch
schönes Gefühl und manchen wichtigen Gedanken auf.

4. Nun kommt auch der Abschluss des
Chaos anbey, woran manches Sie interessiren
wird. Mit dem 52 Stück ward der erste Band
geschlossen, und es fragt sich: ob die anmuthige Societät, wie sie jetzt ist, bey schnell-
wechselnden Theilnehmenden, bey flüchtigen
Gesinnungen, Neigungen und Grillen, unter-
nehmen wird in diesem Flusse zum zweytenmal
zu schwimmen; einige Herzenserleichterungen
von unsrer Schottischen Freundin mitgetheilt,

würden die Entschlüsse wahrscheinlich u. hoffentlich befördern.

5. Meine Metamorphose der Pflanzen mit
einigen Zusätzen, alles übersetzt von Herrn
Soret, liegt denn endlich auch bey. Da dieses
Heft Ursache der retardirten Sendung ist, so
wünsch' ich denn doch dass der Inhalt auch
Ihnen möge von Bedeutung seyn. Gewinnen
Sie dem Ganzen etwas ab, so wird es Sie nach
manchen Seiten hin fördern, auch das Einzelne
wird Ihre Gedanken auf erfreuliche Wege hin-
weisen. Es waren die schönsten Zeiten meines
Lebens da ich mich um die Naturgegenstände
eifrig bemühte und auch in diesen letzten Tagen
war es mir höchst angenehm die Untersuchun-
gen wieder aufzugreifen. Es bleibt immer ein
herzerhebendes Gefühl wenn man dem Uner-
forschlichen wieder einige lichte Stellen abge-
winnt.

Auch liegt ein Blatt bey, von Herrn Hitzig
unterschrieben, die Anerkennung Ihrer Berliner
Fellowship. Von jenen werthen Freunden
habe ich unmittelbar lange nichts vernommen.
Die fortwährende Bemühung mein Haus zu

bestellen und meinen nächsten Mitfühlenden und Mitwirkenden das in die Hände zu legen was ich selbst nicht vollbringen kann, nimmt mir alle brauchbare Stunden weg deren uns doch noch manche gute wie schöne gegönnt sind.

Hiemit sey geschlossen; ins Kästchen selbst wird noch ein Blatt gelegt. Von mir und Ottilien die schönsten Grüsse und treusten Wünsche dem lieben Eremitenpaare. Die Ankunft des Kästchens bitte baldigst zu melden.

Also sey es!

J. W. v. GOETHE.

WEIMAR, den 2 Juni 1831.

[TRANSLATION.]

[*2d June* 1831.]

With the coming of Spring, which by this time will have visited you also, I find it pleasant once more to greet you and to assure you that we have often thought of you during the last winter as snow-bound friends. If I say *we*, it is because of Ottilie, with her children, who, since her Husband, the bond of union between

us, has chosen to remain behind in the Ancient
Capital of the World, naturally and properly
clings more closely to me.   As this brings sufficient interest and entertainment to both of us,
we are sometimes on account of it so secluded
from the rest of the world, that we have been
like to form a kind of Craigenputtock in the
midst of Weimar.

I am sending off this present letter, which will
reach you soon enough, while I still withhold a
package, which I intend for you.

The contents of my last five volumes are for
the most part known to you, and what they
may contain that is new, will, as in former cases,
prove of some interest to you.   Since they were
published, several things relating to me and
Schiller have appeared, which I should now like
to collect and put in order, so that you may at
the same time receive something of importance.

I am even inclined to await your answer
to this Letter to learn from you whether you
have not perhaps noticed anything that has
appeared in Germany which you might by
chance wish to see, and which could be sent

from here. These things might all go to you at once, and now, when we have the time of the year in our favour, it seems to me, one should have no delays.

The good Eckermann has happily returned, cheerful and after his fashion gay. His delicate, and at the same time lively, one might say passionate, feeling is of great value to me; since I communicate to him in confidence much unprinted matter, hitherto lying by unused; while he has in return, as a sympathetic reader, the happy gift of cordially appreciating what is before him; and he knows how to express clearly with tact and discrimination, what may be suggested by feeling and taste.

The preceding was intended to be sent long ago, but remained waiting, till I had collected what other things might be worth going to you across the sea. Thus you now receive—

1. Four Parts of Marginal drawings by Neureuther, to my Parables and some of my other poems. Some years ago an old Prayer-book was found in Munich, in which the text

took up the smallest part of the page, but the margins were adorned, in the most wonderful way, with figures and ornaments by Albert Dürer. The above-named young man was so fired by this example, that, with the most surprising skill, he set about making marginal drawings for many of my poems, and furnishing a comment upon them with pleasingly appropriate pictures. How this has succeeded, one must see with one's own eyes, because it is something new, never seen before, and therefore not to be described. May this charming work afford our hermits of the county of Dumfries oft-repeated, cheerful vistas of life![1]

[1] Eckermann in his *Conversations*, under date of 5th April 1831, reports Goethe as saying: "In Art one does not easily meet with a more pleasing talent than Neureuther's. It is rare that an artist confines himself to what he is able to do well; most of them are anxious to do more than they can, and are eager to overstep the limits which nature has set to their talents. But of Neureuther one may say that he stands above his talent. Objects from all the kingdoms of nature are easily at his command. He draws, equally well, valleys, rocks, trees, animals, and men. He has taste, and is in a high degree, inventive and artistic; while lavishing such wealth on slight marginal drawings, he seems to play with his talent, and the pleasure which usually accompanies the careless, free spending of ample riches is transferred to the spectator. . . . No

T

2. The last Section of my Works; pray turn, with friendly feeling, to what you already know in it. I have closed with a mass of poetry, for, after all, poetry, intervening as it does, between the first dim error and the last chilling doubt, endeavouring to change the one to clearness, and compelling the other to become intelligible and sympathetic, will remain the happy refuge for mankind; and few more effectual means will be found for occupying a man worthily in his own sphere.

3. The two small volumes of *Schiller Redivivus* will please you; they awaken many a noble sentiment and weighty reflection.

4. There is also the conclusion of the *Chaos*, in which various things will interest you. The first volume ended with the 52nd number, and the question arises, whether this pleasant one has surpassed him in marginal drawing, even the great talent of Albert Dürer served in this less as a model to him than an incitement.—I will send a copy of these drawings to Mr. Carlyle in Scotland, and I hope to make with them no unwelcome present to that friend."—Albert Dürer's marginal drawings on the Prayer-Book of Kaiser Maximilian I., here referred to, have since been published (Munich, 1850).

Society as it now exists, with its quickly changing sympathies, with its fickle dispositions, inclinations and whims, will undertake to swim a second time in this stream. Some contribution from our Scotch lady-friend to encourage their fainting hearts, would, it is to be hoped, be likely to advance its resolutions.

5. Finally, my *Metamorphosis of Plants*, with some additions, all translated by M. Soret, is added to the package at last. Since this book has been the reason of the delay, I trust the contents of it may be of importance to you also. If you gain anything from it as a whole, it will be of service to you on various sides, while the details will direct your thoughts in pleasant channels. The happiest time of my life was when I was eagerly at work on the works of Nature, and now in these last days it has been extremely delightful to me to resume those researches. There is after all a feeling of exaltation in once again throwing light on any part of the Impenetrable.

There is with the rest, a sheet, signed by Herr Hitzig, the certificate of your Berlin

"Fellowship." I have heard nothing directly from those worthy friends for a long time. The continual effort to set my house in order and to put in the hands of my fellow-workers, and those nearest me in sympathy, what I myself cannot complete, occupies all my available hours, of which after all many good and beautiful ones are still granted to us.

With this I must end : still another sheet will be put in the box. The fairest greetings from me and Ottilie, and most faithful wishes for the dear pair of hermits. Pray inform me of the arrival of the box as soon as possible.

So let it be!

J. W. v. GOETHE.

WEIMAR, *2d June* 1831.

XXXVII.—GOETHE to CARLYLE.

[*15th June* 1831.]

Eben als ich schliessen will findet sich noch Raum in den Kästchen und ich komme auf einen Gedanken den ich längst hätte haben sollen. Ich lasse Ihnen die fünf verflossenen Monate dieses Jahres von einer unsrer beliebtesten Zeitschriften : dem *Morgenblatt*, einpacken, nebst seinen Beyblättern über Kunst und Literatur. Sie werden dadurch mitten ins Continent versetzt, erfahren wie man sich unterhält, wie man über mancherley denkt und Sie können Sich dabey vorstellen wie es klänge, wenn Sie eine unsrer guten Gesellschaften besuchten. Auch liegt ein Exemplar von dem übersetzten Leben Schillers bey, der Freundin gewidmet, damit sie erfahre wie sich auch die Buchbinder des Continents aller Genauigkeit und Anmuth befleissen.

Und so sey es denn hiermit geschlossen unter den besten Wünschen, und in Hoffnung baldiger Erwiederungen.

G.

WEIMAR, *den* 15 *Juni* 1831.

[TRANSLATION.]

Just as I am about to close it, I find there is still room in the little box ; and a notion which I ought to have had long ago, has struck me. I am having packed up for you the numbers belonging to the five past months of this year, of one of our most popular journals, the *Morgenblatt*,[1] together with its supplements on Art and Literature. You will by its means be transported into the heart of the Continent, will learn what people are interested in there and what they are thinking on a variety of subjects, and can thus imagine what you would hear if you took part in one of our intellectual assemblies. There is also in the box a copy of the translation of the *Life of Schiller*, an offering to my lady-friend, that she may learn how even the bookbinders of the Continent study neatness and elegance.

And so now with this let us close it, amid our best wishes, and in the hope of speedy replies.

G.

WEIMAR, 15*th June* 1831.

---

[1] Carlyle, in 1833, wrote on this volume of the *Morgenblatt* : " Part of the last Present I had from Goethe.—These Newspaper-leaves had been read or looked over by Goethe the year before he left this world."

XXXVIII.—CARLYLE to GOETHE.

CRAIGENPUTTOCK, DUMFRIES,
10th June 1831.

MY DEAR AND HONOURED FRIEND—If kind thoughts spontaneously transformed themselves into kind messages, you had many times heard from me since I last wrote. Here in our still solitudes, where the actual world is so little seen, and Memory and Fancy must be the busier, Weimar is not distant but near and friendly, a familiar city of the Mind. Daily must I send affectionate wishes thither; daily must I think, and oftenest speak also, of the Man to whom, more than to any other living, I stand indebted and united. For it can never be forgotten that to him I owe the all-precious knowledge and experience that Reverence is still possible, nay, Reverence for our fellow-man, as a true emblem of the Highest, even in these perturbed, chaotic times. That you have carried and will yet carry such life-giving Light into many a soul, wandering bewildered in the

eclipse of Doubt; till at length whole generations have cause to bless you, that instead of
Conjecturing and Denying they can again
Believe and Know: herein truly is a Sove-
reignty of quite indisputable Legitimacy, and
which it is our only Freedom to obey.

In anxious hours, when one is apt to figure
misfortune for the absent and dear, I often
look timorously into the Foreign Column of
our Newspapers, lest it bring evil tidings of
you, to me also so evil; again, I delight to
figure you as still active and serene; busy at
your high Task, in the high spirit of old
Times.—*Wie das Gestirn, Ohne Hast, Aber
ohne Rast!*[1]—May I beg for my own behoof,
some few of those moments which belong to
the world? It is chiefly in the hope of drawing
a Letter from Weimar that I now write in the
Scottish wilderness, where there can be so
little to communicate. Our promised Packet
has been detained longer than we looked for,
and diminished in contents; by a circumstance,
however, which, we hope, will render it the

[1] Goethe's *Werke* (Cotta, 1827), vol. iii. p. 259.

welcomer when it comes.   We send it, this
time, by London, where also it will have to
linger, and be finally made up under the eye of
a Proxy.   For in that city, let me announce,
there is a little poetic *Tugendbund* of Philo-
Germans forming itself, whereof you are the
Centre; the first public act of which should
come to light at Weimar, on your approaching
Birthday.   That the Craigenputtock Packet
might carry any little documents of *this* along
with it, was the cause of our delay, and of the
new route fixed on.   In London, with which
I can only communicate by writing, matters
move slower than I could wish : nevertheless,
it is confidently reckoned, the whole will be
ready in time, and either through the hands of
Messrs. Parish at Hamburg, or of the British
Ambassador at Berlin, appear at Weimar before
the 28th of August, where doubtless it will
meet with the old friendly reception.

Of this little Philo-German Combination,
and what it now specially proposes, and
whether there is likelihood that it may grow
into a more lasting union, for more complex

purposes,—I hope to speak hereafter. The mere fact that such an attempt was possible among us, would have seemed strange some years ago ; and gives one of many proofs that what you have named *World-Literature* is perhaps already not so distant. To the Berlin Friends from whom lately came a friendly Note, I purpose communicating some intelligence of this affair : it may be, we too in London shall have a little *Society for Foreign Literature ;* which, in these days, I should regard as of good promise.

The chief item in our Packet for Weimar will be the Proof-sheets of my poor contributions as a Foreign Reviewer ; the most of which I have had stitched up into a volume for your acceptance, till I can offer the whole in another form. If the last number of the *Edinburgh Review* has fallen into your hands, you have already seen the newest of these, the *Criticism of Taylor ;* likewise in the same number, an Essay on the *Correspondence with Schiller.* This latter is by a Mr. Empson,[1] a

[1] See *supra*, p. 255 *n.*

man of some rank and very considerable talent
and learning; in whose spiritual progress, as
manifested in his study of German, I see a
curious triumph of Truth and Belief over
Falsehood and Dilettantism.   He was the
Reviewer of *Faust* in a former number; and
on this occasion, still leaving somewhat to
desire, he has greatly surpassed my expecta-
tions.   Of young men that have an open sense
for such Literature as the German, or of
mature men that from youth upwards have been
acquiring an open sense, there are now not a
few in Britain : but the Critic here in question
started at middle age, as I understand, and only
a few years ago, from quite another point ; is an
English Whig Politician, which means generally a man of altogether mechanical intellect,
looking to Elegance, Excitement, and a certain
refined Utility, as the Highest; a man halting
between two Opinions, and calling it Tolerance; to whom, on the whole, that Precept,
Im Ganzen, Guten, Wahren resolut zu leben,[1]

---

[1] Goethe writes *Schönen*, not *Wahren*.   Carlyle's words at
the end of his Essay on the *Death of Goethe* are : " Could each

were altogether a dead letter. How in this
case the dry bones, blown upon by Heavenly
Inspiration, have been made to live; and a
naturally gifted spirit is freeing itself from that
death-sleep,—is to me an interesting Pheno-
menon.   It is on such grounds that the study of
the best German writings is so incalculably important for us English at this Epoch.   I am
happy to report anew, that we make rapid progress in the matter; that the ultimate recognition
and appropriation of what is worthy in German
literature by all cultivated English minds, may
be considered as not only indubitable, but even
likely to be speedy.

For myself, though my labours in that pro-
here vow to do his little task, even as the Departed did his
great one ; in the manner of a true man, not for a Day, but
for Eternity !   To live as he counselled and commanded, not
commodiously in the Reputable, the Plausible, the Half, but
resolutely in the Whole, the Good, the True : ' *Im Ganzen,
Guten, Wahren resolut zu leben !*' "—This is the verse, from
Generalbeichte, in which these words of Goethe occur :

> Willst du Absolution
> Deinen Treuen geben,
> Wollen wir nach deinem Wink
> Unablässlich streben
> Uns vom Halben zu entwöhnen,
> Und im Ganzen, Guten, Schönen,
> Resolut zu leben.—(*Werke*, i. 140.)

vince have of late been partially suspended,
I hope they are yet nowise concluded. The
History, when it sees the light, may be no
worse for having waited; already, simply by
the influence of Time, various matters have
cleared up, and the form of the whole is much
more decisively before me. As occasion serves,
I can, either at once, or gradually as hitherto,
speak out what further I have to say on it.
But for these last months I have been busy
with a Piece more immediately my own: of
this, should it ever become a printed volume,
and seem in the smallest worthy of such honour,
a copy for Weimar will not be wanting. Alas!
It is, after all, not a Picture that I am painting;
it is but a half-reckless casting of the brush,
with its many frustrated colours, against the
canvas: whether it will make good Foam is
still a venture.[1]

In some six weeks I expect to be in London:
I wish to look a little with my own eyes at
the world; where much is getting enigmatic to
me, so rapid have been its vicissitudes lately.

[1] The Piece was *Sartor Resartus.*

The mountain-solitude, with its silent verdure and foliage, will be sweeter for the change ; and my efforts there more precisely directed.

Here, however, are the limits of my paper, when there was scarcely a beginning of my utterance. How poor is all that a Letter, how poor were all that words, could say, when the heart is so full ! Do you interpret for me, and of broken stammerings make speech.

Think now and then of your Scottish Friends ; and know always that a Prophet is not without honour, that we love and reverence our Prophet. My wife unites with me in every friendliest wish. May all Good be with you and yours !—Ever your affectionate

T. CARLYLE.

All mute and dim as Shadows gray,
　His Scottish Friends the Friend descries ;
Let Love evoke them into day,
　To questions kind, shape kind replies.

CRAIGENPUTTOCK, 16*th June* 1831.

XXXIX.—CARLYLE to GOETHE.

6 WOBURN BUILDINGS, TAVISTOCK SQUARE,
LONDON, 13*th August* 1831.

MY MUCH HONOURED FRIEND—I send you a
word of remembrance from this chaotic whirlpool of a city, where I arrived three days ago ;
where the confusion in which I and all things
are carried round must be my excuse for brevity
and almost unintelligibility. Often do I recal
to myself that saying of poor Panthalis in
Helena, "the soul-confusing spell of the
Thessalian Hag," and feel as if I too were a
Shade ; for in truth this London life looks more
like a Mephistopheles' Walpurgis Night, than a
real Heaven-encircled Day, where God's kind
sun were shining peaceably on industrious men.

Our last two Letters must have crossed each
other about Rotterdam ; for yours was in
Craigenputtock about a week before mine could
be in Weimar. A thousand thanks for your
remembrance of us ! Never was letter more
gladly welcomed : it reached us in the calm

summer twilight, and was itself so calm and
pure, even like the Summer Evening, with mild
sun-rays and the sheen of an everlasting Morning already peering through !   Endless gratitude
I owe you ; for it is by you that I have learned
what worth there is in man for his brother-
man ; and how the "open secret," though the
most are blind to it, is still open for whoso has
an eye.

Since then two things have occurred which I
must now notify.   The first is the departure of a
little packet from Craigenputtock which had to
go round by London, and lie waiting there ;
but was finally put to sea by my Brother, on
the 5th of this month, with impressive charges
to the Messrs. Parish of Hamburg that they
would have it in Weimar before your Birthday.
As it went by the Steam-ship, and our Hamburg Merchants are the most courteous and
punctual of men, I can still hope that in spite of
so many delays, all will be well.   The Craigenputtock articles were insignificant enough, and
might arrive fitly at any time : solely some
Books and printed Lucubrations of mine, which

I hoped might not be quite uninteresting to
you. But along with these went another
article, from others as well as from myself, the
significance of which required that you should
see it on the 28th of August. It is a birthday
gift from a certain select body of English Disciples, who in this way seek to testify their
veneration for you. Perhaps to make the feeling still purer, I find, they have withheld their
names and merely signed themselves, " Fifteen
English Friends."[1] I may mention now that
among our number are some of our most noted
men, our three highest Poets, certain Diplomatic characters, and men of rank, as well as
humbler but not less faithful and honourable
labourers in the vineyard. Let me hope that
it will arrive in due season ; and the sight of
it give you some gratifying moments.

My second thing to be announced is the
arrival of your Weimar Packet at Craigenputtock. I could not but take it as a good
omen of my journey hither that this friendliest
of messengers reached me some two hours

[1] See *infra*, p. 292 *n.*

U

prior to my departure. A hasty glance through the contents was all that could be permitted me : I must leave my wife to assort and admire those printed Poems, and beautiful *Randzeichnungen*, in her mountain loneliness, as I find yesterday by a Letter from her, she is actually doing. For my own part I snatched up the *Metamorphosis of Plants* and *Schiller Redivivus*, with intent to read them as the Steamboat shot along with me to Liverpool, whither the first stage of my journey lay. In a calmer hour, a more deliberate word may be spoken of them.

I have come hither chiefly to dispose of the Piece which I lately described myself as writing.[1] Whether, or how well, I shall succeed seems questionable : for the whole world here is dancing a Tarantula Dance of Political Reform, and has no ear left for Literature. Nevertheless, I shall do my utmost to get the work, which was meant to be a "word spoken in season," actually emitted : at lowest I shall ascertain that it cannot be emitted, and study

[1] *Sartor Resartus.*   See *supra*, p. 85.

to do what duty that situation also will call for.
Probably I shall be here for a month.[1]   On
returning to the Scottish wilderness, you shall
hear from me again.   Meanwhile, figure me
and mine as thinking of you, loving you; as
present especially on that 28th with wishes as
warm as loving hearts can feel.   Salute Ottilie
from my wife and me.   Think sometimes of
those that are yours in this Island, especially
among the Nithsdale Mountains.—All Good be
yours always !

T. CARLYLE.

THE following letter was printed, not long after its
date, in *Fraser's Magazine*, xxii. 447, and afterwards
in a note to Carlyle's Essay, originally published in
the *Foreign Quarterly Review* on *Goethe's Works*.
The words prefixed to it in *Fraser* may still serve
as a sufficient introduction :—

" ' A fact,' says one of our fellow-labourers in this
German vineyard, ' has but now come to our knowledge,
which we take pleasure and pride in stating.   Fifteen
Englishmen, entertaining that high consideration for the

---

[1] Carlyle afterwards decided to spend the winter in London ;
Mrs. Carlyle joined him there, and they did not return to
Craigenputtock until the following April.

Good Goethe, which the labours and high deserts of a long life usefully employed so richly merit from all mankind, have presented him with a highly wrought Seal, as a token of their veneration.' We must pass over the description of the gift, for it would be too elaborate ; suffice it to say, that amid tasteful carving and emblematic embossing enough, stood these words engraven on a golden belt, and on four sides respectively : *To the German Master: From Friends in England:* 28*th August:* 1831 ; finally, that the impression was a star encircled with a serpent-of-eternity, and this motto : *Ohne Hast Aber Ohne Rast."*

The suggestion was due to Carlyle, as well as the design of the Seal, and the choice of the motto for it (from one of Goethe's *Xenien.* See *supra,* p. 280).

XL.—FIFTEEN ENGLISH FRIENDS[1] to GOETHE, on the 28TH AUGUST 1831.

SIR—Among the friends whom this so interesting Anniversary calls round you, may we

---

[1] The names of the " Fifteen English Friends " are given in *Zelter* in the following order, some of them very oddly spelt : Thomas Carlyle, Dr. Carlyle, W. Fraser (editor of the *Foreign Review*), Dr. Maginn, Heraud (editor of *Fraser*), G. Moir (translator of *Wallenstein*), Churchill (author of· a Translation of *Wallenstein's Lager*), Jerdan (editor of the *Literary Gazette*), Professor Wilson (editor of *Blackwood*), Sir Walter Scott, Lockhart (editor of the *Quarterly*), Lord Francis Levison-Gower (translator of *Faust*) : the Poets, Southey, Wordsworth and Procter (Barry Cornwall).—*Briefwechsel zwischen Goethe und Zelter* (Berlin, 1834), Sechster Theil, 256-7.

'English Friends,' in thought and symbolically, since personally it is impossible, present ourselves, to offer you our affectionate congratulations. We hope you will do us the honour to accept this little Birthday Gift; which as a true testimony of our feelings, may not be without value.

We said to ourselves: As it is always the highest duty and pleasure to show reverence to whom reverence is due, and our chief, perhaps our only benefactor is he who by act and word, instructs us in wisdom,—so we undersigned, feeling towards the Poet Goethe as the spiritually-taught towards their spiritual teacher, are desirous to express that sentiment openly and in common. For which end we have determined to solicit his acceptance of a small English gift, proceeding from us all equally, on his approaching Birthday; that so, while the venerable man still dwells among us, some memorial of the gratitude we owe him, and think the whole world owes him,. may not be wanting.

And thus our little tribute, perhaps among

the purest that men could offer to man, now stands in visible shape, and begs to be received. May it be welcome, and speak permanently of a most close relation, though wide seas flow between the parties!

We pray that many years may be added to a life so glorious—that all happiness may be yours, and strength given to complete your high task, even as it has hitherto proceeded, "like a star, without haste, yet without rest."[1]

We remain, Sir, your friends and servants,

FIFTEEN ENGLISH FRIENDS.

[1] Zelter, writing to Goethe on the 17th of August 1831, remarks that Goethe has told him nothing about the Seal from the "Nineteen" Englishmen and Scotchmen. Goethe replies, on the 20th of August: "Since I have received your valuable gift for my approaching birthday, I may now give you tidings of the notable present which I have received from across the Channel. *Fifteen English Friends*, so they subscribe themselves, have had a seal prepared by their most famous goldsmiths; of a size to be easily contained in the hollow of the hand, and in shape like a longish vase. The highest skill of the goldsmith, aided by the enameller, is here displayed. It reminds one of the descriptions in which Cellini is wont to extol his own achievements, and it is obvious that they have worked after the model of the sixteenth century. The English seem to think the saying, ' Ohne Rast, doch ohne Hast' [*sic*] of considerable significance, and essentially it very well expresses

XLI.—GOETHE to CARLYLE.

DEN FUNFZEHEN ENGLISCHEN FREUNDEN.

Worte die der Dichter spricht,
Treu in heimischen Bezircken,
Wircken gleich, doch weiss er nicht
Ob sie in die Ferne wircken.

Britten ! habt sie aufgefasst !
"Thätigen Sinn ! das Thun gezügelt ;
Stetig Streben, ohne Hast."
Und so wollt Ihr es besiegelt.[1]

Vorstehendes habe, gleich nach Empfang des
anmuthigsten Geschenkes, durch Herrn Fraser
an die verbündeten Freunde nach London
gelangen lassen. Ihnen, mein Theuerster, send'
ich das Duplum, das vielleicht früher als jene
Mittheilung von dorther zu Ihnen gelangt.

Ich füge nur hinzu dass die begleitenden
Bücher und Hefte schon von mir angegangen

their own mode of procedure. These words are engraved
round a star, the well-known serpent encircling all, unfortunately in Old German Capitals, which do not bring out the
sense quite clearly." [The words, in a circle, are without full
stop or distinctive initial letter, and are indeed very difficult to
read.] "It is a gift in every sense worthy of thanks, and I
have written some friendly rhymes to them in return."

[1] These "friendly rhymes" are in Goethe's own handwriting, and the Letter bears an impression of the new seal.

worden sind, und dass ich darin manches Erfreuliche gefunden habe. Worüber nächstens
mehr. Auch eine Betrachtung der Schattenrisse
und deren unglaubliche Vergegenwärtigung des
Abwesenden.

Die zu Ende Juni von Hamburg, durch Hn.
Parish abgesendete Kiste, ist nun schon, oder
bald in Ihren Händen ; lassen Sie mich deshalb
ein Wort vernehmen.

Wie ich denn hier, nur mit den wenigsten
Worten, wiederhole : dass mir die Gabe der
verbündeten Freunde ein so ausserordentliches,
als unerwartetes Vergnügen gemacht hat und
nicht mir allein, sondern gleichmässig Freunden
und Bekannten, die eine so kunstreiche Arbeit
zu schätzen wissen.

Den theuren Gatten glückliche Stunden !

GOETHE.

WEIMAR, *19. Aug. 1831.*

[TRANSLATION.]

TO THE FIFTEEN ENGLISH FRIENDS.

The words the Poet speaks swiftly and
surely work within the compass of his land

and home ; yet knows he not if they do work afar.   Britons, ye have understood !   " The active mind, the deed restrained : steadfast striving, without haste."   And thus ye will that it be sealed.

———

The above I sent through Mr. Fraser of London, for the associated friends immediately after receiving their most charming gift.   To you, my dearest Sir, I send this duplicate, which will perhaps reach you before that missive comes thence to you.

I now merely add that I have already read here and there in the books and pamphlets which accompanied the gift, and that I find in them much that is delightful.   Of this more next time, as well as of the silhouettes and the inconceivable way in which they bring the absent before one.

The box, sent from Hamburg, through Messrs. Parish, at the end of June, is ere now, or will soon be, in your hands ; let me have a word from you concerning it.

I now repeat here, but in the fewest words :

the gift of the associated friends has afforded me a pleasure as unusual as unexpected ; and not me alone, but likewise friends and acquaintances, who know how to appreciate so artistic a piece of work.

To the dear Pair, happy hours !

GOETHE.

WEIMAR, 19*th August* 1831.

———

Goethe died on the 22d of March 1832. Carlyle has written in his *Journal,* under a newspaper cutting announcing Goethe's death :

" This came to me at Dumfries, on my first return thither. I had written to Weimar, asking for a Letter to welcome me home ;[1] and *this* was it. My Letter would never reach its *address :* the great and good Friend was no longer *there ;* had departed some seven days before."

CRAIGENPUTTOCK, 19*th April* 1832.

---

[1] After his long stay in London. No such letter has been found in the Goethe archives ; it is probably in the archives of Chancellor von Müller, the Executor of Goethe's Will.

APPENDIX I

To the Honourable Society for
Foreign *Belles Lettres* in Berlin.

When towards the end of last year, I received
the welcome intelligence that a Society with
which I was already in friendly relation, and
which had till then devoted itself to German
Literature, proposed in future to turn its attention also to that of foreign countries, I could
not, as I was then situated, record at sufficient
length and with due clearness my appreciation
of this enterprise, on occasion of which, moreover, much goodwill has been shown to myself.

Even now in this public expression of my

gratitude and interest, I can only present in a fragmentary manner what I should have liked to set forth with greater coherence. However, I will not neglect the present opportunity, since I hope to attain by it my principal object, that of bringing my friends into relation with a man whom I count among those who have in late years become actively attached to me, and who by their close sympathy have encouraged me to exertion and action, while by their noble, pure, and well-directed efforts, they have made me feel young again, and I, who attracted them, have been carried forward with them. This gentleman is the Author of the Work which is translated here, Mr. Thomas Carlyle, a Scotchman, whose labours and superior attainments, as well as his personal environment, the following pages will make known.

If I am right in my estimate of him and my Berlin friends, a pleasant and useful intercourse will be brought about, and both parties alike will, as I venture to hope, for many years rejoice in this legacy of mine and its fruitful results; and in order that I may, in pleasing anticipa-

tion, enjoy a lasting memorial, I would in conclusion request you to grant it me.

In faithful attachment and sympathy,

J. W. v. GOETHE.

WEIMAR, *April* 1830.

There has for some time been question of a
Universal World - Literature, and indeed not
without reason : for all nations, after having
been clashed together by the most dreadful
wars, and then severally settled down again,
could not but notice that they had imbibed
many a foreign thing, and here and there
become conscious of spiritual needs hitherto
unknown. Hence arose a sense of their relationship as neighbours, and instead of shutting
themselves up as heretofore, the desire gradually
awoke within them to become associated in a
more or less free intellectual commerce.

This movement has, it is true, existed but a
short time, but still long enough to admit of
our making some observations upon it, and of
our deriving from it, as quickly as possible,

as must be done to carry on commerce in material things, some profit and enjoyment.

———

The translation of the present Work, written in memory of Schiller, can bring us scarcely anything new. The Author obtained his knowledge from documents long since familiar to us; and in general the matters here treated of have frequently been subjects of discussion and dispute among us. What must be highly gratifying, however, as may be confidently asserted, to those who honour Schiller, and therefore to every German, is to learn at first hand, how, across the sea, an earnest, aspiring, discriminating man of sensitive feeling has, in his best years, been affected, influenced, and stirred by Schiller's productions, and thus impelled to the further study of German Literature.

To me, at least, it was touching to see how, even in the earliest, often harsh, almost crude productions of our departed friend, this clear and tranquil-hearted foreigner never failed to recognise the noble, right-minded, right-intentioned man; and was thus able to form for himself the ideal of a mortal of the highest excellence.

I therefore consider this Work, written by a young man, one to be commended to the youth of Germany; for if lightsome youth may legitimately form a wish, it were surely this: to discern in every performance what is praiseworthy, good, fair, aspiring, in a word, the Ideal, and even in what is not typical, to discern the universal type and exemplar of man.

————

This Work may further be of importance to us, if we seriously consider how Schiller's Works, to which we owe such varied culture, are valued and honoured by a foreigner too, as a source of his own, and how he, without definite intention of doing so, calmly and clearly shows this.

Again, it may not be out of place to remark here, that writings which with us have nearly completed their work, are now, at the very moment when the omens are propitious to

German Literature abroad, beginning to exert their powerful influence anew ; thereby showing how, at a certain stage of Literature, they will always be useful and effective.

Thus, Herder's *Ideas*, for example, have so permeated the minds of the mass of readers with us, that only a few who now read the *Ideas*, are instructed by it for the first time, for by a hundred channels and in other connections they have become thoroughly familiar with what was, at the time of its publication, of great importance. This Work was recently translated into French, from the conviction that a multitude of educated men in France still required to be enlightened by these ideas.

———

With respect to the Frontispiece of the present Volume, let this be noted : our friend, when first we began our correspondence with him, was living in Edinburgh, where, in quietude, he was seeking, in the best sense, to educate himself; and we may say without vainglory, that he found in German Literature his chief

furtherance.   Later on he betook himself to a
property of his, some ten German miles southwards, in the County of Dumfries, in order that
he might, while turning it to account, choose his
own mode of life, and thus in independence
pursue his honest literary studies.   Here, in a
mountainous district, through which the River
Nith flows to the neighbouring sea, not far
from the Town of Dumfries, at a place called
Craigenputtock, he, with a beautiful and highly-
accomplished Consort, established his simple
country home, faithful drawings of which have
been the immediate occasion of these words.

Accomplished geniuses, sympathetic souls
who yearn after the good that is far away, and
feel disposed to do good from afar, can
scarcely refrain from the wish to have brought
before their eyes the portrait of honoured, beloved, and far-distant persons, and also a picture
of their dwelling-place and of their immediate
environment.

How often are pictures of Petrarch's abode

in Vaucluse, or Tasso's dwelling at Sorrento
reproduced even to this day! And is not
the island in the Lake of Bienne, which
afforded shelter to Rousseau, a locality which
can never be too often represented for his
admirers?

With this same feeling, I sought to obtain
a picture of the surroundings of my distant
friends, and I was the more desirous to have
one of the dwelling of Mr. Thomas Carlyle,
because he had chosen his abode, under the
55th degree of Latitude, in an almost wild,
mountainous region.

I trust that by means of the accompanying
faithful reproduction of the original drawings
recently sent to me, an ornament may be added
to this Volume, and that a congenial feeling of
pleasure may be given to the present, perhaps
still more to the future reader; and thus, as
well as by extracts inserted from the letters
of the honoured writer, the interest in a noble,
general intercourse between all nations of the
world may be increased.

[Here follows a translated extract from

Carlyle's Letter to Goethe of 25th September 1828. It begins, " You inquire with such affection touching our present abode and employments," and ends with the last sentence but one in the letter,—" Surely you will write to me again, and ere long, that I may still feel myself united to you." (See *supra*, pp. 124-126.)]

We Germans, well-disposed to those on every side of us, and aiming at the most comprehensive culture, have for a long time past valued the services of eminent Scotchmen. We are not ignorant of what they formerly accomplished in Natural Science, through which the French afterwards acquired such great superiority.

In more recent times, we have not failed to recognise the praiseworthy influence which their Philosophy has had in diverting the course of Thought among the French, by leading them, from a stubborn sensualism to a more tractable state of mind, in the direction of Common Sense. We have been indebted to them for much profound insight concerning the most important aspects of British life and tendencies.

On the other hand, we have, until recently, been compelled to see our own ethical and æsthetic endeavours treated in their Journals in such a way that it remained doubtful whether want of insight, or simple ill-will predominated ; whether it was a question of a superficial and shallow view or of unfriendly prejudice. Nevertheless we regarded this circumstance with patience, having indeed always had enough of the like to endure in our own country. In late years, however, we have been rejoiced by the most friendly recognition from those regions, which we feel in duty bound to return, and concerning which we propose in these pages to give information, so far as may be needful, to our well-disposed countrymen.

Mr. Thomas Carlyle had already translated *Wilhelm Meister*, when, in 1825, he published the present *Life of Schiller*. In 1827 there appeared in four Volumes *German Romance*, in which from the Novels and Tales of such German Authors as Musäus, La Motte Fouqué, Tieck, Hoffmann, Jean Paul and Goethe, he gave such selections as were likely to be best suited to his Nation.

The accounts of the life, writings, and tendency of these Poets and Prose-writers, prefixed to their respective sections, bear witness to the diligent and sympathetic manner in which this friend sought to inform himself, as far as possible, concerning the personality and position of each writer, and to the fact that he thus found the right way of further perfecting his own knowledge.

In the Edinburgh Periodicals, particularly in those specifically devoted to Foreign Literature, are to be found, in addition to the German Authors already named, Ernst Schulz, Klingemann, Franz Horn, Zacharias Werner, Count Platen, and many others, all of whom have been introduced, and had judgment passed upon them, by various critics, but chiefly by our friend.

And here it is most important to remark that these writers take each particular work as a text and occasion for expressing their opinions, and giving their verdict, in a masterly manner, on the whole field of investigation, as well as on the individual work.

These Edinburgh Reviews, whether devoted to domestic or general topics, or to Foreign Literature especially, deserve the attentive consideration of the friends of knowledge, for it is extremely noteworthy that in these Articles, a profound earnestness goes hand in hand with the freest survey, and a stern patriotism with a clear unmixed spirit of liberal thought.

———

As now from that region we enjoy, in what so closely concerns us here, a sincere and pure sympathy in these ethic and æsthetic efforts of ours, which may be regarded as a special trait in the German character, we must now on our part look about for whatever of the same sort lies near their own hearts. I refer at once to the name of Burns, concerning whom a letter of Mr. Carlyle's contained the following passage.

"The only thing of any moment I have written since I came hither is an Essay on Burns. Perhaps you have never heard of this *Burns,* and yet he was a man of the most decisive genius; but born in the rank of a Peasant, and miserably wasted away by the complexities of his strange situation; so that all he effected was comparatively a trifle, and he died before middle age.

"We English, especially we Scotch, love Burns more than any other Poet we have had for centuries. It has often struck me to remark that he was born a few months only before Schiller, in the year 1759; and that neither of these two men ever heard the other's name; but that they shone as stars in opposite hemispheres, the little Atmosphere of the Earth intercepting their mutual light." [1]

Yet Robert Burns was better known to us than our friend conjectured. The charming Poem *John Barley-Corn* had come to us

[1] From Carlyle's Letter of 25th September 1828. See *supra,* p. 123.

anonymously, and being deservedly prized, led
to many attempts to appropriate it in our own
language. John Barley-Corn (*Hans Gersten-
korn*), a valiant man, has many enemies, who
incessantly persecute and harm him, at length
even threaten to kill him outright. From all
these injuries, however, he finally emerges
triumphant, for the special blessing and cheer
of eager beer-drinkers. In this lively, happy
anthropomorphism Burns is at once seen to be
a genuine Poet.

On further investigation, we found this
Poem in the Edition of his Works of 1822, to
which a Sketch of his Life is prefixed, instruct-
ing us, in some measure at least, as to his
outward circumstances. Those of his Poems
that we have made our own, convinced us of
his extraordinary talent, and we regretted that
the Scottish dialect proved a hindrance precisely
where he must have attained his finest and most
natural expression. On the whole, however, we
have carried our studies so far that we can subscribe to the laudatory statement quoted below,
as agreeing with our own conviction.

For the rest, how far this Burns of ours may be known in Germany beyond what the *Con-versations-Lexicon* reports of him, I should be unable to say, being ignorant of the new literary movements in Germany; still I would at any rate set the friends of Foreign Literature upon the right road, by mentioning the *Life of Robert Burns*, by J. G. Lockhart, Edinburgh, 1828,—criticised by our friend in the *Edin-burgh Review*, December 1828.

The following passages translated from this Article will, it may be hoped, arouse an eager desire to become thoroughly acquainted with this Work, and with the man himself.

———

" Burns was born in an age the most prosaic Britain had yet seen, and in a condition the most disadvantageous, where his mind, if it accomplished aught, must accomplish it under the pressure of continual bodily toil, nay of penury and desponding apprehension of the worst evils, and with no furtherance but such knowledge as dwells in a poor man's hut, and the rhymes of a Ferguson or Ramsay for his standard of beauty, he sinks not under all these impediments : through the fogs and darkness of that obscure region, his lynx eye discerns the true relations of the world and human life ; he grows into intellectual strength, and trains himself into intellectual expertness. Impelled by the expansive movement of his own irrepressible soul, he struggles forward into the general view ; and with haughty modesty lays down before us, as the fruit of his labour, a gift, which Time has now pronounced imperishable.

"A true Poet, a man in whose heart resides some effluence of Wisdom, some tone of the 'Eternal Melodies,' is the most precious gift that can be bestowed on a generation : we see in him a freer, purer development of whatever is noblest in ourselves ; his life is a rich lesson to us ; and we mourn his death as that of a benefactor who loved and taught us.

"Such a gift had Nature, in her bounty, bestowed on us in Robert Burns ; but with queenlike indifference she cast it from her hand, like a thing of no moment ; and it was defaced

and torn asunder, as an idle bauble, before we
recognised it.   To the ill-starred Burns was
given the power of making man's life more
venerable, but that of wisely guiding his own
life was not given.   Destiny,—for so in our
ignorance we must speak,—his faults, the faults
of others, proved too hard for him ; and that
spirit, which might have soared could it but
have walked, soon sank to the dust, its glorious
faculties trodden underfoot in the blossom ;
and died, we may almost say, without ever
having lived.   And so kind and warm a soul ;
so full of inborn riches, of love to all living and
lifeless things !   The ' Daisy ' falls not unheeded
under his ploughshare ; [nor the ruined nest of
that ' wee, cowering, timorous beastie,' cast forth,
after all its provident pains, to ' thole the sleety
dribble and cranreuch cauld '[1]].   The hoar visage
of Winter delights him ; he dwells with a sad
and oft-returning fondness in these scenes of
solemn desolation ; but the voice of the tempest

---

[1] Goethe translates the words in brackets : ' *So wenig als
das wohlbesorgte Nest der furchtsamen Feldmaus, das er her-
vorwühlt.*'

becomes an anthem to his ears; he loves to walk in the sounding woods, for ' it raises his thoughts to *Him that walketh on the wings of the wind.*' A true Poet-soul, for it needs but to be struck, and the sound it yields will be music!

" What warm, all-comprehending fellow-feeling; what trustful, boundless love; what generous exaggeration of the object loved! His rustic friend, his nut-brown maiden, are no longer mean and homely, but a hero and a queen, whom he prizes as the paragons of Earth. The rough scenes of Scottish life, not seen by him in any Arcadian illusion, but in the rude contradiction, in the smoke and soil of a too harsh reality, are still lovely to him: Poverty is indeed his companion, but Love also, and Courage; the simple feelings, the worth, the nobleness, that dwell under the straw roof, are dear and venerable to his heart: and thus over the lowest provinces of man's existence he pours the glory of his own soul; and they rise, in shadow and sunshine, softened and brightened into a beauty which other eyes discern not in the highest.

" He has a just self-consciousness, which too often degenerates into pride ; yet it is a noble pride, for defence, not for offence ; no cold suspicious feeling, but a frank and social one. The Peasant Poet bears himself, we might say, like a King in exile : he is cast among the low, and feels himself equal to the highest ; yet he claims no rank, that none may be disputed to him. The forward he can repel, the supercilious he can subdue ; pretensions of wealth or ancestry are of no avail with him ; there is a fire in that dark eye, under which the ' insolence of condescension ' cannot thrive. In his abasement, in his extreme need, he forgets not for a moment the majesty of Poetry and Manhood. And yet, far as he feels himself above common men, he wanders not apart from them, but mixes warmly in their interests ; nay, throws himself into their arms, and, as it were, entreats them to love him. It is moving to see how, in his darkest despondency, this proud being still seeks relief from friendship ; unbosoms himself, often to the unworthy ; and, amid tears, strains to his glowing heart a heart that knows only the name of friendship. And yet he was 'quick to learn'; a man of keen vision, before whom common disguises afforded no concealment. His understanding saw through the hollowness even of accomplished deceivers; but there was a generous credulity in his heart. And so did our Peasant show himself among us; 'a soul like an Æolian harp, in whose strings the vulgar wind, as it passed through them, changed itself into articulate melody.' And this was he for whom the world found no fitter business than quarrelling with smugglers and vintners, computing excise-dues upon tallow, and gauging ale-barrels! In such toils was that mighty Spirit sorrowfully wasted: and a hundred years may pass on, before another such is given us to waste." [1]

And as we wish the Germans joy on their Schiller, so, with the same feeling, will we

[1] It will be observed that in this extract several passages have been omitted by Goethe. Compare Carlyle's *Essay on Burns*,—*Miscellanies* (Library edition, 1869), vol. ii. pp. 8-12.

congratulate the Scotch. They have indeed
bestowed on our friend Schiller so much attention and sympathy, that it would be but just if
we, in like manner, should introduce their Burns
to our people. Some young member of the
honourable Society to which as a whole the
present pages are dedicated, would find his
time and labour abundantly rewarded, should
he determine to perform this friendly service in
return, to a Nation so worthy of honour, and
faithfully carry out his undertaking. We
esteem this highly - praised Robert Burns
amongst the first poetical spirits which the
past century has produced.

———

In the year 1829, a very neat and attrac-
tively printed little octavo Volume came to our
hands : *Catalogue of German Publications,
selected and systematically arranged for W. H.
Koller and Jul. Cahlmann*, London.

This little book, compiled with special
knowledge of German Literature, in a manner
to facilitate the survey of it, does honour to

the compiler as well as to the publishers, who seriously undertake the important office of introducing foreign literature to their own country; and who do this, indeed, not only in such wise that one can see what it has produced in every department, but also so as to attract and satisfy the scholar and the thoughtful reader, as well as those who merely seek for sentiment and entertainment. Every German writer and man of letters who has distinguished himself in any department, will be eager to open this catalogue to see if there is mention of him, and if his Works have been courteously admitted with others of a similar sort. It will be to the interest of all German Publishers to learn how their wares are regarded across the Channel, what value is set on each, and they will neglect no means of establishing and actively maintaining relations with men of such serious purpose.

———

As now I introduce and bring into light the *Life of Schiller*, written so many years ago, by our Scottish friend, and upon which he looks back with a becoming modesty, may he permit me to add some of his most recent utterances, which shall best show our common progress up to this time.

———

THOMAS CARLYLE to GOETHE.

22d December 1829.

" I have read the *Briefwechsel* a second time with no little satisfaction, and even to-day am sending off an Essay on Schiller, grounded on that Work, for the *Foreign Review.* It will gratify you to learn that a knowledge and appreciation of Foreign, especially of German, Literature, is spreading with increased rapidity over all the domain of the English tongue ; so that almost at the Antipodes, in New Holland itself, the wise of your country are by this time preaching their wisdom. I have heard lately that even in Oxford and Cambridge, our two English universities, which have all along been regarded as the strongholds of Insular pride

Y

and prejudice, there is a strange stir in this
matter.   Your *Niebuhr* has found an able translator in Cambridge ; and in Oxford two or
three Germans already find employment as
teachers of their language ; the new light contained in which may well dazzle certain eyes.
Of the benefits that must in the end result from
all this no man can be doubtful : let nations,
like individuals, but know one another and
mutual hatred will give place to mutual help-
fulness ; and instead of natural enemies, as
neighbouring countries are sometimes called,
we shall all be natural friends." [1]

If, now, in view of all that precedes, the
hope flatters us, that a harmony of Nations, a
universal goodwill, will by degrees come into
existence, by means of a closer acquaintance
with different languages and ways of thinking,
I venture to speak of an important influence of
German Literature, which, in a special case,
may perhaps prove of great effect.

[1] See *supra*, pp. 161-163.

Namely this, It is well enough known that the inhabitants of the Three British Kingdoms do not live in quite the best mutual understanding ; but that, on the contrary, one neighbour finds in the other ground of censure sufficient to justify himself in a secret aversion.

I am convinced that, as the German ethic and æsthetic Literature spreads through the Three Kingdoms, there will, at the same time, arise a quiet community of Philo-Germans, the members of which, in their affection for a Fourth, nearly-related Nation, will feel themselves united, nay blended together.

APPENDIX II

THE following little note by Goethe, which he had intended to accompany the *Kästchen*, announced in his Letter to Carlyle of the 6th of June 1830 (Letter XXVII., see p. 194), had evidently never reached its destination; the original being now in private hands in Weimar. It was printed in the *Grenzboten* (*Goethiana: Zu Goethes Verhältnis zu Carlyle*, von Ewald Flügel), iii. 1885; but it did not reach us in time to permit of its being inserted in its proper place.

SENDUNG AN HERRN CARLYLE.

[14*th June* 1830.]

1. Goethe's Farbenlehre, zwey Bde. in 8., u. ein Heft Tafeln, in 4°; in letzterem finden sich:

2. Zwey Kupferstiche beygelegt: (*a*) von Goethe's Gartenhaus im Ilmthale und (*b*) dessen Haus in der Stadt. Beym ersteren wird man sich der Bemerkung nicht enthalten dass solches gleichfalls drey Fenster, wie das zu Craigenputtock hat, und mir mehrere Jahre zur Sommer-und Winterwohnung diente. Nur ungern verliess ich es, um mancher Sorge und Mühe des Städtischen Aufenthaltes entgegen zu gehen.

3. Hrn. Dr. Wachler's Vorlesungen über die Geschichte der deutschen National Literatur. Zwey Bände. 8. 1818-19.

4. Ueber Werden und Wirken der Literatur zunächst in Beziehung auf Deutschlands Literatur unserer Zeit v. Dr. Wachler.   Breslau 1819.

5. Schillerisch-Goethescher Briefwechsel 3-6. Bd. incl. und das ganze also abgeschlossen.

6. Das Chaos, Wochenblatt, Manuscript für Freunde. Gesellige Scherze einer geistreichen Weimarischen Gesellschaft, wie aus dem Inhalt des mehreren zu ersehen ist. Es darf eigentlich Niemanden mitgetheilt werden als wer dazu Beyträge liefert, da nun aber wie zu ersehen ist, auch Mitarbeiter von Edinburg datiren, so ist es billig dass auch ein Exemplar nach Schottland wandere.   Man bittet die Freunde in der Grafschaft Dumfries ihre bisherige Gunst fortzusetzen.   Leider kann man kein vollständiges Exemplar schicken, die Gesellschaft war im Anfang sehr klein und werden nur wenig Exemplare gedruckt um das Abschreiben zu vermeiden; nach und nach wuchs der Antheil, die Auflage ward stärker aber die ersten Blätter stufenweise nicht mehr zu haben.   Mögen diese sibyllinischen [Blätter [1]] Productionen, entstanden auf den spätesten Kalkflözen des Continents, den übermeerischen Freunden auf ihrem Urgranit einige anmuthige Stunden verleihen. Von Ottilien habe ich die herzlichsten Grüsse beyzufügen, sie ist ganz eigentlich der Redacteur dieses Blattes und dirigirt mit einigen treuen verständigen Freunden die ganze mitunter bedenkliche Angelegenheit.

!7. Der Abschluss der Uebersetzung Ihrer Schillerischen Biographie.   Mit der nächsten Sendung hoffe das ausgestattete Werklein zu überschicken.   Schon einiges deshalb habe in meinem letzten Briefe vom 7. Juni vermeldet.

8. Auch liegt eine gar löbliche Trauerrede auf unsre

---

1 Written and crossed out in MS.

jüngst verstorbene, höchst geschätzte und geliebte Frau
Grossherzogin bey.

> *Soviel treulichst u. eiligst*
> *damit kein Aufenthalt sey,*
> *um baldige Nachricht der Ankunft bittend*
>
> GOETHE·

WEIMAR, *den* 14. *Juni* 1830.

[TRANSLATION.]

Contents of Packet for Mr. Carlyle.

1. Goethe's *Farbenlehre*, two vols. 8vo, and a set of
plates, in 4to ; along with the latter are :

2. Two Copper-plate Engravings : (*a*) of Goethe's
Garden-house in Ilmthal and (*b*) his House in town.   As
to the first, it may be remarked that it has three windows,
like the house at Craigenputtock ; and that it served me
for several years as dwelling-place both in summer and in
winter.   I was loath to leave it and to encounter the many
cares and troubles of a residence in town.

3. Dr. Wachler's *Lectures on the History of German
National Literature.*   Two vols., 8vo, 1818-19.

4. *Concerning the Growth and Influence of Literature,*
especially of the German Literature of our time, by Dr.
Wachler.   Breslau 1819.

5. Schiller - Goethe Correspondence.   Vols. 3-6 (the
whole being thus completed).

6. *The Chaos,* a weekly paper, for private circulation,
in manuscript.   Social pleasantries of an intellectual
Weimar Society, as is obvious from the contents of most of

the numbers. Strictly speaking, its circulation is confined to contributors ; but as it appears that certain of the fellow-labourers date from Edinburgh, it is surely fair that at least one copy should find its way to Scotland. A request is made that the favours from our friends in the county of Dumfries may be continued. Unfortunately a complete copy cannot be sent. It was at first a very small society and only a few copies were printed, merely to save transcribing. Gradually the interest in it increased, and the issue became larger, but by degrees the early numbers were exhausted. May these Sibylline products, sprung from the most recent Chalk Deposits of the Continent, afford some pleasant hours to our friends, who are across the sea on their Primary Granite. I am to add kindest greetings from Ottilie. She is in reality the sole Editor of this Periodical, and, with the aid of a few faithful intelligent friends, takes the whole direction of the, at times, ticklish concern.

7. The conclusion of the translation of your *Life of Schiller*. By the next despatch I hope to send the little work complete ; I have already given you some news of it in my Letter of the 7th of June.

8. There is also enclosed a much to be commended Funeral-oration on our recently deceased, most esteemed and beloved Grand Duchess.

No more lest I delay the Packet. Hoping for speedy news of its arrival,

Most faithfully, and in greatest haste,

GOETHE.

WEIMAR, 14*th June* 1830.

ECKERMANN to CARLYLE.

WEIMAR, *d.* 20 *Octbr.* 1832.

MEIN THEURER FREUND—Ihr lieber Brief hat mir die Versicherung gegeben dass unsere schon seit Jahren bestehende Verbindung fortbestehen und vielleicht noch inniger geknüpft werden wird.

Ihren ersten Artikel über Goethe in dem *Magazine* habe ich auf Verlangen vieler Freunde übersetzt; und [er] wird in diesen Tagen im Morgenblatt erscheinen. Ueber den zweyten bedeutenderen Artikel redet man viel in Deutschland und ich würde ihn auch sogleich übersetzt haben, wenn nicht meine ganze Zeit mit der Redaction der nachgelassenen 15 Bände hingenommen wäre. Doch höre ich dass Herr v. Cotta ihn wird übersetzen lassen.

Heute sende ich Ihnen zwey bedeutende Dinge : 1. Eine vorzügliche Schrift über Goethe von Herrn Canzler v. Müller, der Ihnen ein Exemplar dedicirt hat. Herr v. Müller ist ein vieljähriger Freund von Goethe weshalb er auch von ihm zum Executor des Testaments ernannt worden. Er hat bey seiner trefflich geschriebenen Schrift Quellen benutzen können die jedem anderen nicht frey standen. Das Büchlein wird für Sie von hohem Interesse seyn und Sie werden es sicherlich zu einem ferneren Artikel über Goethe benutzen. 2. Sende ich Ihnen das letzte Heft von Kunst und Alterthum das am 6n. Bande noch fehlte und das von uns Freunden herausgegeben worden. Auch dieses Heft wird für Sie brauchbar und von manchem Interesse seyn.

Ich bin sehr beschäftigt mit der Herausgabe der nachgelassenen Werke Goethes wovon die ersten 5 Bände in wenig Monaten erscheinen. Diese erste Lieferung wird enthalten :

1. Den zweyten Theil des Faust.
2. Erstes Manuscript v. Götz v. Berlichingen.
3. Schweizer Reise von 1797.
4. Ueber Kunst.
5. Theater und Deutsche Literatur.

In die zweyte Lieferung welche Ostern erscheint wird kommen:

6. Ausländische Literatur.
7. Gedichte.
8. Aus meinem Leben (die Zeit von 1775).
9. Verschiedene einzelne Sachen.
10. Allgemeines über Natur.

Dann die 3te. Lieferung welche Michaeli 1833 erscheint wird alle naturwissenschaftlichen Werke enthalten, wodurch denn auch die Farbenlehre sich nach England verbreiten wird.

Ich bin nun mit der Redaction dieser bedeutenden Schriften Tag und Nacht beschäftigt, und habe keinen anderen Gedanken als dieses so gut zu machen als in meinen Kräften steht.

Ist dieses geschehen so werde ich meine Conversationen mit Goethe herausgeben wovon ich hoffentlich einen guten Namen und etwas Geld haben werde.

Stunden an junge Engländer habe ich schon seit zwey Jahren nicht mehr gegeben. Ich hatte bloss den Zweck das unentbehrliche Englisch dabey zu lernen.

Ich zweifle dass ich künftig in Weimar bleiben werde. Wohin ich aber mich wenden soll weiss ich noch nicht.

Mr. Reeve ist zwey Tage hier gewesen. Er ist ein wohlunterrichteter sehr liebenswürdiger junger Mann. Er ist fast die ganze Zeit bey Frau v. Goethe gewesen, denn ich war zu beschäftigt um viel mit ihm zu seyn. Er ist nach München zurückgegangen.

Ein hiesiger berühmter Kupferstecher, Herr Schwerdgeburth, hat vorigen Winter kurz vor Goethes Tode ein Portrait
von ihm gemacht das zu den vorzüglichsten gehört die je
erschienen. Er sendet Ihnen ein Blatt, das der Abhandlung des Herrn v. Müller beyliegt. Der Künstler hat die
Absicht einige hundert Abdrücke von diesem Bilde an den
Kunsthändler Ackermann nach London zu senden um sie
an die englischen Freunde Goethes in den drey König-
reichen zu verkaufen. Vielleicht haben Sie Gelegenheit
durch ein günstiges Wort in öffentlichen Blättern auf dieses
Bild aufmerksam zu machen.

Ich hoffe Sie werden von Frau v. Goethe bald einen
Brief selber sehen. Ich bitte um meine herzlichen Grüsse
an Madame Carlyle ; und verbleibe, Ihr treu verbundener
Freund,

ECKERMANN.

[TRANSLATION.]

WEIMAR, 20*th October* 1832.

MY DEAR FRIEND—Your valued letter has given me
the assurance that the connection between us, which has
already existed for years, will continue, and perhaps become still more closely knit.

At the desire of many friends I have translated your
first Article on Goethe,[1] and it will appear very shortly in
the *Morgenblatt.* There is much talk in Germany about
the more important second Article, and this also I should

---

[1] " Death of Goethe," in the *New Monthly Magazine,*
No. CXXXVIII. (see *Miscellanies,* vol. iii. 385). The more
important article " Goethe's Works " appeared in the *Foreign
Quarterly Review,* No. XIX. (see *Miscellanies,* vol. iv. 109).

have translated immediately, had not my whole time been taken up with editing the fifteen posthumous Volumes. I hear, however, that Herr von Cotta is about to have it translated.

I send you to-day two things of importance :

1. An excellent Essay on Goethe by the Chancellor von Müller, who has inscribed a copy to you. Herr von Müller was for many years a friend of Goethe, and was appointed by him the Executor of his Will. In his admirably written Essay, he has been able to make use of sources of information which were not available to others. The little work will be of great interest to you, and you will surely make use of it for another Article on Goethe. 2. I send you the last part of *Kunst und Alterthum*, which was still wanting to the sixth volume, and which has been published by us, his friends. This part will also be useful, as well as exceedingly interesting, to you.

I am very busy with the publication of Goethe's *Posthumous Works*, of which the first five volumes will appear in a few months. This first Section will contain :

1. The second part of Faust.
2. The first manuscript of Götz von Berlichingen.
3. Swiss Journey of 1797.
4. Concerning Art.
5. The Theatre ; German Literature.

The second Section, which will appear at Easter, will include :

6. Foreign Literature.
7. Poems.
8. "From my Life" [*Dichtung und Wahrheit*] (the period of 1775).
9. Miscellaneous detached Pieces.
10. General Views of Nature.

Then the third Section, which is to appear at Michaelmas 1833, will contain all the works on Natural Philosophy, by means of which the *Farbenlehre* also will now become known in England. I am busy day and night with the editing of these important papers, and have no other thought than to do this as well as lies in my power.

This done, I shall publish my Conversations with Goethe, from which I hope to obtain both good repute and a little money.

For these last two years past I have not given any lessons to young Englishmen. My only object in giving them was to learn the, to me indispensable, English language. I doubt if I shall remain in Weimar for the future. But in what direction I shall turn my steps, I do not yet know.

Mr. [Henry] Reeve has been here for two days. He is a well-informed and very charming young man. He has spent almost the whole time with Madame von Goethe, for I was too busy to be much with him. He has gone back to Munich.

Herr Schwerdgeburth, an engraver of repute here, did a portrait of Goethe last winter shortly before his death, one of the best that has ever appeared. He sends you a copy, which accompanies Herr von Müller's Essay. The artist intends to send some hundred impressions of this portrait to the Picture-dealer Ackermann in London, that they may be sold to Goethe's English friends in the Three Kingdoms. Perhaps you may have an opportunity to draw attention to this portrait, by a favourable word in the public papers.

I hope you will soon receive a letter from Madame von Goethe herself. Pray give my cordial greetings to Mrs. Carlyle. I remain, your faithful, obliged friend,

ECKERMANN.

On the 2d of December 1832 Carlyle writes to his brother Dr. Carlyle, then at Rome :

"I get more earnest, graver not unhappier, every day : the whole Creation seems more and more Divine to me, the Natural more and more Supernatural. Out of Goethe, who is my near neighbour, so to speak, there is no writing that *speaks* to me (*mir anspricht*) like the Hebrew Scriptures, though they lie far remote. Earnestness of Soul was never shown as there. *Ernst ist das Leben ;* and ever to the last, soul resembles soul.—Here, however, speaking of Goethe, I must tell you that last week, as our Mother and I were passing Sundaywell, a little parcel was handed in which proved to be from Eckermann at Weimar. It made me glad and sad. There was a medal in it, struck by Bovy since the Poet's death : Ottilie had sent it me. Then a gilt cream-coloured Essay on Goethe's *Practische Wirksamkeit* by one F. von Müller, a Weimar *Kunstfreund* and intimate of deceased's, with an inscription on it by him. Finally the third *Heft* of the sixth volume of *Kunst und Alterthum*, which had partly been in preparation and now posthumously produced itself ; to me a touching kind of sight. Eckermann wrote a very kind letter, explaining how busy he was with redacting the fifteen volumes of *Nachgelassenen Schriften*, the titles of all which he gave me. There is a volume of *Dichtung und Wahrheit*, and the completion of *Faust*. These are the most remarkable. I have read Müller's Essay ; which is sensible enough ; several good things also are in the *Heft ;* towards the last page of which I came upon these words (by Müller speaking of Goethe) : ' *Unter den jüngern Britten ziehen Bulwer* (?) *und Carlyle ihn ganz vorzüglich an, und das schöne reine Naturell des letztern, seine ruhige, zartsinnige Auffassungsgabe steigern Goethe's*

Anerkennung bis zur liebevollsten Zuneigung.'[1] This of
liebevollste Zuneigung was extremely precious to me.   Alas,
und das Alles ist hin!   Ottilie promises to write, but I
think *not*."

ECKERMANN to CARLYLE.

WEIMAR, *d.* 10*n. Novbr.* 1833.

Dieses, mein werther Freund, ist nun der dritte Brief
den ich Ihnen schreibe, ohne erfahren zu haben, dass irgend
etwas in Ihre Hände gekommen ist.   Im vorigen Winter
ging ein Paket an Sie durch die Herren Parish et Comp.
in Hamburg.   Wir sendeten Ihnen das letzte Heft von
Kunst und Alterthum, nach Goethe's Tode von uns hinter-
bliebenen Freunden herausgegeben.   Auch hatte ich eine
sehr bedeutende kleine Schrift beygelegt : *Goethe in seiner
practischen Wirksamkeit,* von Herrn Geheimenrath v. Müller.
Da der Verfasser ein langjähriger Freund Goethe's und ihm
überdiess als Testaments-Vollstrecker Quellen zu Gebote
standen woraus kein Anderer schöpfen konnte, so ist jene
kleine Schrift voll der bedeutendsten Details ; und ich hatte
die Hoffnung dass Sie daraus für die literarische Welt in
England angenehme Schätze ziehen würden.   Auch hatte
ich das letzte Portrait von Goethe beygelegt.   Wir haben
nun keine Nachricht dass diess alles bey Ihnen angekommen
ist ; auch scheint es dass Sie meinen Brief vom Anfang des
letzten Sommers nicht erhalten haben.   Unterdess sind

---

[1] Translation : " Among the younger Englishmen, Bulwer
and Carlyle quite especially attract him.   The beautiful, pure
nature of the latter, with his calm delicate faculty of perception,
raises Goethe's recognition of him to the warmest affection."
(See *Kunst und Alterthum,* Cotta, 1832, *Band* vi., 3*tes Heft,*
640.)

nun Goethe's Nachgelassene Werke bis zum 1on. Bande
erschienen und wir erwarten die letzten 5 in einigen
Wochen. Wir·möchten Ihnen diese 15 Bände schicken,
aber vorher möchten wir erfahren, ob sie nicht vielleicht
schon durch den englischen Buchhandel in Ihren Händen
sind, und ob die Transportkosten nicht vielleicht mehr
betragen als der Preis dieser Werke im englischen Buchhandel.

Heute sende ich Ihnen die Ankündigung und den
Vorbericht des Briefwechsels zwischen Goethe und
Zelter. Es sind bereits in diesen Tagen die beyden ersten
Bände davon erschienen, und ich mache Sie aufmerksam
auf dieses höchst bedeutende Werk, das für Sie, wie für alle
übrigen Freunde Goethe's in England, von nicht geringem
Interesse seyn wird.

Nun möchte ich bald etwas von Ihnen hören, besonders
auch was Sie jetzt arbeiten, und ob in dem Laufe des
letzten Jahres nicht irgend eine Abhandlung in Bezug auf
Goethe und die deutsche Literatur, in einem der englischen
Reviews von Ihnen erschienen ist. Da die vorzüglichsten
englischen Journale nach Weimar kommen, so würden Sie
hier eifrige Leser finden.

Ich sage die herzlichsten Grüsse an Madame Carlyle,
und schliesse mit dem Wunsch eines baldigen Briefes von
Ihnen.

Ihr treuer Freund,

ECKERMANN.

[TRANSLATION.]

WEIMAR, 10*th November* 1833.

This, my esteemed friend, is now the third letter I
write to you, without having learnt if any one of them has

reached you.　Last winter a parcel went to you by Messrs.
Parish and Co. of Hamburg.　We sent you the last part of
Kunst und Alterthum, published after Goethe's death by us,
his surviving friends.　I also added a very important little
paper :　"Goethe, in his Official Capacity," by Herr von
Müller, Privy-Counsellor.　As the author was a friend of
Goethe's of many years' standing, as well as Executor of
his Will, sources of information were at his command,
which were not available to any one else ; his little paper
is full of the most important details, and I had the hope
that you would draw from it welcome treasures for the
English literary world.　I also sent the last portrait of
Goethe.　We have up to this time no information that
all this has reached you, and it also seems that you have
not received my letter of the beginning of last summer.
Meanwhile Goethe's *Posthumous Works* as far as the tenth
volume have appeared, and we expect the last five in a few
weeks.　We should like to send you these fifteen volumes,
but we want first to learn whether, by chance, they have
not already reached you through the English booksellers,
and whether the cost of carriage will not perhaps amount
to more than the price of the books in England.

I send you to-day the announcement of the *Correspondence between Goethe and Zelter*, and the Preface to it.
The first two volumes of this have already appeared within
these last days, and I call your attention to this most important work, which will be of no small interest to you as
well as to Goethe's other friends in England.

I trust that I may soon hear something from you,
especially of what you are at present at work upon, and
whether in the course of the last year, some essay by you
on Goethe and German Literature has not appeared in one
of the English Reviews ?　As the leading English Journals

come to Weimar, you would find eager readers here. I send my most cordial greetings to Mrs. Carlyle, and close with the hope of receiving a letter from you very soon.

Your faithful friend,
ECKERMANN.

The original of the following Letter is said to be lost ; in any case it is not discoverable. Eckermann printed a translation of it ; and from his translation [1] it is here rendered back into English.

CARLYLE to ECKERMANN.

CRAIGENPUTTOCK, *6th May* 1834.

MY DEAR ECKERMANN——Your kind Letter of the 10th of November 1833 reached me at last, after our long stormy winter, a few days ago,——a belated but highly welcome arrival. It is painful to think how our Correspondence has gone astray of late : your Letter of last summer never arrived here and two of mine seem to have been lost. My last from you was the Weimar Packet of the previous winter, which, as I very well remember, reached me (by the hands of a rustic on his way to us) one stormy day, among the mountains, in the valley of Glenessland. I hurriedly opened it, and in spite of the wind, took a hasty glance. I found there the things you mention : a Letter from you, the last part of *Kunst und Alterthum*, Herr von Müller's interesting Brochure, both of these with an extremely friendly inscription in his own hand, and lastly Herr Schwerdgeburth's

---

[1] Republished in the *Grenzboten*, iii. 562-564, 1885.

Z

Engraving and the Medal from Frau von Goethe. A
grateful, copious answer failed not to leave by the next post ;
which, it seems, was an answer spoken to the winds.   In
truth, you Weimar friends have had need of faith, and I
am most happy to see it has certainly not been wanting.
And now, dear Eckermann, will you, after such an interval,
accept yourself and present to the others, all the thanks
you can imagine me to have expressed.   Say to Frau von
Goethe that her Medal, still wrapped in your handwriting and
reposited in a little Roman porphyry box . . . lies on our
mantelpiece, and daily reminds us of her, moreover that we
have not forgotten her promise of a Letter, and we hope it
is likewise remembered by herself.   Say to the Geheimrath
[von Müller] that I have read, and am again reading in more
than one language, his valuable piece of writing, with real
pleasure, and that I feel myself richer by his regard.   And
now let us hope that no such interruption and delay in our
Correspondence will occur again as long as there is nothing
to divide us but mere physical distance : nay, I am about
to come nearer to you, if not a great deal nearer in actual
miles, much nearer in social facilities.

    For this, my friend, is in all probability the last letter
you will receive from Craigenputtock.   With Whitsuntide
we are to be in London ; in two days I set out to make
our arrangements on the spot : and there in future we are
to have our habitation.   That this will make a great differ-
ence in our external affairs you can imagine, but you can
hardly realise how very great this change will be : from the
deepest, stillest solitude in this world to the most huge,
tumultuous, never-resting Babel that ever the sun looked
down upon.   The thought fills me with a nameless, vague
foreboding, but the step is unavoidable, indeed is plainly
necessary.   I comfort myself, however, with the saying of

our Goethe, grounded on clear insight and ever again recurring to one's mind with a new application : " We look upon our scholars as so many swimmers who in the element which threatened to swallow them, feel with astonishment that they are lighter, that it bears and carries them forward."[1] True, how true ! Let us swim then, so long as life lasts, in this or other water, with more room or less, and, provided our course be right, bless our fate. I used to call the London stream *Phlegethon Fleetditch ;* but I find, however delirious the condition of Literature is becoming and has become, that it cannot be carried on by an Englishman in any other place than London. So through *Phlegethon Fleetditch* lies our way, and, with God's help, we will follow it as blamelessly as possible. Thus henceforth the old stone mansion of Craigenputtock is to be left deserted, or inhabited only by men, with double-barrelled guns, intent on shooting the moorfowl, and who know nothing of Weimar. So now you will have to figure us in quite another kind of environment.

Add to all these external confusions, that I have for a long time been in a kind of spiritual crisis,—of which condition you will no doubt have had experience and will know how horrible it is to speak of it until its issue has become clear,—and you will not think it singular that I should this year have written less than in any of the last ten, and that of what I have written I should have been able to publish nothing. But when Heaven favours me, I shall still have one and another thing to say. With German Literature in particular I have had as good as no concern ; the few books that have reached me are nothing of more consequence than Heyne and Börne and the like, of no worth or of less

---

[1] *Wilhelm Meister's Travels* (Library Edition, 1871), p. 267.

than none. My Goethe on the other hand, with all that pertains to him, grows greater and ever truer the more I attain to clearness in myself. And yet he stands there, a completed subject, as one might say, to which there will be nothing further added,—like a granite promontory, high and serene, stretching far out into the waste chaos, but not through it. *Through* it the world seems to be seeking out for itself another path, or else to have given up all zeal after such. To me highly significant! With him and his work, it appears that my labours in the field of German Literature may with advantage be brought to an end, or at any rate, to a pause. And moreover, as to my own England, my mission, in so far as it can be called my mission, may be regarded as fulfilled; as witness merely this, that we have had within the last twelve months no fewer than three new translations of *Faust*, of which two appeared in Edinburgh on one and the same day. In truth the fire is kindled, and we have enough of smoke, and more than enough—there is here and there, even a little flame, as in Mrs. Austin's *Characteristics of Goethe* which you will no doubt have seen. All this is in the common course of things; it will at some time be all flame and clear light, on which account we will for the present cheerfully welcome the smoke. "And do thou take thy bellows and go elsewhere!" This is one of the aspects of the spiritual crisis I spoke of. How it will end, or if it is already ending, I will give you some signal when I have succeeded in putting together, in London, some patchwork of recent Essays; which latter are likely for a long time to be our only vehicle of publication, at least the only one for me, much as I hate it.

In such an attitude towards my old favourites, you may judge whether the Correspondence of Goethe and Zelter, which you announce in your last communication, is likely to be welcome to me. Zelter himself, the solid man and mason, is a figure on whom I look with almost filial love. That Goethe so loved him is to me another beautiful proof of his universal geniality. The book will, I think, have already come to England; but this I shall not learn for certain till I get to London. Of the *Nachgelassene Werke* I possess no copy and have only seen the first Section,—in which I read the continuation of *Faust*, with deeper reflections than I have yet been able to express. Many thanks for your kind offer to send it to me; I shall receive the packet with pleasure, no matter what the cost of carriage may be. The whole of the *Werke* which I have here, are a present from him; and I should like to have all the volumes uniform. But in any case I should think the cost of carriage will not be much. What our address in London will be we do not yet know; meanwhile, that of Messrs. Black, Young and Young, Foreign Booksellers, Tavistock Street, Covent Garden, London, will always find me; and for everything, except post-letters, is probably the best. They have an agent in Leipzig (a certain Herbig, I think, probably known to your Weimar Bookseller); once in his hands any parcel will reach me in a few weeks.

When we have cast anchor in London you shall hear from me again. Let us hope that the present letter may not go astray also!

If you think of writing to me soon, as I hope you will do, the above address may be employed, or better still, the following : " Care of Mrs. Austin, 5 Orme Square, Bayswater, London." Tell me, I beg of you, fully and minutely, what you are about and what your outlooks are. Are we not to see you face to face in the modern Babel? A bedroom and a hearty welcome will await you there. From your letters I gather that I shall see you.—You told me also of Conversations with Goethe, which you were about to write down. *Falk*, I should think, was a failure, almost a scandal : but yours will certainly be one of the most interesting books ever written. Do you know our English *Boswell's Life of Johnson ?* If not, read it. There are not ten books of the eighteenth century so valuable. Farewell, my friend. The lady returns your kind greeting. Think of me as yours most faithfully,

T. CARLYLE.

P.S.— London, 14th May.—Have arrived safe ; expect amongst other things to see Mrs. Jameson here, and to hear from her a great deal about Weimar. No house found as yet. *Ora pro nobis.*

SUMMARY AND INDEX

SUMMARY OF THE CHIEF CONTENTS OF
EACH LETTER

Carlyle to Goethe, 24th June 1824.—Permit me, in soliciting your acceptance of this Translation (*Wilhelm Meister's Apprenticeship*), to return you my sincere thanks for the profit which, in common with many millions, I have derived from the Original. I have long hoped that I might one day see you, and pour out, as before a Father, the woes and wanderings of my heart. (Pages 1, 2.)

Goethe to Carlyle, 30th October. — Accept my sincere thanks for your hearty sympathy in my literary work. Perhaps I may hereafter come to know much of you. I send copy of a set of poems which you can hardly have seen. (2-5.)

Carlyle to Goethe, 15th April 1827.—Above two years ago I received your kind letter and present, which I value with a regard which can belong to nothing else. If I have been delivered from darkness into any measure of light, it is to you more than any other man that I am indebted. I now take the liberty to offer you some further poor products of my endeavours (*Schiller* and *German Romance*). Ere long your name and doctrines will be English as well as German. If there be any gift in me, I may yet send you some work of my own. My young wife, who sympathises with me in most things, agrees also in my admiration of you ; and begs you to accept the accompanying purse, the work of her own hands. May I hope to hear from you again ? (6-11.)

Goethe to Carlyle, 17th May.—Let me hastily announce the

arrival of your welcome packet and kind letter. Most sincere thanks to the dear husband and wife. A packet will speedily be despatched in testimony of my sympathetic interest. (11, 12.)

The same, 20th July.—Let me, first of all, commend most highly your Biography of Schiller. It is evident that the efforts of the best writers in all nations are now being directed to what is universal in humanity. Every translator is a kind of middle-man in this universal spiritual commerce. Gratify me soon with some reply ; and permit me to greet your dear wife, for whom I give myself the pleasure of adding some trifles, in return for her charming gift. Accept my thanks for the pains expended on my Works. (13-27.)

Carlyle to Goethe, 20th August.—No royal present could have gratified us more than yours. This little drawing-room may now be said to be full of you. For your ideas on the tendency of modern poetry to promote freer intercourse among nations, I must also thank you. You are kind enough to inquire about my bygone life ; and often I have longed to pour out the whole history before you. I was once an unbeliever, not in religion only ; but now, thank Heaven, all this is altered. I can now look forward with cheerfulness to a life spent in Literature, hoping little and fearing little from the world. Postscript, by Mrs. Carlyle, of heartfelt thanks. (30-35.)

Goethe to Carlyle, 1st January 1828.—Another packet of books, etc., goes to you, *viâ* Hamburg. What may be the merit of Des Voeux's English translation of *Tasso?* It is precisely the bearing of an orignal to a translation, which most clearly indicates the relations of nation to nation. Be so good as give your dear wife the parcel addressed to her. I send also six Medals, two for Sir Walter Scott ; the others please distribute to my well-wishers. Am greatly interested in the English appreciation of, and contact with, German Literature. " Little children, love one another ! " (36-45.)

The same, 15th January.—Message to Sir Walter Scott, and admiration of his *Life of Napoleon*. Cultured society in

Weimar: such free bondage perhaps hardly exists anywhere else. Contents of parcel sent. (48-59.)

Carlyle to Goethe, 17th January.—I have now to solicit a favour of a more practical, and as I may justly fear, of a more questionable nature; that of a testimonial of fitness for the Professorship of Moral Philosophy at St. Andrews. Have just heard of your intended enlargement of the *Wanderjahre*, but confess I see not well what improvements could be made. Will Ottilie von Goethe accept the friendly compliments of Jane Welsh Carlyle? We even paint day-dreams of spending next winter, or the following summer, in Weimar. (63-68.)

Goethe to Carlyle, 14th March.—I shall be glad if the enclosed (the Testimonial), unfortunately delayed, should arrive in time. A little box was sent from here on the 20th of January, and I hope proved welcome. Let me have news of it, and greet your dear wife from me and mine. (68-70.)

Carlyle to Goethe, 18th April.—The box was long delayed by the severe winter, but is now here in perfect safety: our best thanks are heartily yours. I have already written to Sir Walter Scott, announcing your delightful message. Within the last six years, the readers of your language here must have increased tenfold. Sorry am I to tell you that Des Voeux's translation of *Tasso* is unequivocally trivial: instances of its insufficiency. I shall never cease to value your Testimonial, although for the present occasion it was too late. A Captain Skinner called here with your card, and delighted us by singing *Kennst du das Land.* (81-90.)

Mrs. Carlyle to Goethe, 10th June.—I embrace the opportunity of sending you by Mr. May the continued assurance of our affection and grateful regard. (91.)

Goethe to Carlyle, 15th June.—Your richly filled letter reached me in due time. Mr. Skinner is again with us, and gives us good and pleasant news of you and your surroundings. Perhaps never before did one nation take such pains to understand another as Scotland now does in respect to Germany.

The unlucky Werner. Am greatly pleased with your treatment of *Helena*. Dr. Eckermann almost one of my family. The translation of *Wallenstein* has made a quite peculiar impression upon me : pray tell me the name of the translator. A translator works not only for his own nation, but also for the one from whose language he translates. A letter enclosed from the good Eckermann. Alas, as I close this letter, there comes upon us the sad news of our excellent Prince's death. (91-104.)

Eckermann to Carlyle, 15th June.—You live much in our thoughts at this moment, through your criticism of *Helena*. French and Russian criticisms of the same. Your translation convinced me, for the first time, that it may be possible to render *Faust* perfectly in a foreign language. It could, I am sure, find no better translator than yourself. You will go on prospering in your studies, and England will owe you gratitude for them. I hope soon to hear direct from you how you and your amiable lady have settled yourselves in your new home in the country. (104-111.)

Goethe to Carlyle (continuation of preceding letter).— Ottilie sends her most cordial greetings to Mrs. Carlyle. A piece of embroidery should have gone with this despatch. We Germans, like you, are occupying ourselves with foreign literature. Greet your dear wife from me, and give me soon some clear idea of your present abode (Craigenputtock). (111-115.)

The same, 8th August. — The most sad calamity has befallen us in the death of our estimable Prince, as I have already announced. You will sympathise with me in the condition in which, after more than fifty years of life together, I am left by the loss. Meanwhile it is a necessity diligently to maintain all my remaining connections with life. Fare you well, and let me hear from you soon. (115-117.)

Carlyle to Goethe, 25th September 1828.—The book-parcel arrived last night : all in perfect safety, Books, Music, and Manuscript. One dainty little article I already notice, your translation of our ancient Scottish "Schwank," *Get up and bar the door.* Scotland is very rich in popular songs. In trying bereavements, when old friends are snatched away from you, it must be a consolation to think that, neither in this age nor in any other, can you ever be *alone.* Sir Walter Scott received the Medals several months ago. George Moir is the name of the translator of *Wallenstein.* Articles on German Literature. Burns. Description of Craigenputtock. Jane unites with me in affectionate respects to your Ottilie, whom in many a day-dream we still hope to see and know in her Father's circle. Pray assure Dr. Eckermann of my regard, and purpose to express it directly. (117-127.)

Goethe to Carlyle, 25th June 1829.—Were an echo to reach you as often as we think and speak of you, you would often be aware of a friendly presence. I am now addressing a written conversation from my "fireside" to yours. When I visit distant friends in thought, I do not like to let my imagination wander in space. I therefore beg for myself a sketch of your dwelling and its surroundings. With your countryman, Burns, I am sufficiently acquainted to prize him, but the Scotch dialect is very perplexing to us. I now announce the speedy despatch of a box, containing the Fourth and Fifth Sections of my Works, with something pleasant from the ladies of my household. (127-138.)

Eckermann to Carlyle, 2d July.—Your valued letter of December last gave me much pleasure. Your article on Goethe in the Foreign Review has excited great interest in Germany. I could say a great deal about the new and extended edition of the *Wanderjahre.* If you had courage to pull your volume to pieces, and, on this new basis, reconstruct the whole, one might hope your country would be grateful to you. Goethe enjoys most excellent health, and we have the joyful hope that he may live and work amongst us for many years to come. (139-145.)

Goethe to Carlyle, 6th July.—The parcel already announced

is only now being despatched. It contains the final proof-
sheets of a translation of your *Life of Schiller*. On the 28th
of August I beg you quietly to keep my eightieth birthday.
At the bottom of the little box there is lying a gift sent by
the ladies of my family, with the friendliest feelings. (145-
151.)

Carlyle to Goethe, 3d November.—Your much prized letter
and packet have both arrived in perfect safety and entireness.
Six years ago, the possibility of a Letter, of a Present from
Goethe to *me*, would have seemed little less wondrous and
dreamlike than from Shakespeare or Homer. My wife bids
me say that she intends to read your entire Works this winter :
she sends her best thanks to your Ottilie for the beautiful
gift. Thanks also for the volume sent, in which I can already
discover no little matter for reflection. The *Farbenlehre* I
have never seen, and shall thankfully accept and study. I
still remember that it was the desire to read Werner's Mineralogical Doctrines in the original, that first set me on studying
German. A little packet, chiefly for your Ottilie, is getting
ready. In regard to my employments, I am still but an
Essayist, and longing more than ever to be a Writer in a far
better sense. (152-159.)

The same, 22d December.—The promised packet at length
sets out, with true wishes on our part that it may find you
happy and busy, and bring kind remembrances of friends that
love you. The Craigenputtock *Sketches* are from the pencil
of Mr. Moir, the translator of *Wallenstein*, to whom I have
presented the last of the four Medals. The portfolio is of
my wife's manufacture, who sends among other love-tokens a
lock of her hair. She begs and hopes that you will send her
a lock of yours in return. The *Cowper's Poems* you are to
accept as a New-year's gift from me. A knowledge of German
literature is fast spreading over all the domains of the English
tongue. Have almost decided to write a History of German
Literature ; but still purpose to try something infinitely greater.

Alas, the huge formless Chaos is here, but no creative voice to say, " Let there be light." (159-165.)

Carlyle to Eckermann, 20th March 1830.—No spot on the globe is at present so significant to me as Weimar. We are still speculating on a winter's residence there. A little box recently despatched. Was shocked to hear of Müllner's death. Increasing attention amongst us to the Literature of neighbouring nations. My projected History of German Literature. A few words from you might save me much groping. My wife sends her kind regards, and continued hope of one day seeing you. (165-173.)

Goethe to Carlyle, 13th April.—The precious casket, after long delay owing to the extreme severity of the winter, at last arrived safely. I will mention first the incomparable lock of hair. I did not need to touch my skull to become aware that only stubble was left there. The impossibility of making the desired return smote my heart. The elegant Scotch *Bonnet*, I can assure you, has given much pleasure. Ottilie sends her most grateful thanks. Let me announce the despatch of another parcel in return, which will contain, with other books, the final proof-sheets of the translation of your *Schiller*. I trust you will not regard the use I have made of some portions of our correspondence as an indiscretion. Tell me how you propose to introduce German literature amongst your people, and I will gladly give you my thoughts on the sequence of its epochs. Dr. Eckermann is making a journey south with my son. (173-184.)

Carlyle to Goethe, 23d May.—Our long-cherished hope of seeing you in person now assumes some faint shape of possibility. We have been pondering together over that glorious *Mährchen* of yours, and I have promised my wife some day to write a commentary on it. In regard to my History of German Literature, I need not say that no words of yours can be other than valuable. For your guidance in this charitable service, I will try to explain as clearly as I can the scope of my project. My wife unites with me in friendliest wishes.

Few men have been permitted to finish such a task as yours. (184-193.)

Goethe to Carlyle, 6th June.—Your valued letter took only fourteen days in coming, and this incites me to write immediately. No alterations to be suggested in your proposed book : only a few gaps here and there. I will immediately despatch books in aid, and some further works of my own. Illustrations and Preface to the German translation of *Schiller*. To your dear wife my most friendly greetings : by means of the silhouette she has come much nearer to us. May she now send us such another portrait of her husband. I am glad that famous *Mährchen* does not fail in its effect. A normal imagination irresistibly demands from it something logical and consistent, which reason never succeeds in accomplishing. However I possess two interpretations, which I will seek out, and if possible send in the little box. A peerless lock of black hair impels me to add with true regret that the desired return is, alas, impossible. (193-207.)

Carlyle to Goethe, 31st August.—The packet, containing books and other valuables, arrived in perfect order. The bibliopolic fate of that History of German Literature, in which you are pleased to take an interest, has become more dubious than ever. Nor do I much regret it : my first professed appearance in Literature may now take place under some less questionable character than that of a Compiler. A wonderful Chaos within me, full of natural Supernaturalism and all manner of Antediluvian fragments. I see not what is to come of it all, and only conjecture, from the violence of the fermentation, that something strange may come. Goethe-Schiller Correspondence. The promised interpretation of the *Mährchen* still earnestly wanted by the female intellect. I had a strange letter with certain strange books, from the Saint-Simonians in Paris ; if you have chanced to notice that affair, I could like much to hear your thoughts. (207-215.)

Goethe to Carlyle, 5th October.—Once more a little box is

going to you ; and at last the *Life of Schiller* in German translation. May you succeed in making your nation acquainted with the good points of the Germans. Constantly, at all epochs and in every place, the result should be to exhibit, transmit, and if possible establish, something beneficial to mankind. Our Berlin friends (the Society for Foreign Literature) have sent me a Diploma, in which they appoint Mr. Thomas Carlyle of Craigenputtock a foreign honorary member. (215-224.)

The same, 17th October.—I now enclose you the letter from the Berlin Society, in which their resolution concerning you was transmitted to me. From the St. Simonian Society pray hold yourself aloof : more about this on another occasion. (224-227.)

Carlyle to Goethe, 23d October.—From the first sentence of your otherwise most welcome letter, I fear that mine of August may have failed to reach you, but will still hope that it was not so. Schiller and Burns. The peculiar expressiveness of the latter's diction, at all times hard to be seized by a translator : the whole British nation passionately attached to him. Our kindest wishes every way to Ottilie. (227-236.)

The same, 15th November.—The box, with all its precious contents, arrived in perfect order. I now enclose a few lines of thanks to our Berlin friends. Your Introduction to *Schiller* fitter to have stood at the head of some Epic Poem of my writing than here. Am sometimes meditating a translation of *Faust*, for which the English world is getting more and more prepared. Postscript of grateful thanks from Mrs. Carlyle. (236-242.)

Eckermann to Carlyle, 6th December. — I returned to Weimar last week alone. Herr von Goethe, the son, as you perhaps have heard, died at Rome. Goethe also has had so violent a hemorrhage of the lungs that his life was in danger ; but he is now up again and busy in his usual ways. I now look forward to the completion of *Faust*, of which so much is finished.   It is not for me to offer advice, but were I in your place I would employ my best leisure hours on a faithful translation.   One should never ask if a nation is ready for a work : nations are matured by daring works.   Postscript, by Goethe, giving assurance of his improved health ; with greetings and blessings to the dear Pair.   (242-252.)

Carlyle to Goethe, 22d January 1831.—Words of sympathy and comfort.   Your being busy with a Continuation of *Faust* could not be other than great news to me.   Have almost determined upon attempting a translation.   Taylor's *Historic Survey of German Poetry*, which I am reviewing, you may judge of by the fact that the longest article but one is on August von Kotzebue.   I fear you will not like the satirical style, but all the more agreeable will be some concluding speculations, on what after you I have called *World-Literature*, with its "Sacred College and Council of Amphictyons." Meanwhile, I am working at another curious enterprise of my own (*Sartor Resartus*), which is yet too amorphous to be prophesied of.   A little collection of Memorials is getting together for the next 28th of August.   The Saint-Simonians have again communicated with me.   Although wandering in strange paths, I cannot but look upon their Society and its progress as a true and remarkable Sign of the Times.   The world is heavily struggling out into a new era ; but the Sun and Seasons are the only changes that visit this wilderness. (252-260.)

Hitzig to Carlyle, 28th January.—Explaining the objects of the Berlin Society for Foreign Literature.   (260-264.)

Goethe to Carlyle, 2d June.—We have been so secluded of late, that we have been like to form a kind of Craigenputtock in the midst of Weimar.   Another package of books getting ready.   The good Eckermann of great value to me.   Neureuther's Marginal Drawings.   Poetry will always remain the happy refuge of Mankind.   Mrs. Carlyle requested to contribute to Ottilie's Periodical, called *Chaos*.   The *Metamorphosis of Plants.* Many good and beautiful hours are still granted us. The fairest greetings from me and Ottilie for the dear pair of hermits. (264-276.)

The same, 15th June.—Just as I am about to close the box, I find there is still room ; I am therefore having packed up for you some numbers of one of our most popular journals, the *Morgenblatt.* There is also a copy of the translation of *Schiller* for my lady friend, to show her how even the book-binders of the Continent study neatness and elegance. (276-278.)

Carlyle to Goethe, 10th June.—Daily do I send affectionate wishes to the Man, to whom more than any other living, I stand indebted and united. A little poetic *Tugendbund* of Philo-Germans is forming itself in London, whereof you are the Centre ; the first public act of which should come to light at Weimar on your approaching Birthday. Of this little Philo-German Combination ; what it now specially proposes, and whether it is likely to grow into a more lasting union for more complex purposes,—I hope to speak hereafter. Interest-ing phenomena of hopeful significance. In these last months I have been busy with a Piece more immediately my own ; but, alas, it is not a Picture that I am painting, but a half-reckless casting of the brush, with its many frustrated colours, against the canvas : whether it will make good Foam is still a venture. In some six weeks I expect to be in London, wishing to look a little with my own eyes at the world, getting so enigmatic. (279-286.)

The same, 13th August.—I now send you a word of remem-brance from this chaotic whirlpool of a city, where I arrived three days ago. Endless gratitude I owe you, for it is by you that I have learned what worth there is in man for his brother-man ; and how the "open secret" is still open for whoso has an eye. A birthday gift from "Fifteen English Friends" should reach you on your Birthday. Let me hope it may arrive in due season, and the sight of it give you some gratifying moments. I have come hither chiefly to dispose of the Piece which I lately described myself as writing : meant to be a " word spoken in season." But the whole world here is dancing a Tarantula Dance of Political Reform, and has no ear left for Literature. Figure me and mine as thinking of you, loving you ; as present especially on that 28th, with wishes as warm as loving hearts can feel. (287-291.)

Fifteen English Friends to Goethe.—Begging his acceptance of a Birthday Gift, as a true testimony of their feelings of reverence and gratitude towards him. (292-294.)

Goethe to Carlyle, 19th August.—Poetical thanks to "the Fifteen."—Britons ye have understood : The mind active, the deed restrained, the purpose unhastingly steadfast. In the books you sent I find much that is delightful. The silhouettes, in an inconceivable way, bring the absent before one. The gift of the associated friends has afforded us a pleasure as unusual as unexpected. To the dear Pair, happy hours ! (295-298.)

APPENDIX II

Goethe to Carlyle, 14th June 1830.—Contents of packet sent. (See Letter XXVII. p. 193.) *Chaos,* a weekly paper, containing social pleasantries, for private circulation. Ottilie, the sole editor ; further favours from our friends in the county of Dumfries are requested. Hope to send you the translation of *Schiller,* in its complete form by the next despatch. (324-327.)

Eckermann to Carlyle, 20th October 1832.—At the desire of many friends I have translated your first article on Goethe. (The article, *Death of Goethe.*) I send you to-day two books which will interest you. Am very busy with Goethe's Posthumous Works. Doubt if I shall remain in Weimar for the future. Herr Schwerdgeburth sends you his new portrait of Goethe, one of the best that has appeared. Pray give my cordial greetings to Mrs. Carlyle. I hope you will soon receive a letter from Madame von Goethe herself. (328-332.)

The same, 10th November 1833.—This is the third letter I write to you, without knowing whether one of them has reached you. I now send you the announcement of the *Correspondence between Goethe and Zelter,* and the Preface to it. I trust I may soon hear something from you. (334-337.)

Carlyle to Eckermann, 6th May 1834.—Your kind letter of the 10th of November reached me only a few days ago. Your letter of last summer never arrived, and two of mine seem to have been lost. My last from you was the Weimar packet of the previous winter, which arrived in perfect safety, and to which I at once gratefully and copiously replied. And now, dear Eckermann, after such an interval, pray accept yourself, and present to our friends, all the thanks you can imagine me to have expressed. With Whitsuntide we are to be in London. I have for a long time been in a kind of spiritual crisis ; and you will know how horrible it is to speak of it, until its issue has become clear. Have had as good as no concern with German Literature ; although my Goethe, with all that pertains to him, grows greater and ever truer the more I attain to clearness in myself. My mission, if it may be so called, of introducing German Literature here, may now be regarded as fulfilled. Two new translations of *Faust* in one day. The fire is kindled, and we have smoke enough : it will some day be all flame and clear light. " Do thou take thy bellows, and go elsewhere ! " This is one of the aspects of my spiritual crisis. When we have cast anchor in London you shall hear from me again. Are we not to see you face to face in the modern Babel ? The lady returns your kind greetings. *Ora pro nobis.* (337-342.)

INDEX